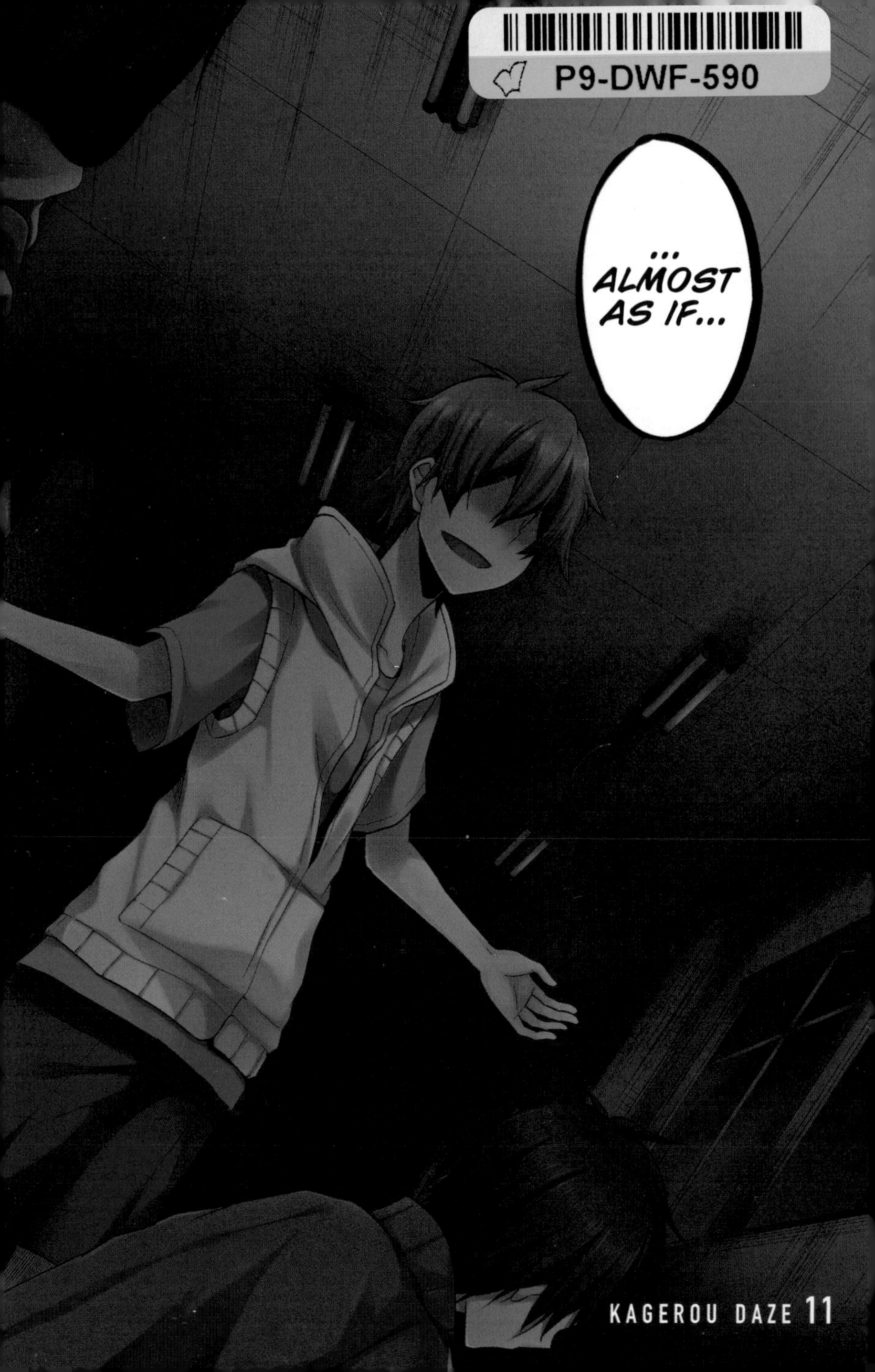
...
ALMOST
AS IF...
KAGEROU DAZE 11

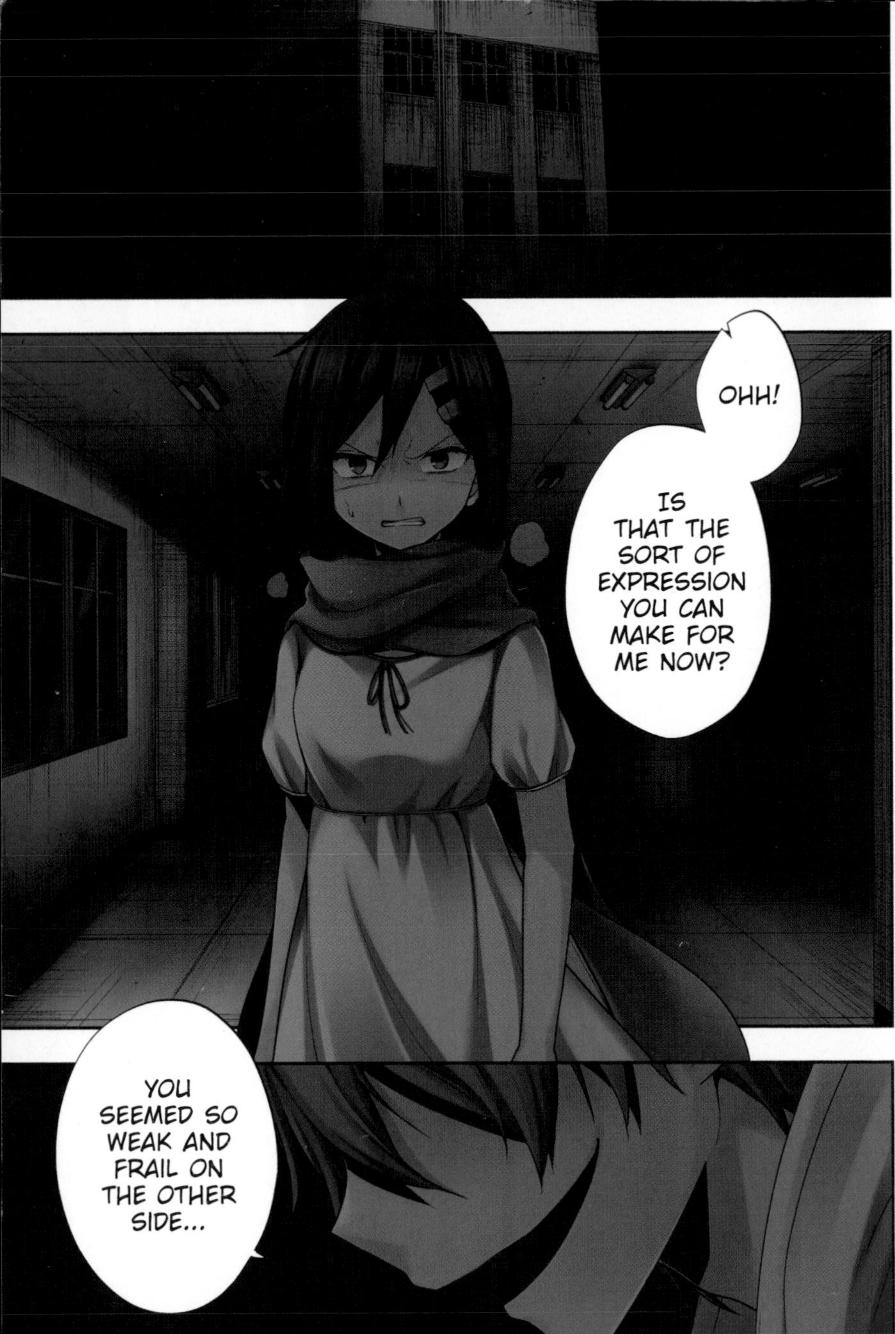
OHH!
IS THAT THE SORT OF EXPRESSION YOU CAN MAKE FOR ME NOW?
YOU SEEMED SO WEAK AND FRAIL ON THE OTHER SIDE...

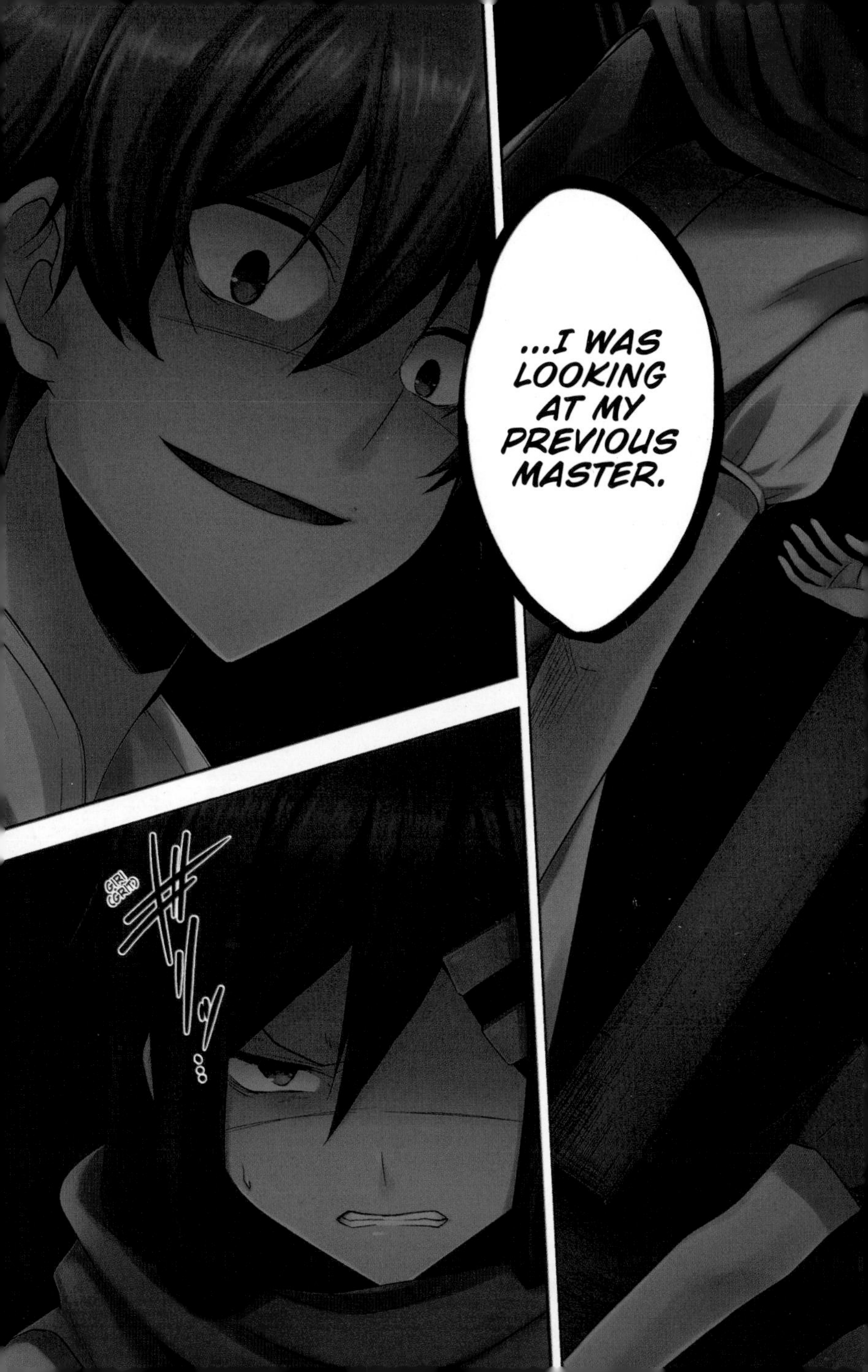
...I WAS LOOKING AT MY PREVIOUS MASTER.
GIRI (GRIT)

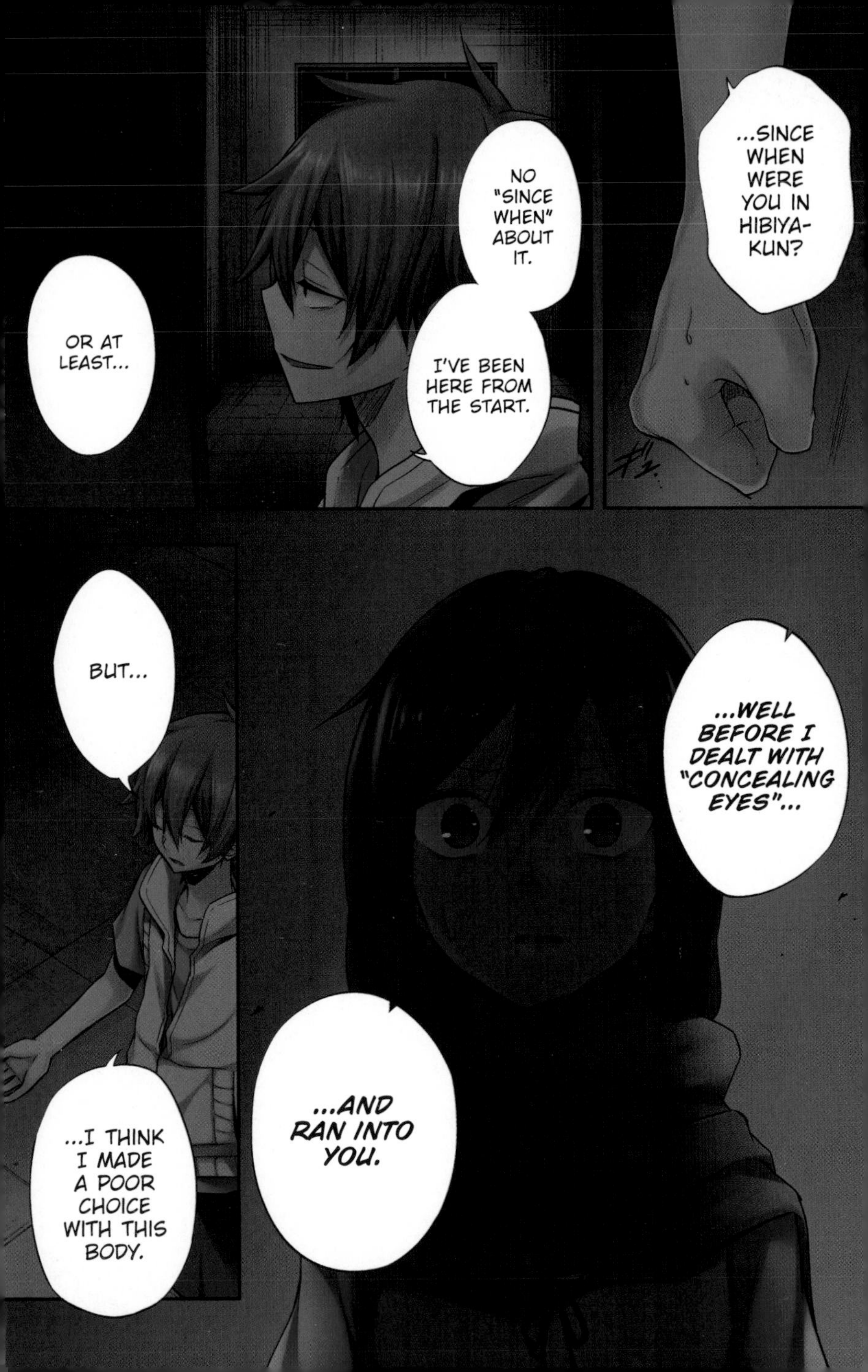
...SINCE WHEN WERE YOU IN HIBIYA-KUN?
NO "SINCE WHEN" ABOUT IT.
I'VE BEEN HERE FROM THE START.
OR AT LEAST...
...WELL BEFORE I DEALT WITH "CONCEALING EYES"...
...AND RAN INTO YOU.
BUT...
...I THINK I MADE A POOR CHOICE WITH THIS BODY.

KAGEROU DAZE 11

CONTENTS

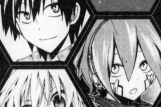

CHARACTERS

>>>

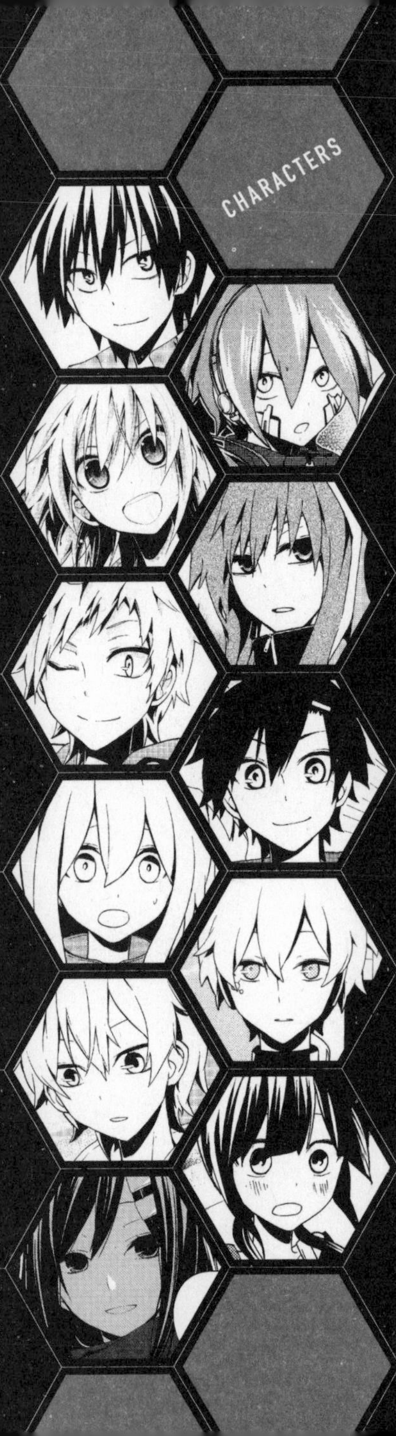

SHINTARO

A teenage boy who's been holed up in his house for the past two years.

<<<

ENE (Takane Enomoto)

An innocent, naive "digital girl" who's taken up residence in Shintaro's computer.

>>>

MOMO

An ultra-popular singer with the "drawing eyes" ability. Shintaro's sister. Died after the "clearing eyes" snake dropped her off a building.

<<<

KIDO

Leader of the Mekakushi-dan. Possesses the "concealing eyes" ability. Killed when attacked by the "clearing eyes" snake.

>>>

KANO

Friends with Kido and Seto since childhood. Possesses the "deceiving eyes" ability.

<<<

SETO

A young man engaged in assorted part-time work. Possesses the "stealing eyes" ability.

>>>

MARIE

A young Medusa whose "locking eyes" ability lets her freeze people in their tracks.

<<<

KONOHA (Haruka Kokonose)

A friend of Takane and Shintaro back when he was still Haruka. After an illness took his life, he worked with the Mekakushi-dan under the name Konoha.

>>>

HIBIYA

A boy who's come to visit the neighborhood with Hiyori. Controlled by the "clearing eyes" snake.

<<<

HIYORI

A girl who's come to visit Shintaro's neighborhood. A big fan of Momo. Infused with the "focusing eyes" ability.

>>>

AYANO

A girl whose "favoring eyes" ability lets her directly transmit feelings and emotions to others. She separated from Kano and the rest after trying to kill Marie.

STORY

The tale of the events of August 14 and 15.

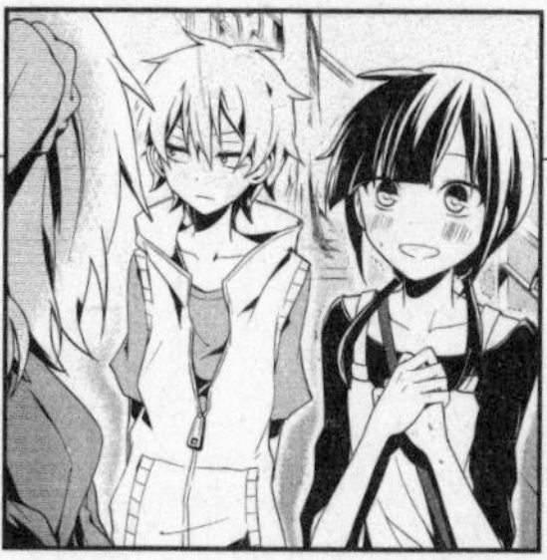

Shintaro and Momo run into a pair of children, Hibiya and Hiyori. They soon become friends, but after relaying a cryptic message to Momo over the phone, Hiyori disappears. They later discover Hibiya alone and unconscious, but he has lost his memory of the recent past. On the same day, Shintaro and Momo come across Kido and Kano, who claim to be part of a secret organization. They are also pursuing Hibiya and Hiyori, and soon, the entire group's goals, destinies, and anxieties crisscross—and it's all connected by a supernatural phenomenon known as "Kagerou Daze."

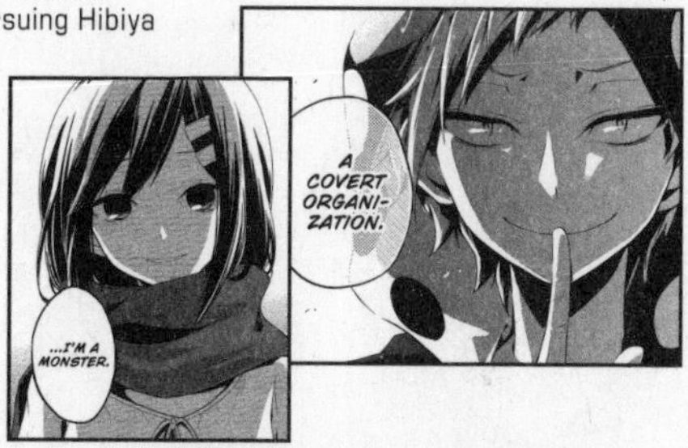
A COVERT ORGANI-ZATION.
...I'M A MONSTER.

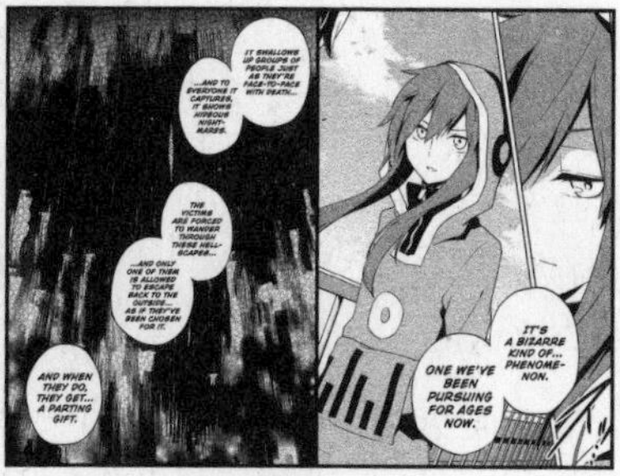
IT'S A BIZARRE KIND OF... PHENOME-NON.
ONE WE'VE BEEN PURSUING FOR AGES NOW.
IT SWALLOWS UP GROUPS OF PEOPLE JUST AS THEY'RE FACE-TO-FACE WITH DEATH...
...AND TO EVERYONE IT CAPTURES, IT SHOWS HIDEOUS NIGHT-MARES.
THE VICTIMS ARE FORCED TO WANDER THROUGH THESE HELL-SCAPES...
...AND ONLY ONE OF THEM IS ALLOWED TO ESCAPE BACK TO THE OUTSIDE... AS IF THEY'VE BEEN CHOSEN FOR IT.
AND WHEN THEY DO, THEY GET... A PARTING GIFT.

As Hibiya searches for the missing Hiyori, a mysterious girl approaches him. Using her ability to impart memories and emotions directly into anyone she wants, she reveals the truth behind the Kagerou Daze. She fears a snake with the "clearing eyes" ability is attempting to unite all the snakes that gave the rest of this group their own eerie skills into a single entity—and now it might be here, in the "worst possible form."

When Kano and Momo do find Hiyori, the scene is like something out of their worst nightmares: Hiyori, covered in blood, standing in front of a lifeless Kido. As he carries the fainted Momo back, Kano tells Ene about the lives of the Mekakushi-dan and how the snake has affected all of them.

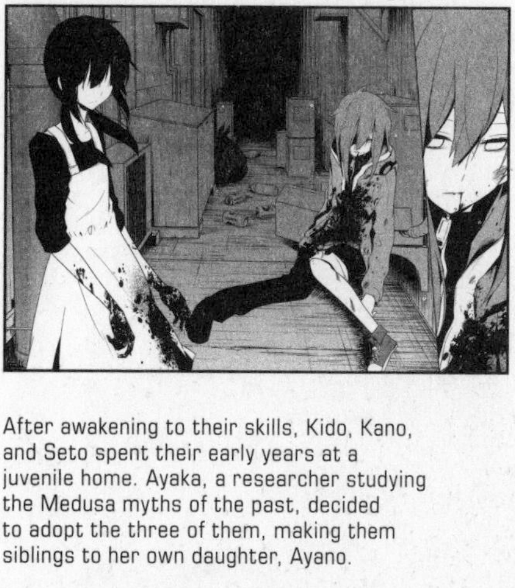

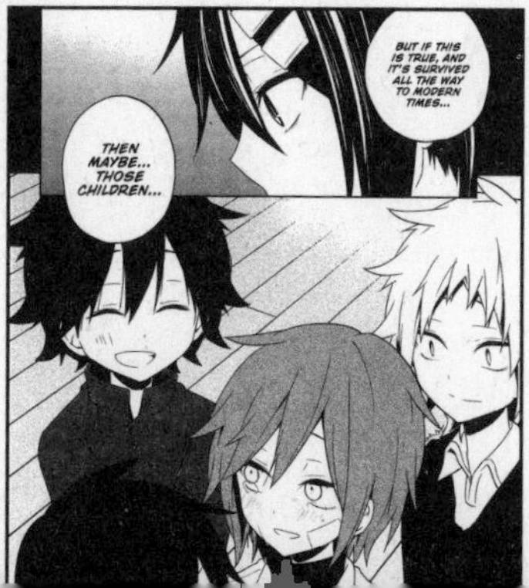
BUT IF THIS IS TRUE, AND IT'S SURVIVED ALL THE WAY TO MODERN TIMES...
THEN MAYBE... THOSE CHILDREN...

After awakening to their skills, Kido, Kano, and Seto spent their early years at a juvenile home. Ayaka, a researcher studying the Medusa myths of the past, decided to adopt the three of them, making them siblings to her own daughter, Ayano.

Kido, Kano, Seto, and Ayano form the Mekakushi-dan, living as brothers and sisters despite any real blood relation. They are later joined by Marie, who stays on after suddenly being brought to their doorstep.

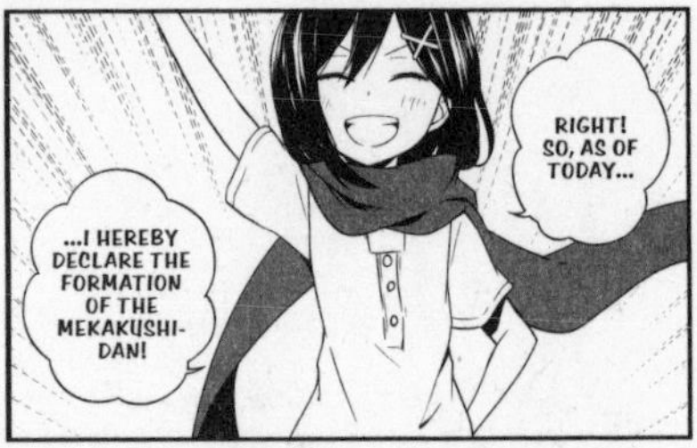
RIGHT! SO, AS OF TODAY...
...I HEREBY DECLARE THE FORMATION OF THE MEKAKUSHI-DAN!

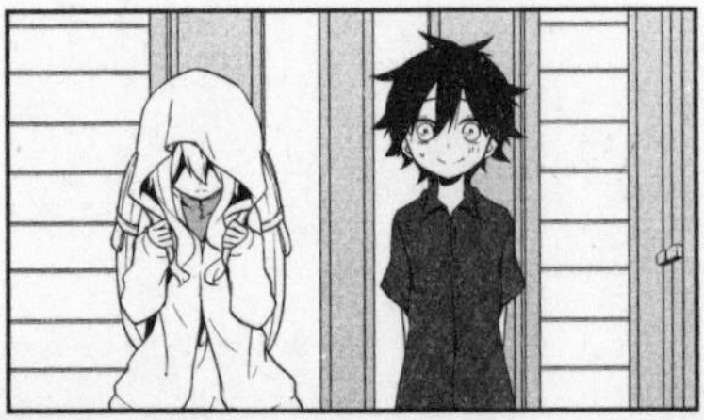

Once she realizes Marie is the child of a Medusa and that the children's abilities might affect their well-being—and their lives—Ayano resolves to protect her brothers and sisters.

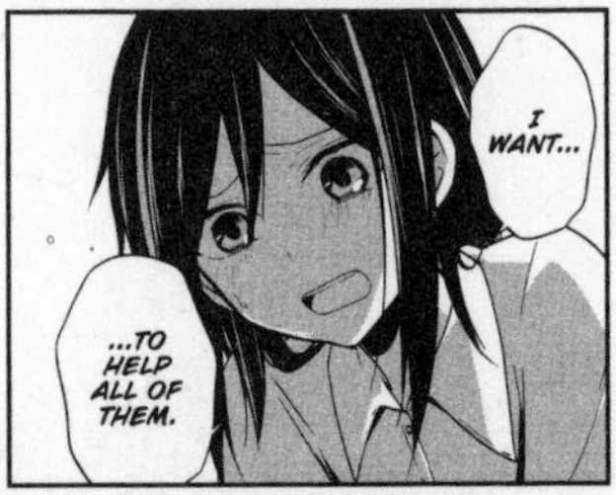
I WANT...
...TO HELP ALL OF THEM.

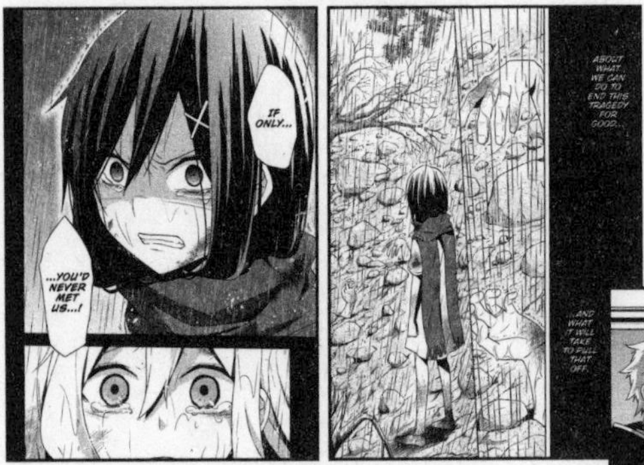
ABOUT WHAT WE CAN DO TO END THIS TRAGEDY FOR GOOD...
...AND WHAT IT WILL TAKE TO PULL THAT OFF.
IF ONLY...
...YOU'D NEVER MET US...!

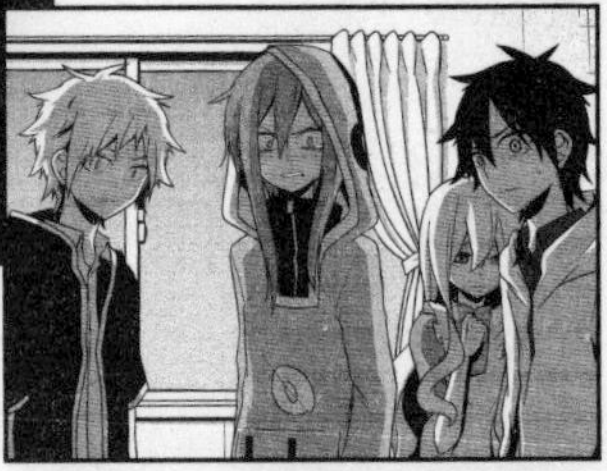

However, en route to Marie's home in search of clues that might explain the children's abilities, Ayano and her parents are killed in an accident. Swallowed up by the Kagerou Daze, Ayano gains her own eye ability along with an insight into the true nature of the Kagerou Daze. In light of what she has learned, Ayano determines the only way to put an end to the tragedy is to kill Marie. The other children vehemently refuse, but she presses on, chasing after the "clearing eyes" snake.

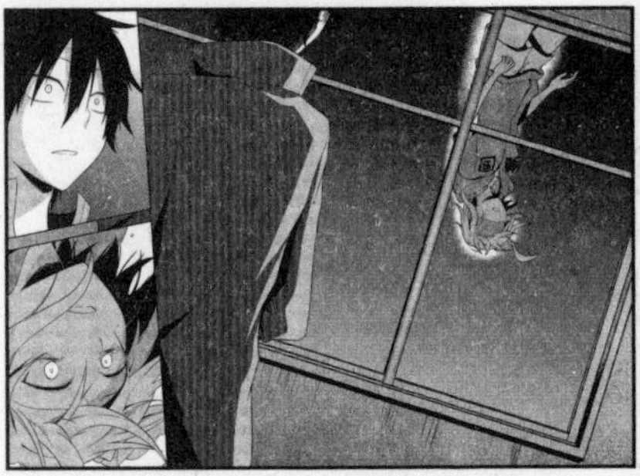

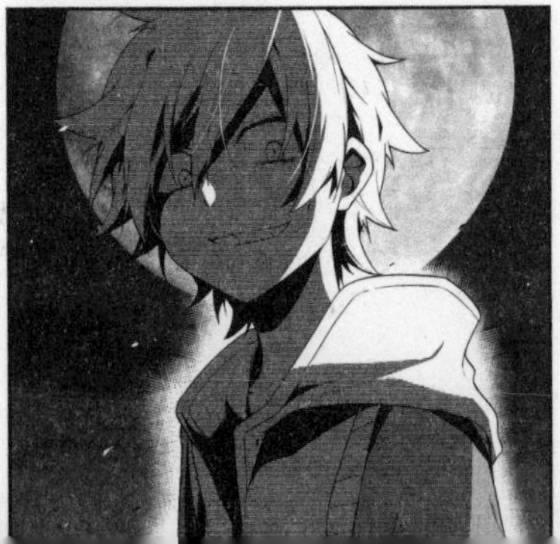

Meanwhile, Shintaro attempts to track down Momo, who has gone off to search for Hiyori. Kano tells him that the "focusing eyes" ability has housed itself within Hiyori, not Hibiya. Just as he does, Shintaro spots Momo falling off the building he's in—as Hibiya's maniacal laughter echoes from up on the roof...

As the group reels from Momo's death, Konoha appears. He apparently doesn't remember Ene, who then reveals that she was once Takane Enomoto, a friend of Konoha's back when he still lived as Haruka Kokonose.

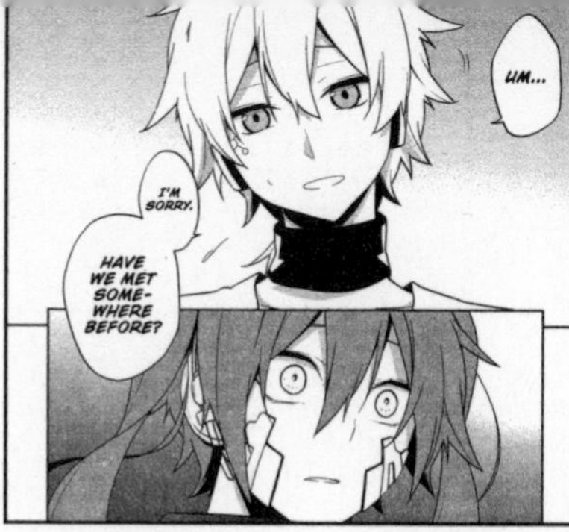
UM...
I'M SORRY.
HAVE WE MET SOME-WHERE BEFORE?

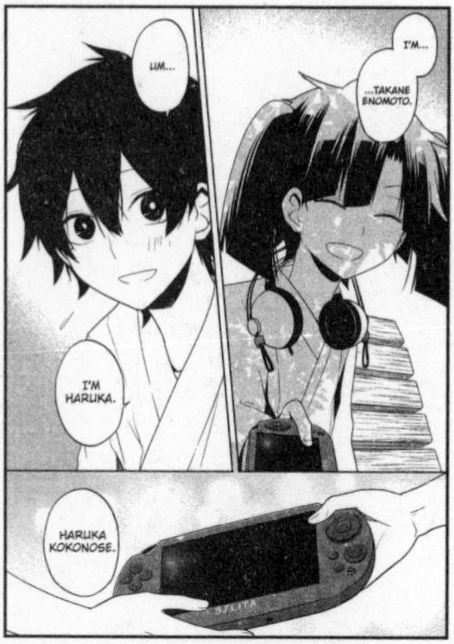
I'M...
...TAKANE ENOMOTO.
UM...
I'M HARUKA.
HARUKA KOKONOSE.

Haruka met Takane at the hospital where he had been admitted for management of his terminal illness. Through video games, they became fast friends, but just as Haruka felt he at last had something to live for, Takane was discharged. Shortly after, her vacancy is filled by Shintaro, who's admitted after a nasty fall. Despite Shintaro's distrust for other people, Haruka suggests they play a game, and the two become friends. Takane, seeing how well they get along, is too emotionally torn to see her friend.

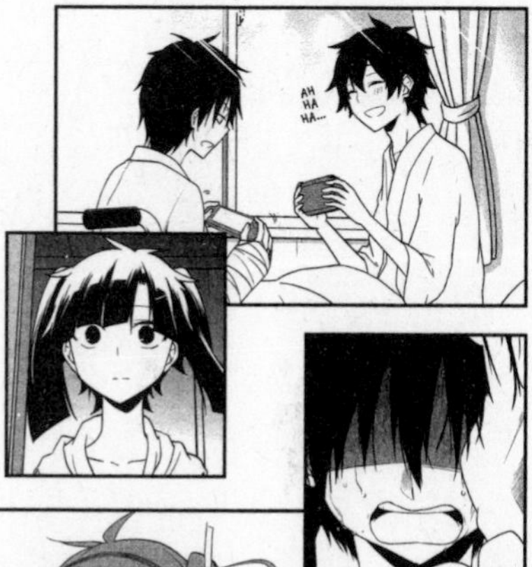
AH HA HA...

Making a promise to attend school together, Shintaro leaves the hospital, but it isn't long before Haruka's illness finally takes him. Takane, who had been unable to see him before his death, is so shocked that she jumps to her death from the hospital roof. Shintaro becomes a recluse in his bedroom, only to be visited by Takane's consciousness (calling itself "Ene") in his computer...

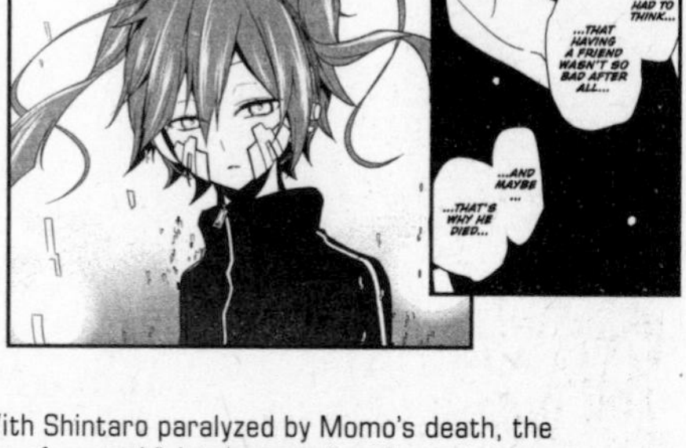
I JUST HAD TO THINK...
...THAT HAVING A FRIEND WASN'T SO BAD AFTER ALL...
...AND MAYBE...
...THAT'S WHY HE DIED...

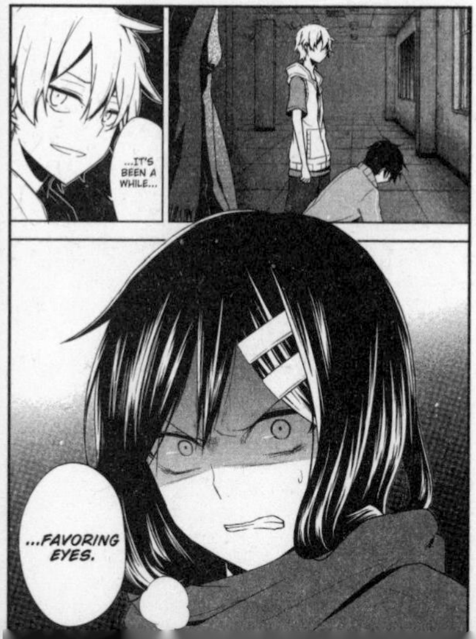
...IT'S BEEN A WHILE...
...FAVORING EYES.

With Shintaro paralyzed by Momo's death, the out-of-control "clearing eyes" snake arranges a fateful encounter with Ayano...!

KAGEROU DAZE

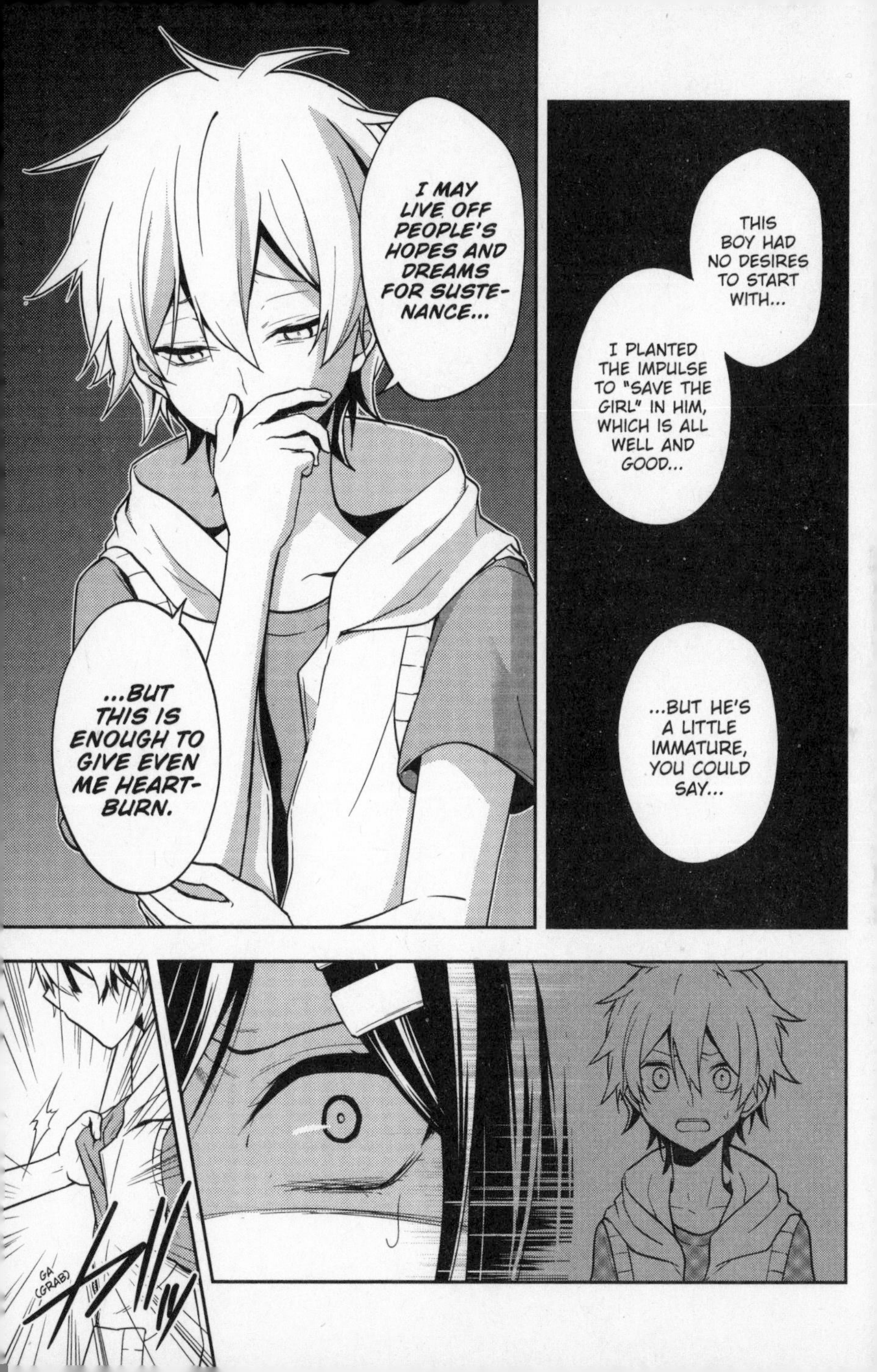
THIS BOY HAD NO DESIRES TO START WITH...
I PLANTED THE IMPULSE TO "SAVE THE GIRL" IN HIM, WHICH IS ALL WELL AND GOOD...
...BUT HE'S A LITTLE IMMATURE, YOU COULD SAY...
I MAY LIVE OFF PEOPLE'S HOPES AND DREAMS FOR SUSTE-NANCE...
...BUT THIS IS ENOUGH TO GIVE EVEN ME HEART-BURN.
GA (GRAB)

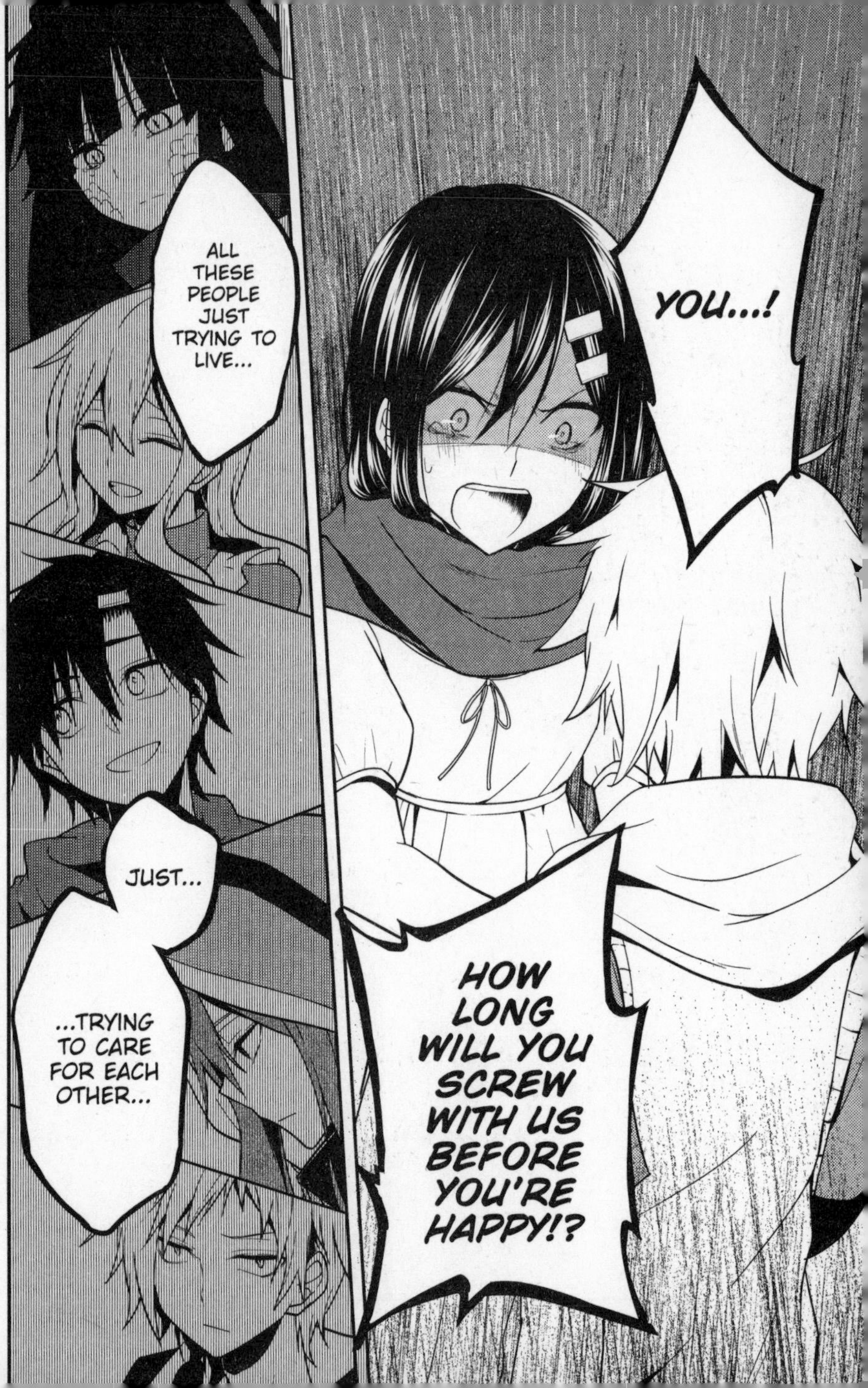
YOU...!
HOW LONG WILL YOU SCREW WITH US BEFORE YOU'RE HAPPY!?
ALL THESE PEOPLE JUST TRYING TO LIVE...
JUST...
...TRYING TO CARE FOR EACH OTHER...

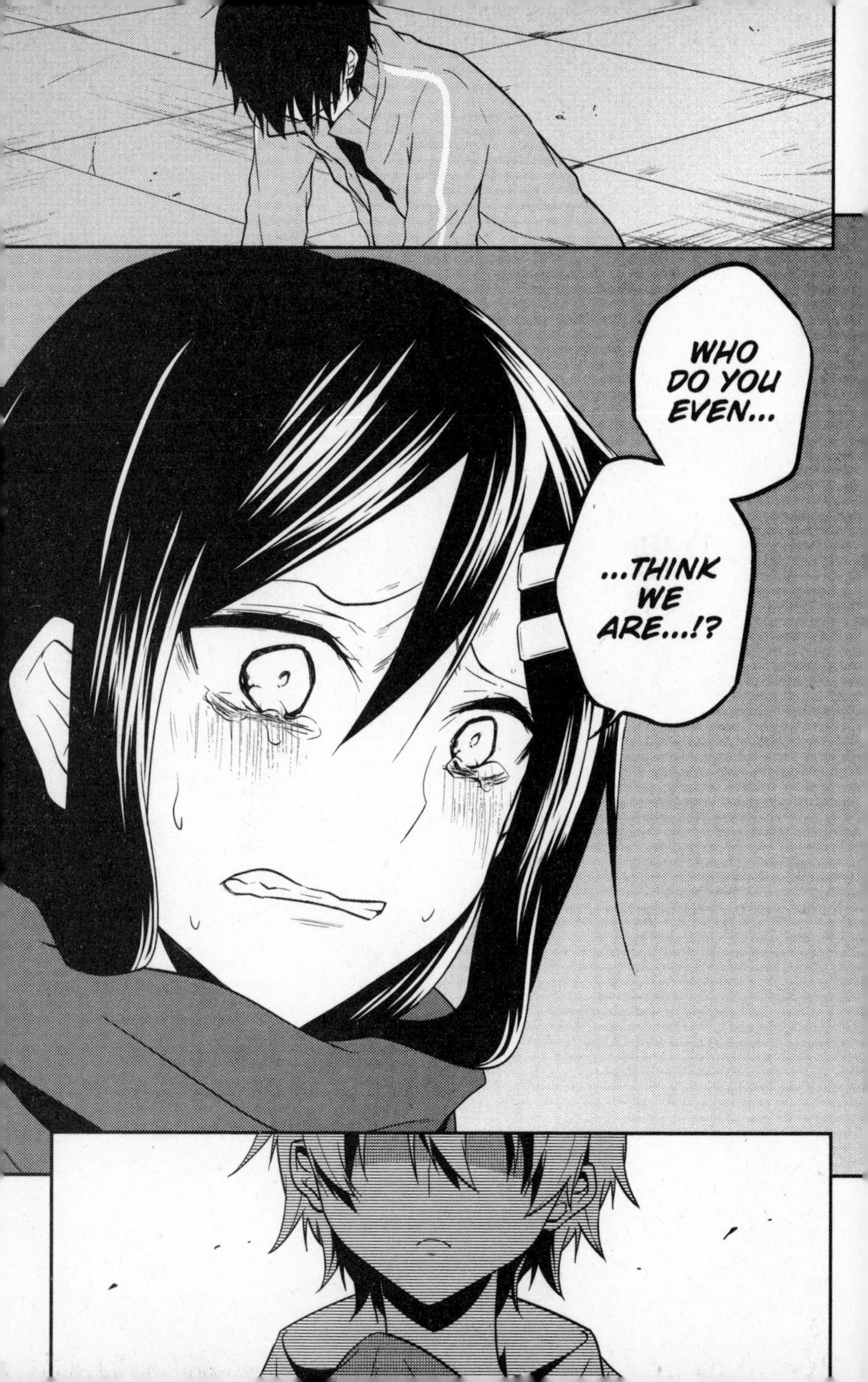
WHO DO YOU EVEN...
...THINK WE ARE...!?

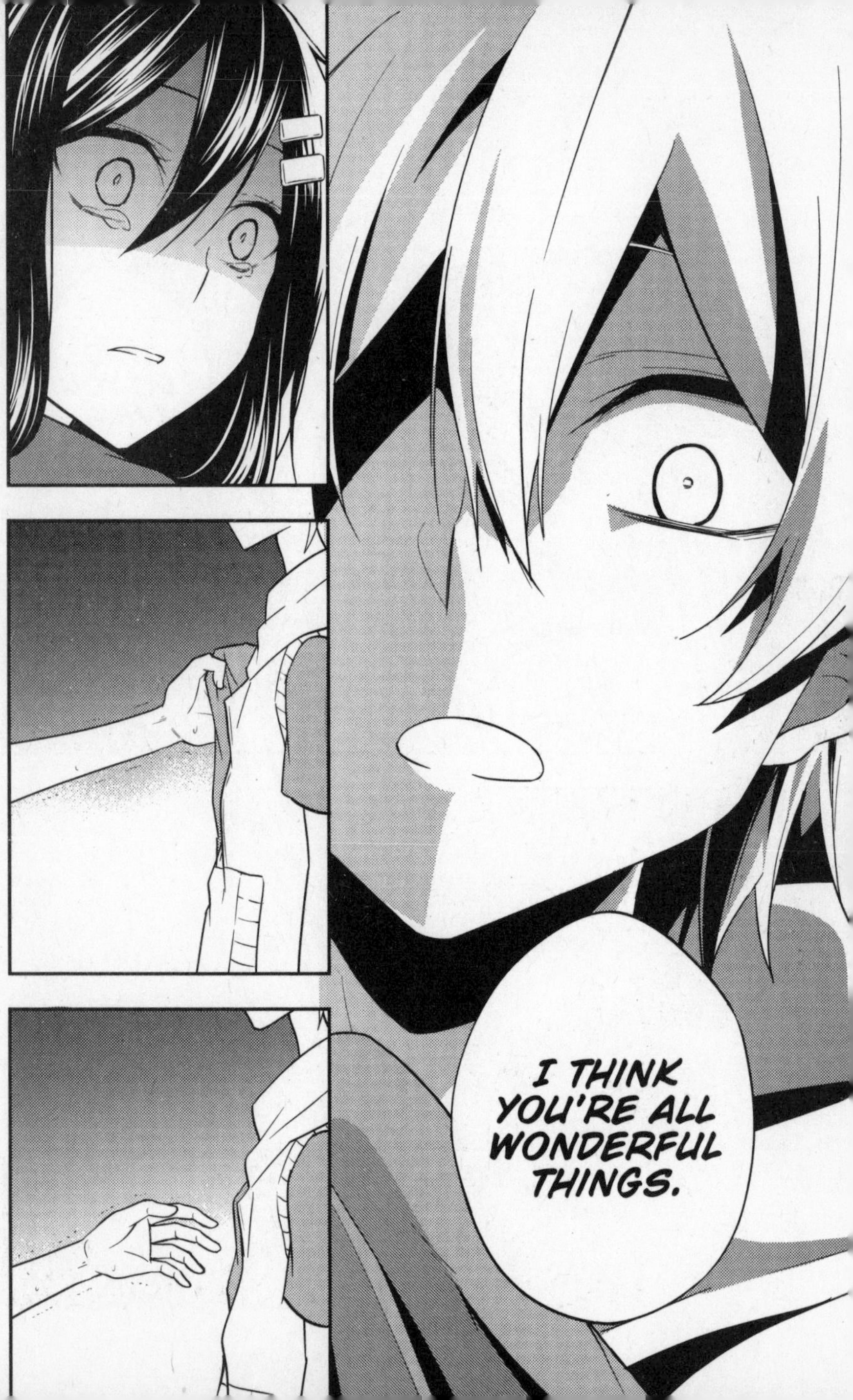
I THINK YOU'RE ALL WONDERFUL THINGS.

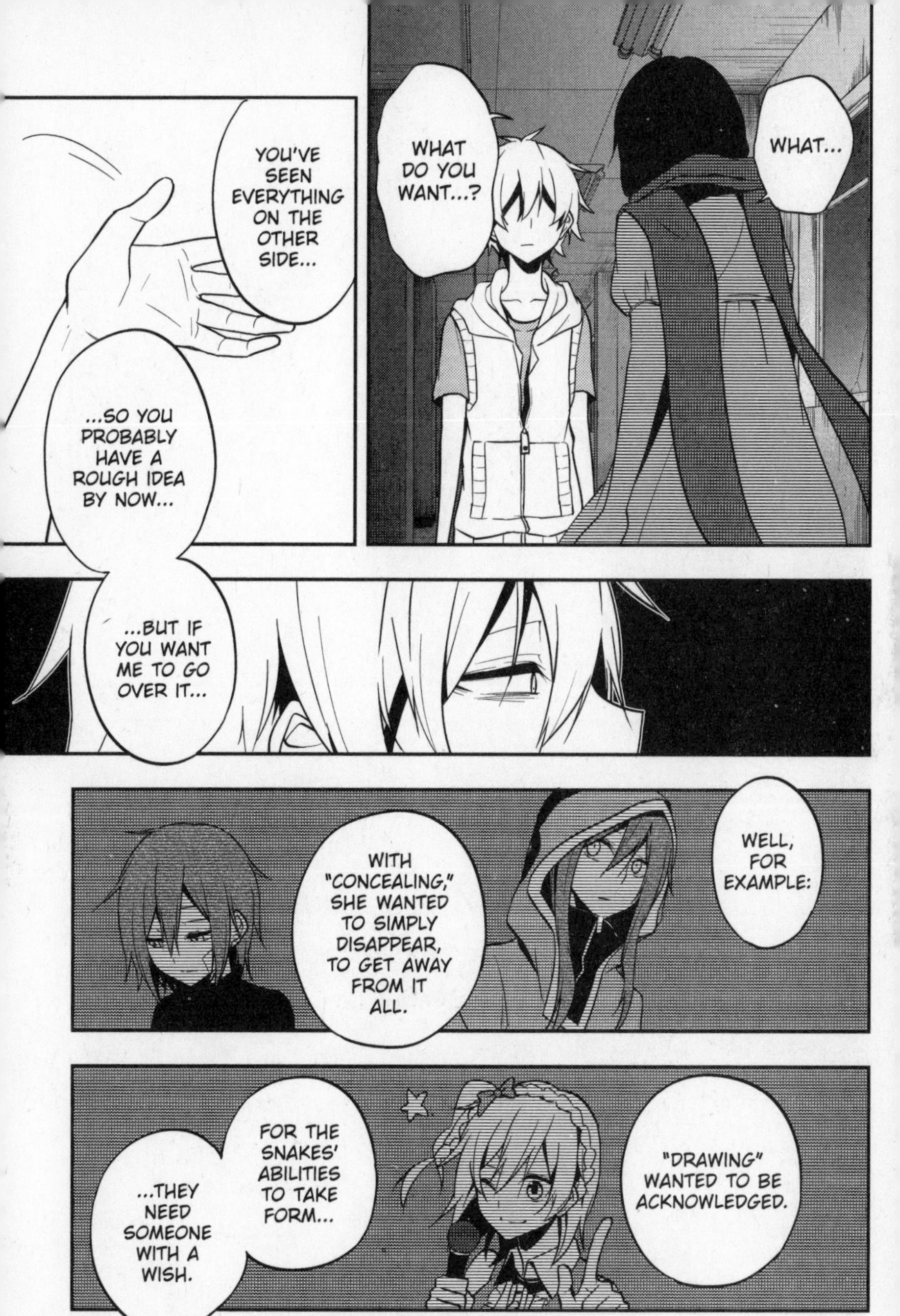
WHAT...
WHAT DO YOU WANT...?
YOU'VE SEEN EVERYTHING ON THE OTHER SIDE...
...SO YOU PROBABLY HAVE A ROUGH IDEA BY NOW...
...BUT IF YOU WANT ME TO GO OVER IT...
WELL, FOR EXAMPLE:
WITH "CONCEALING," SHE WANTED TO SIMPLY DISAPPEAR, TO GET AWAY FROM IT ALL.
"DRAWING" WANTED TO BE ACKNOWLEDGED.
FOR THE SNAKES' ABILITIES TO TAKE FORM...
...THEY NEED SOMEONE WITH A WISH.

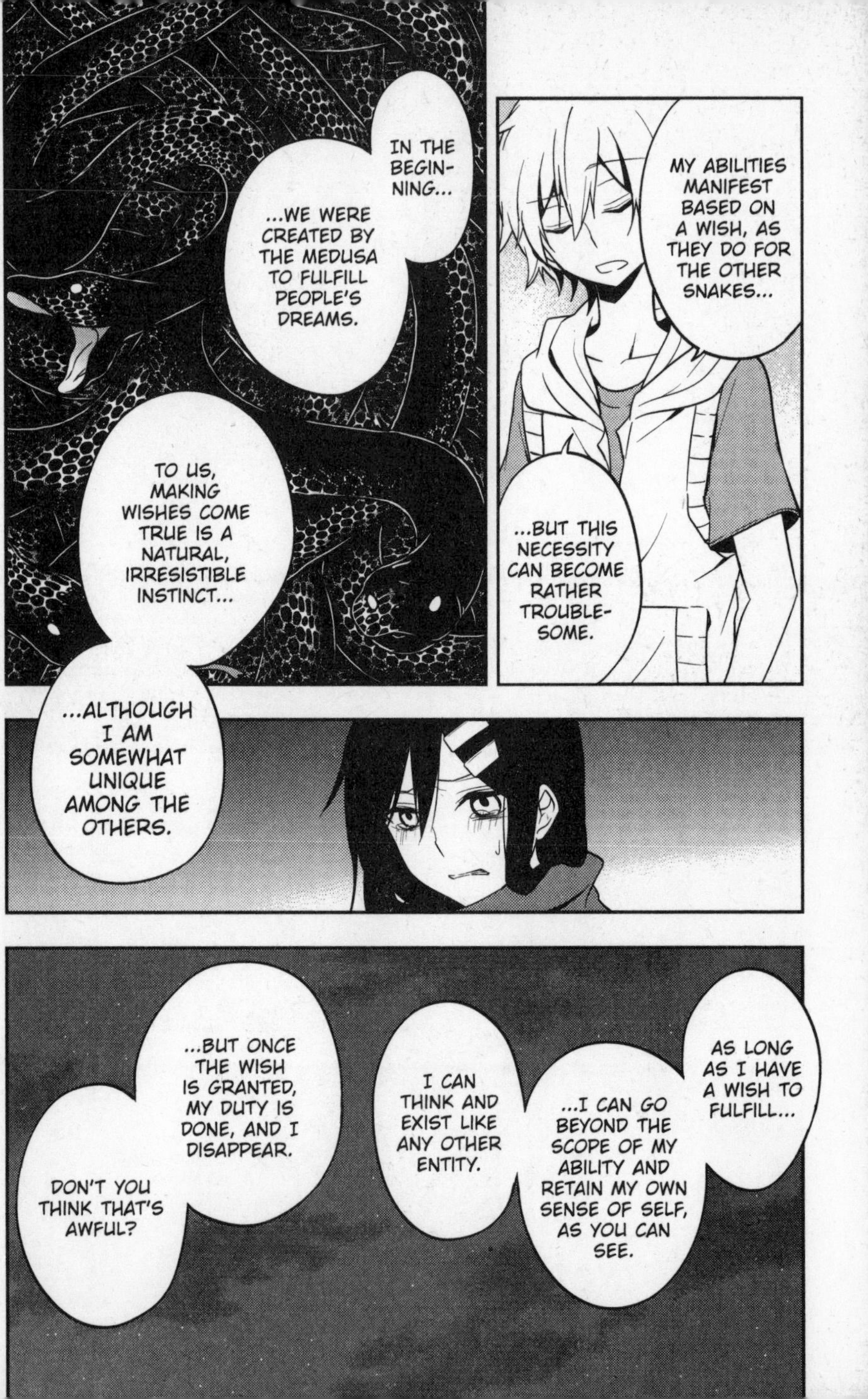
MY ABILITIES MANIFEST BASED ON A WISH, AS THEY DO FOR THE OTHER SNAKES...
...BUT THIS NECESSITY CAN BECOME RATHER TROUBLE-SOME.
IN THE BEGIN-NING...
...WE WERE CREATED BY THE MEDUSA TO FULFILL PEOPLE'S DREAMS.
TO US, MAKING WISHES COME TRUE IS A NATURAL, IRRESISTIBLE INSTINCT...
...ALTHOUGH I AM SOMEWHAT UNIQUE AMONG THE OTHERS.
AS LONG AS I HAVE A WISH TO FULFILL...
...I CAN GO BEYOND THE SCOPE OF MY ABILITY AND RETAIN MY OWN SENSE OF SELF, AS YOU CAN SEE.
I CAN THINK AND EXIST LIKE ANY OTHER ENTITY.
...BUT ONCE THE WISH IS GRANTED, MY DUTY IS DONE, AND I DISAPPEAR.
DON'T YOU THINK THAT'S AWFUL?

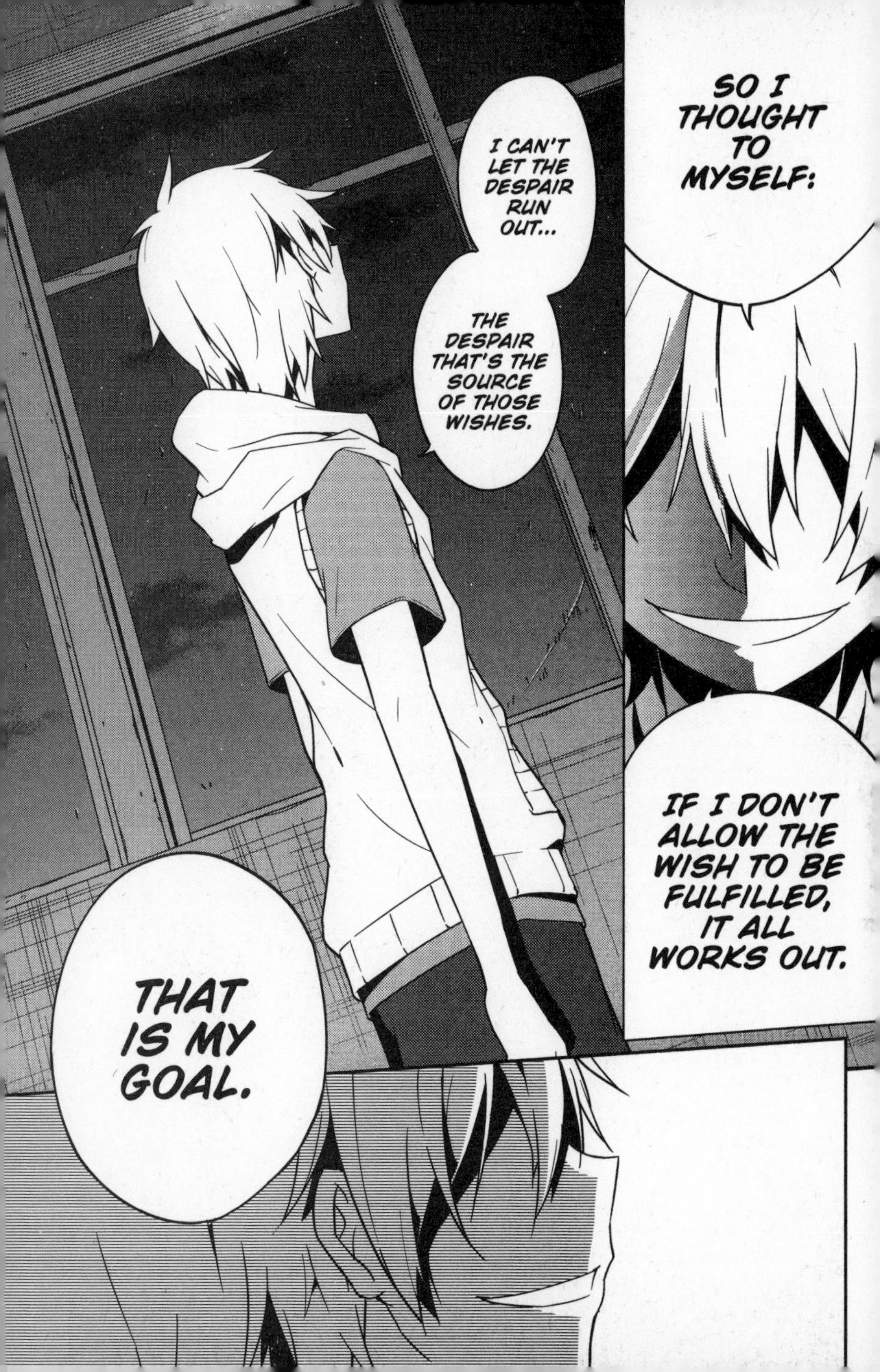
SO I THOUGHT TO MYSELF:
IF I DON'T ALLOW THE WISH TO BE FULFILLED, IT ALL WORKS OUT.
I CAN'T LET THE DESPAIR RUN OUT...
THE DESPAIR THAT'S THE SOURCE OF THOSE WISHES.
THAT IS MY GOAL.

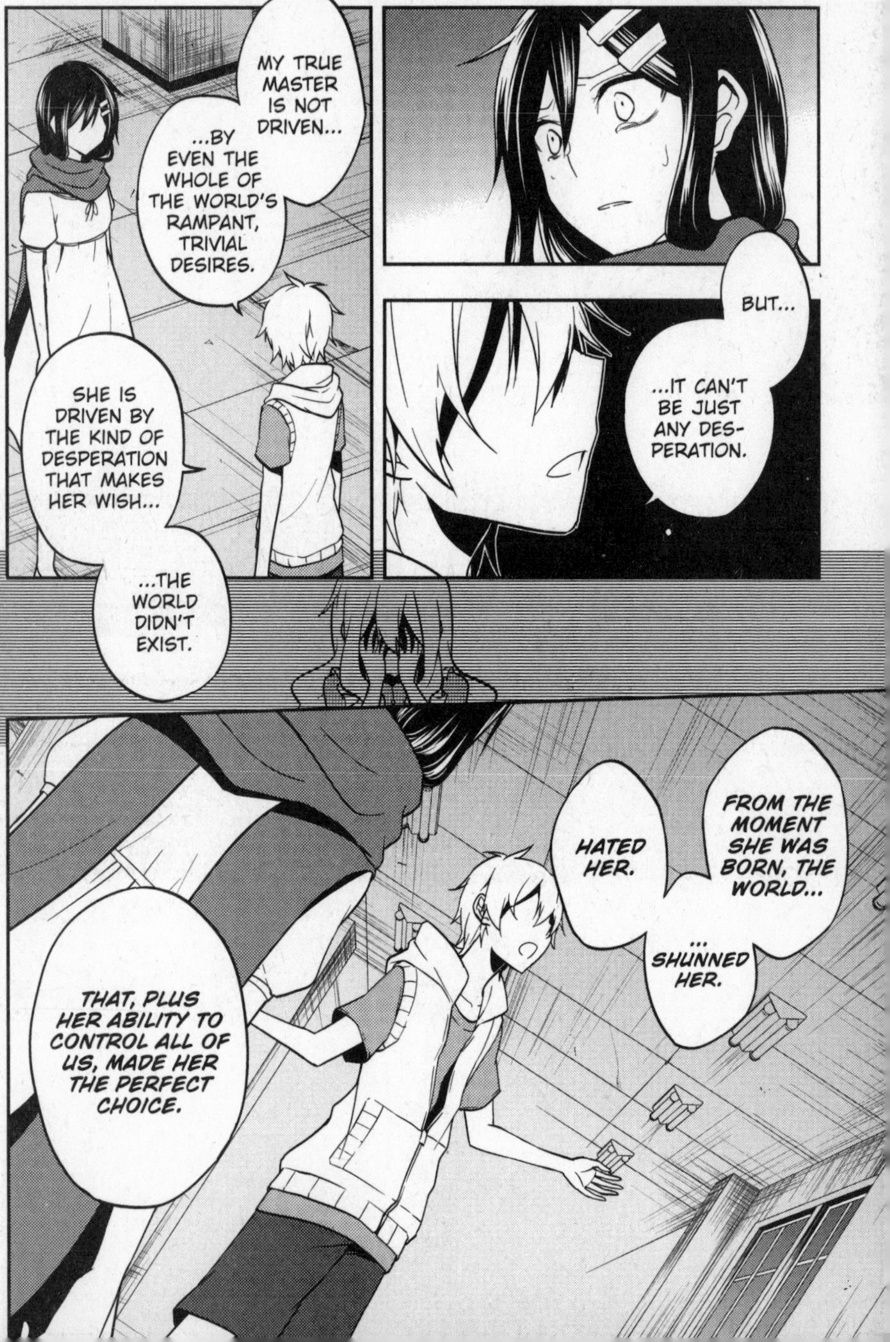
BUT...
...IT CAN'T BE JUST ANY DES-PERATION.
MY TRUE MASTER IS NOT DRIVEN...
...BY EVEN THE WHOLE OF THE WORLD'S RAMPANT, TRIVIAL DESIRES.
SHE IS DRIVEN BY THE KIND OF DESPERATION THAT MAKES HER WISH...
...THE WORLD DIDN'T EXIST.
FROM THE MOMENT SHE WAS BORN, THE WORLD...
HATED HER.
...SHUNNED HER.
THAT, PLUS HER ABILITY TO CONTROL ALL OF US, MADE HER THE PERFECT CHOICE.

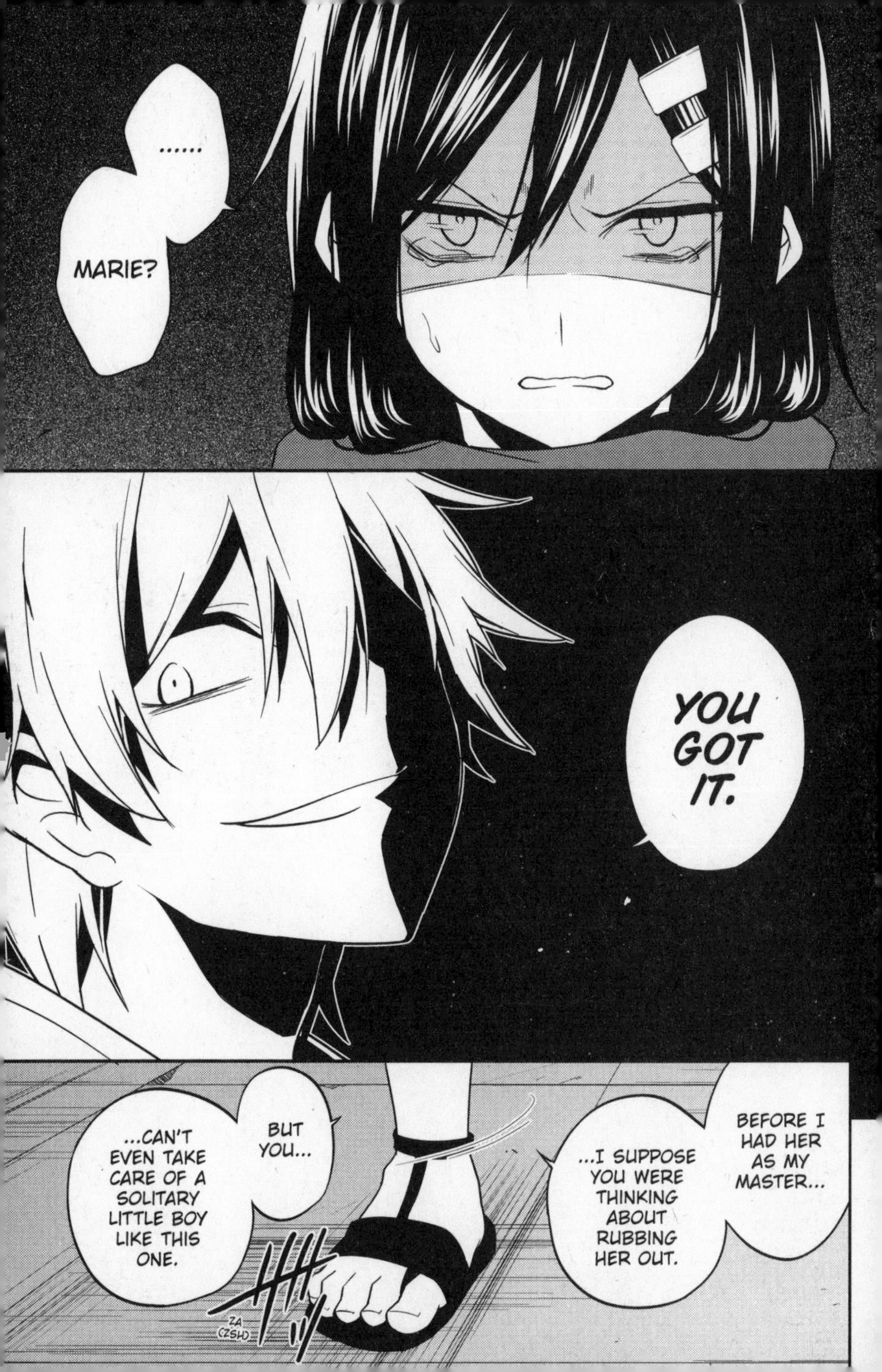
......
MARIE?
YOU GOT IT.
BEFORE I HAD HER AS MY MASTER...
...I SUPPOSE YOU WERE THINKING ABOUT RUBBING HER OUT.
BUT YOU...
...CAN'T EVEN TAKE CARE OF A SOLITARY LITTLE BOY LIKE THIS ONE.
ZA (ZSH)

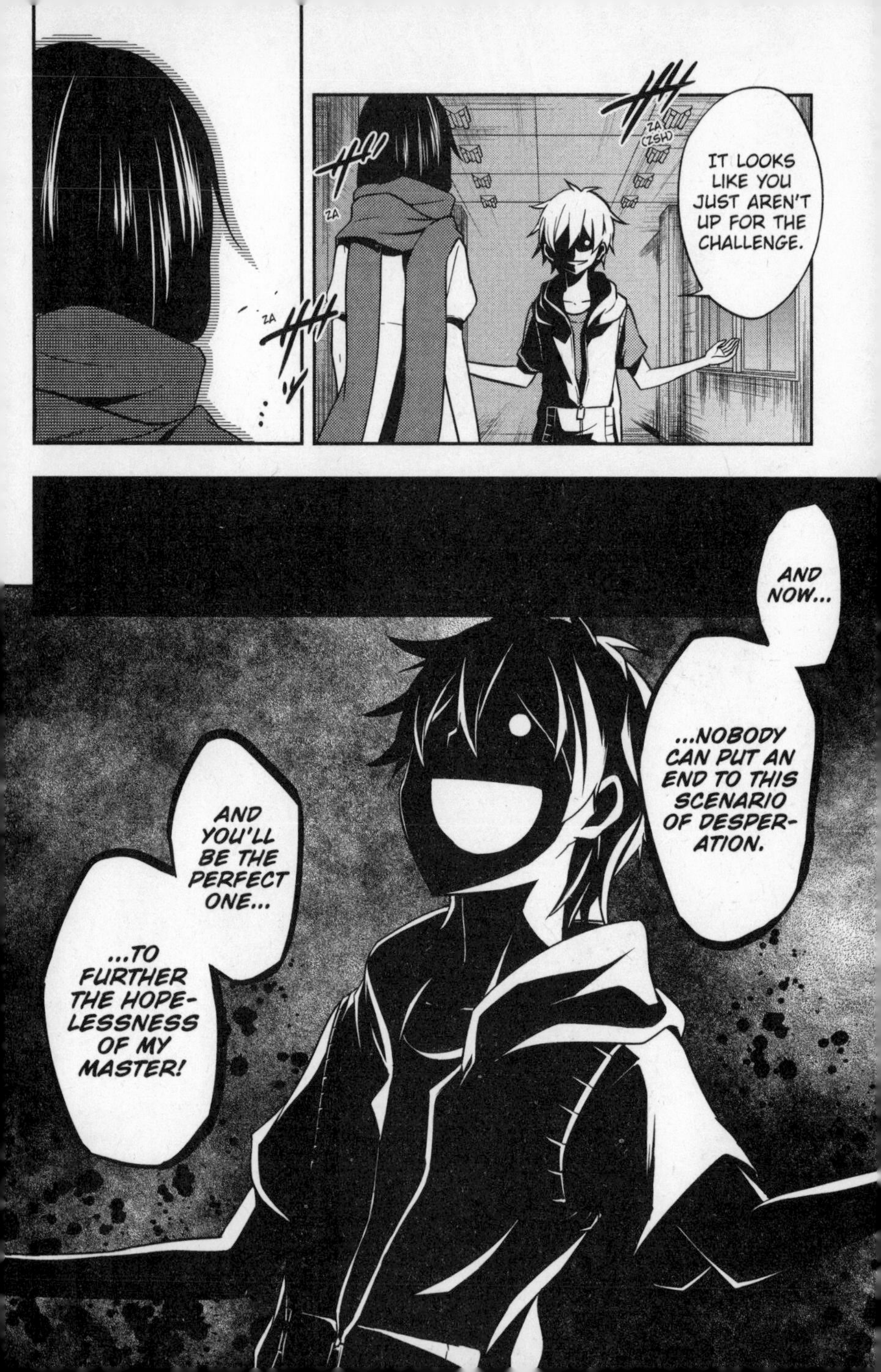
ZA (ZSH)
IT LOOKS LIKE YOU JUST AREN'T UP FOR THE CHALLENGE.
ZA
ZA
AND NOW...
...NOBODY CAN PUT AN END TO THIS SCENARIO OF DESPER-ATION.
AND YOU'LL BE THE PERFECT ONE...
...TO FURTHER THE HOPE-LESSNESS OF MY MASTER!

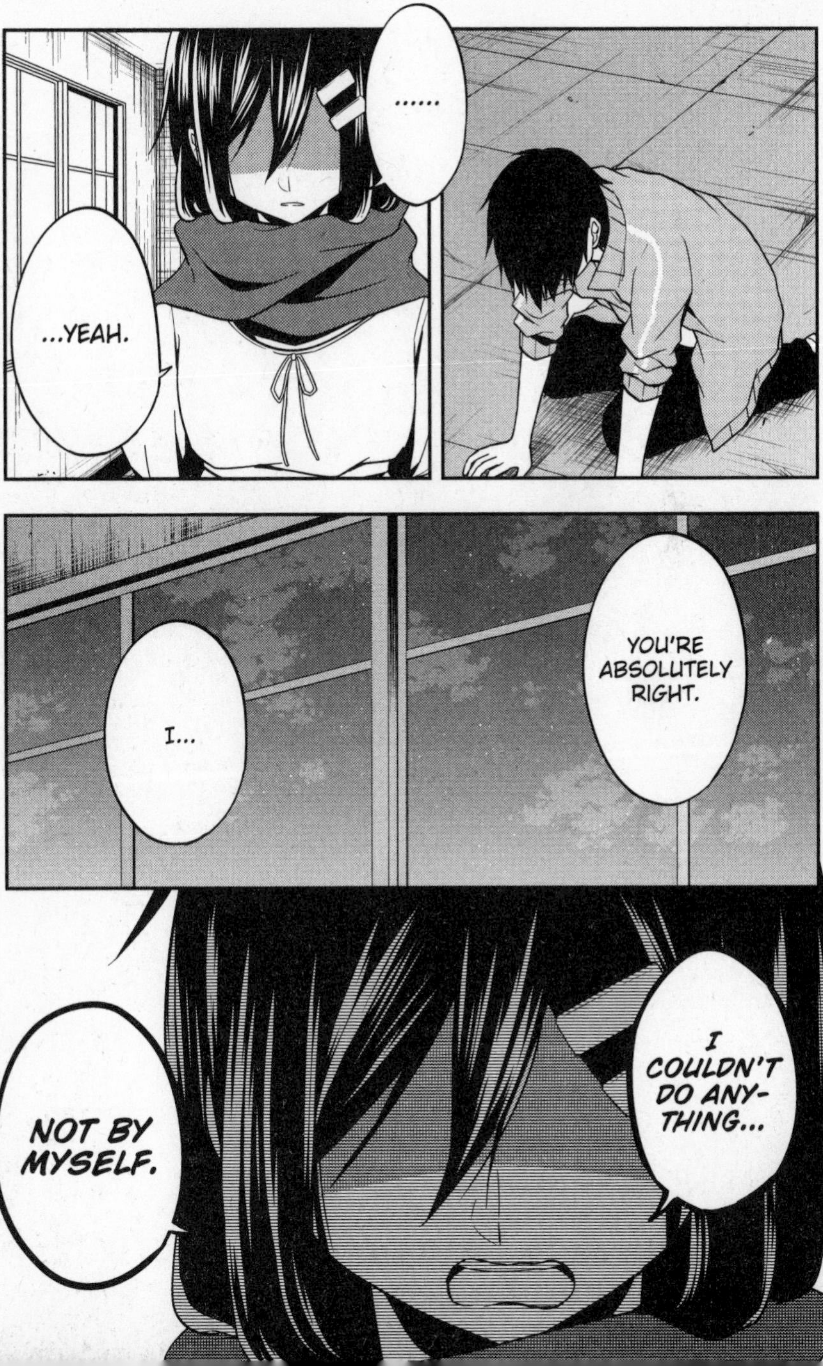
......
...YEAH.
YOU'RE ABSOLUTELY RIGHT.
I...
I COULDN'T DO ANY-THING...
NOT BY MYSELF.

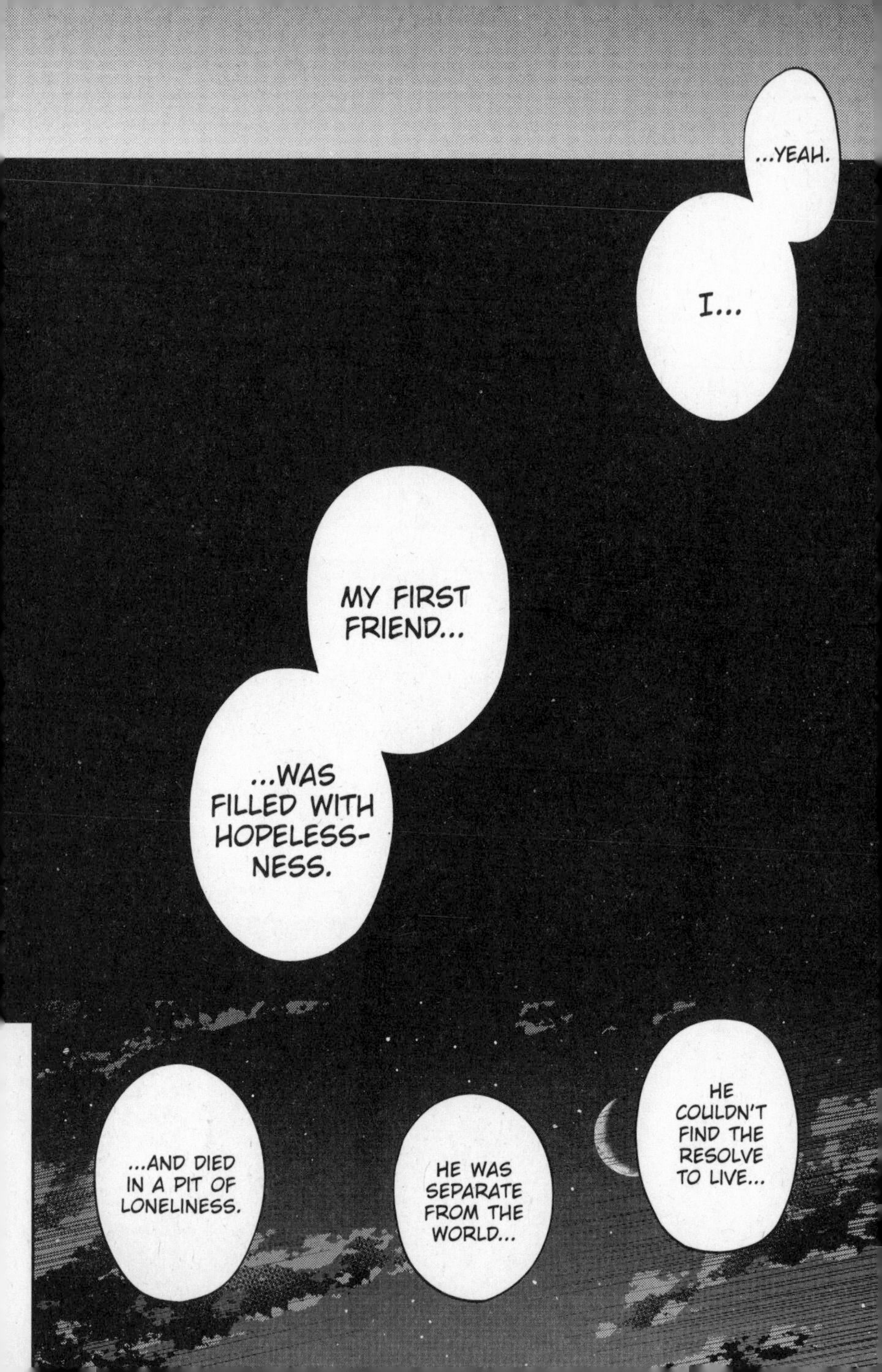
...YEAH.
I...
MY FIRST FRIEND...
...WAS FILLED WITH HOPELESS-NESS.
HE COULDN'T FIND THE RESOLVE TO LIVE...
HE WAS SEPARATE FROM THE WORLD...
...AND DIED IN A PIT OF LONELINESS.

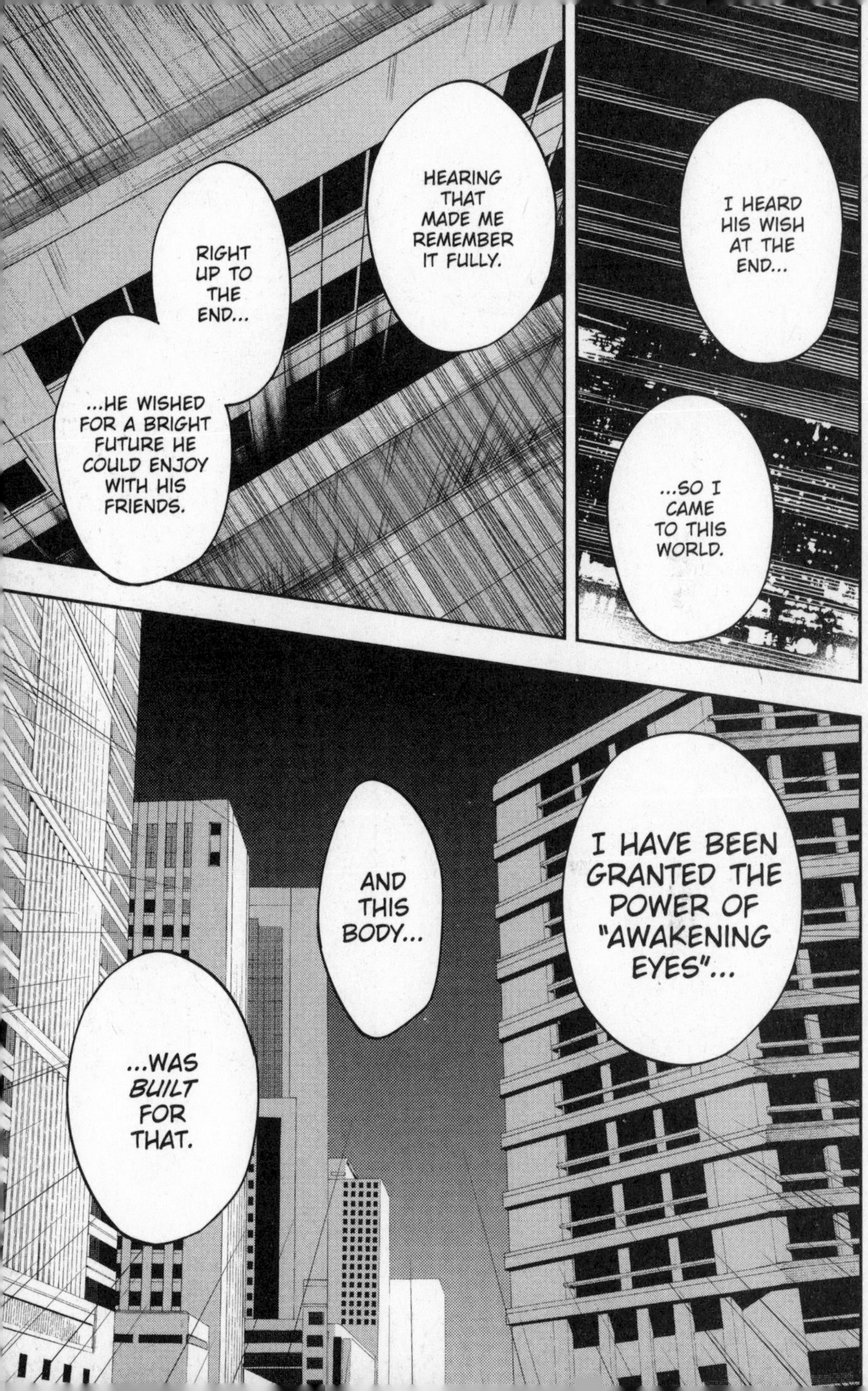
I HEARD HIS WISH AT THE END...
...SO I CAME TO THIS WORLD.
HEARING THAT MADE ME REMEMBER IT FULLY.
RIGHT UP TO THE END...
...HE WISHED FOR A BRIGHT FUTURE HE COULD ENJOY WITH HIS FRIENDS.
I HAVE BEEN GRANTED THE POWER OF "AWAKENING EYES"...
AND THIS BODY...
...WAS *BUILT* FOR THAT.

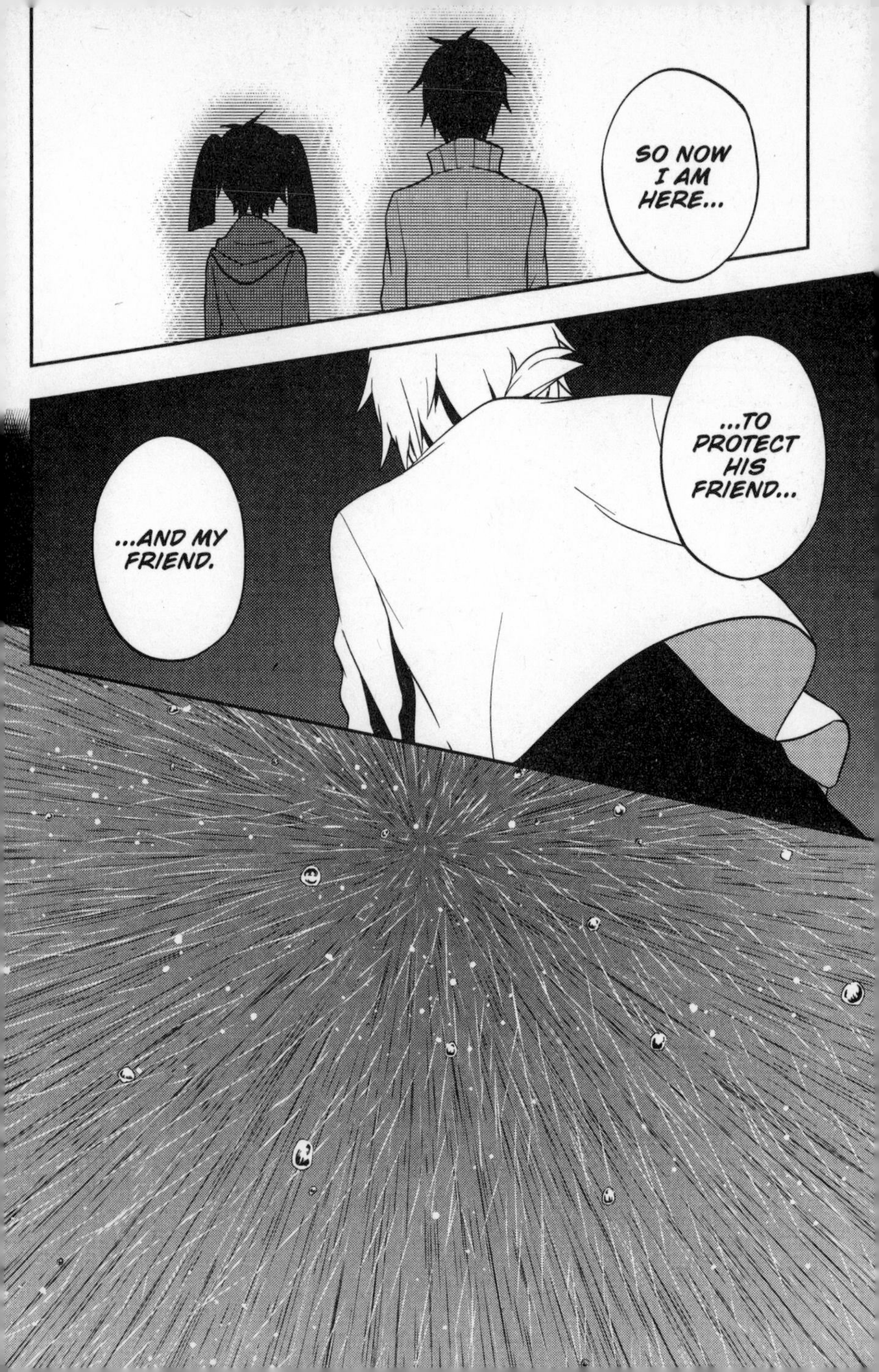
SO NOW I AM HERE...
...TO PROTECT HIS FRIEND...
...AND MY FRIEND.

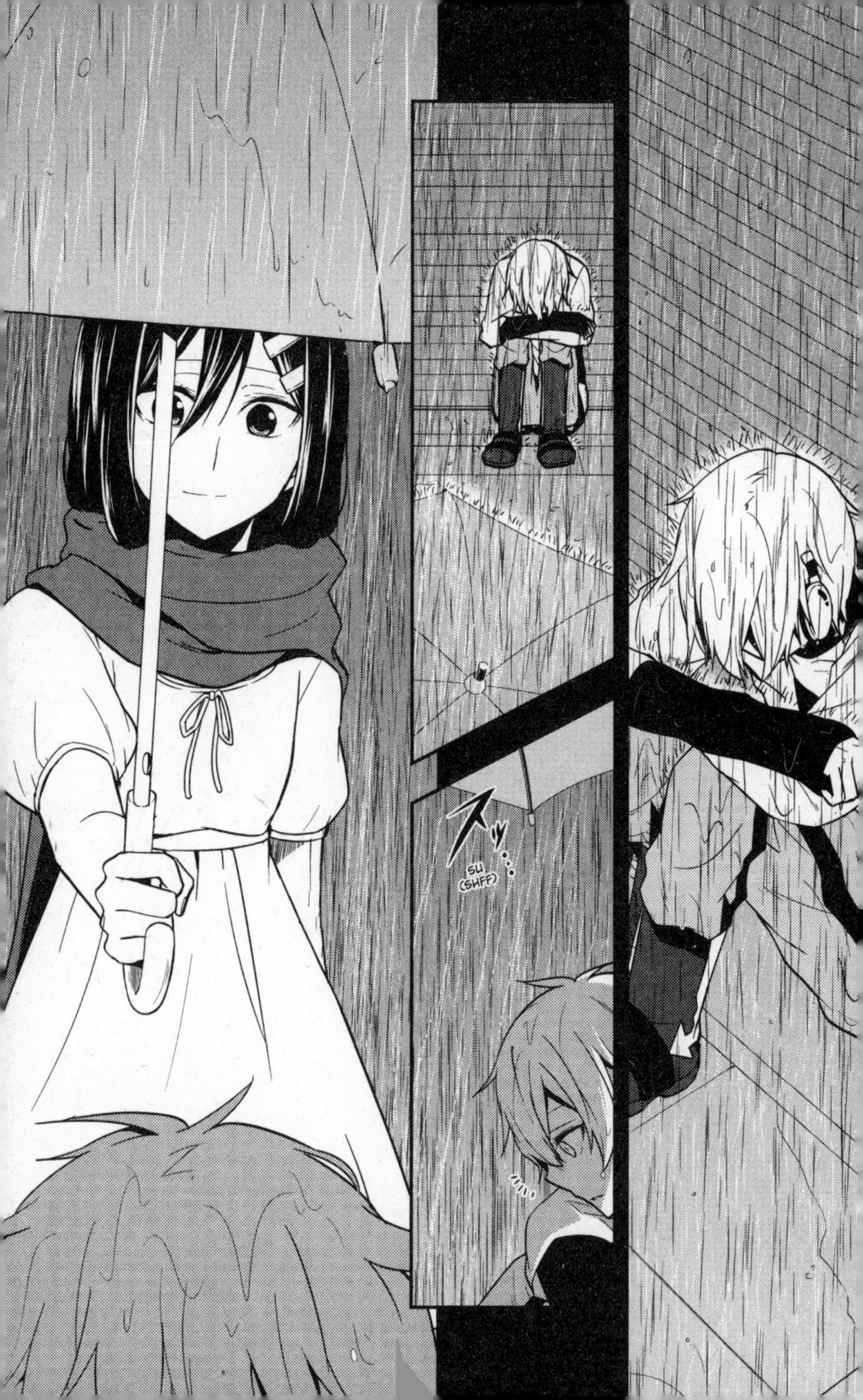
スッ…
SU
(SHFF)

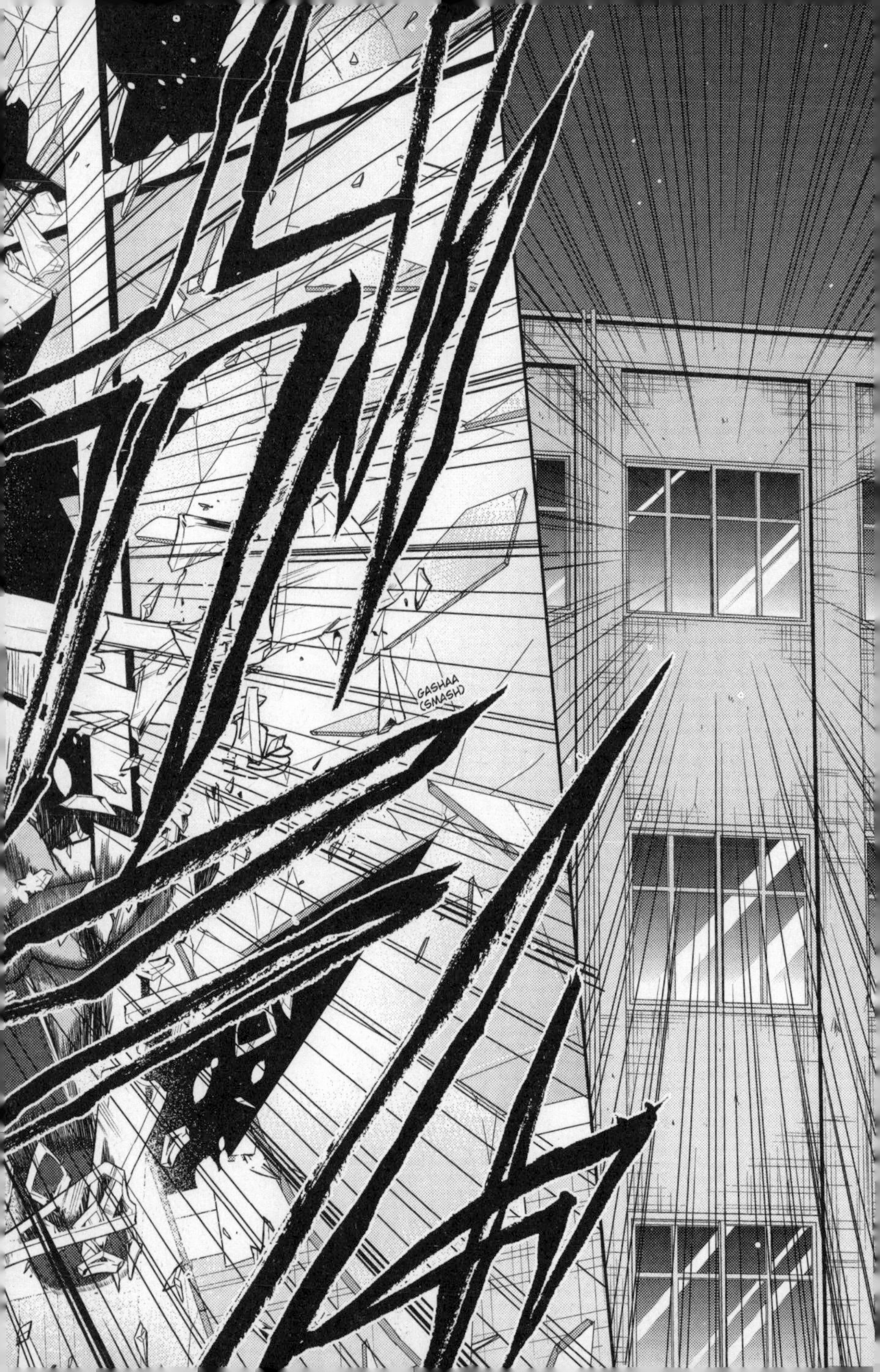
GASHAA
(SMASH)

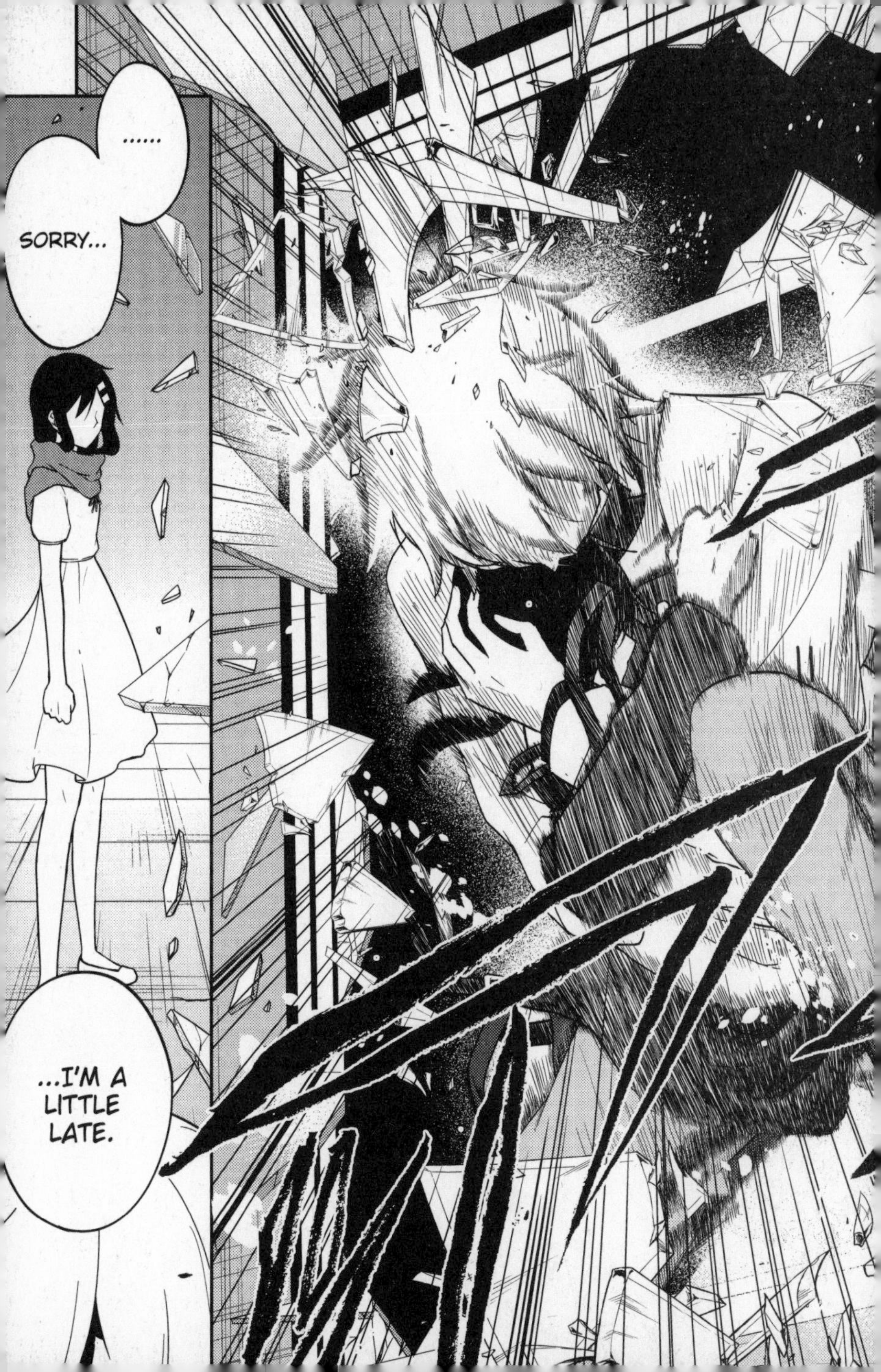
......
SORRY...
...I'M A LITTLE LATE.

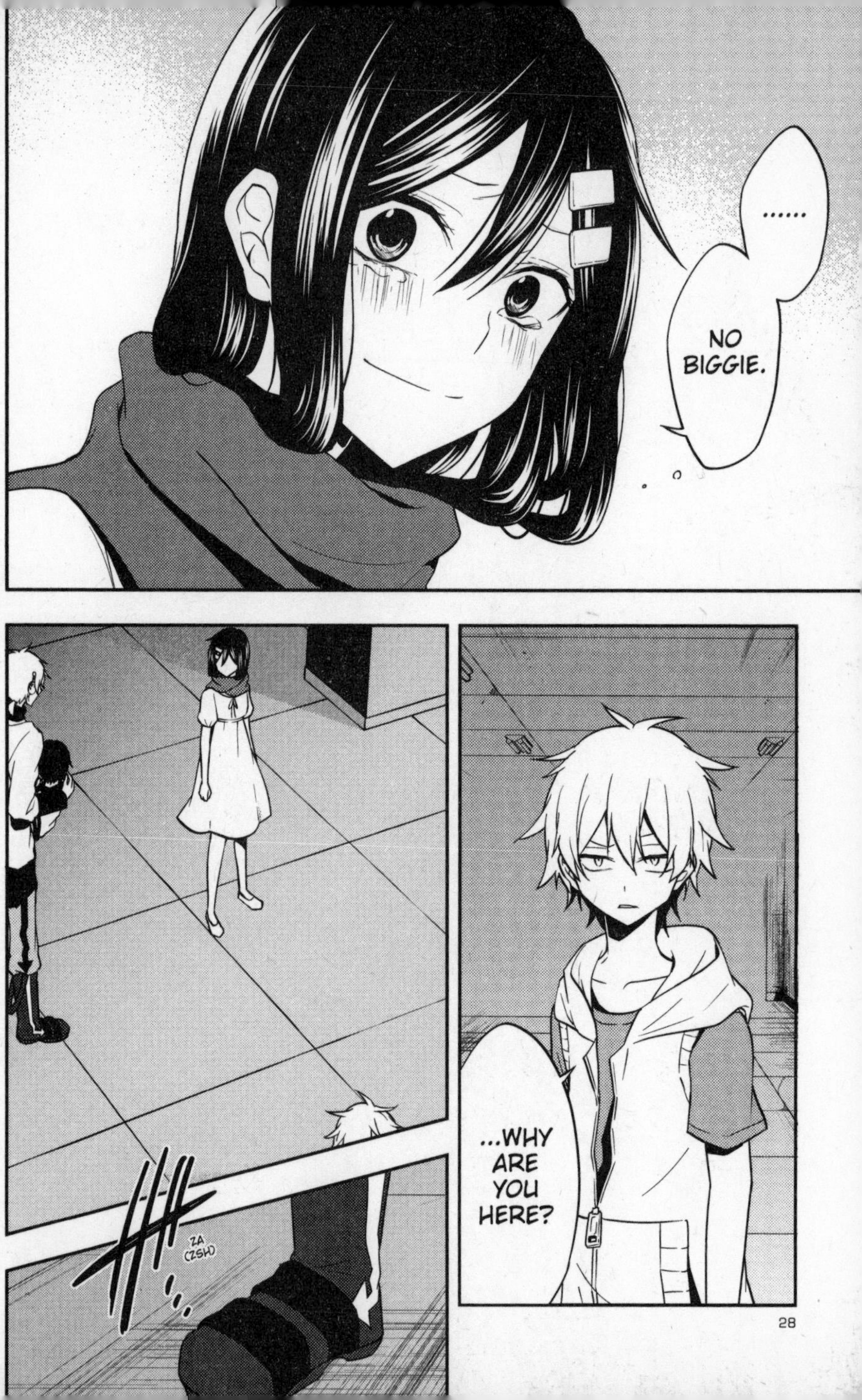
......
NO BIGGIE.
...WHY ARE YOU HERE?
ZA (ZSH)

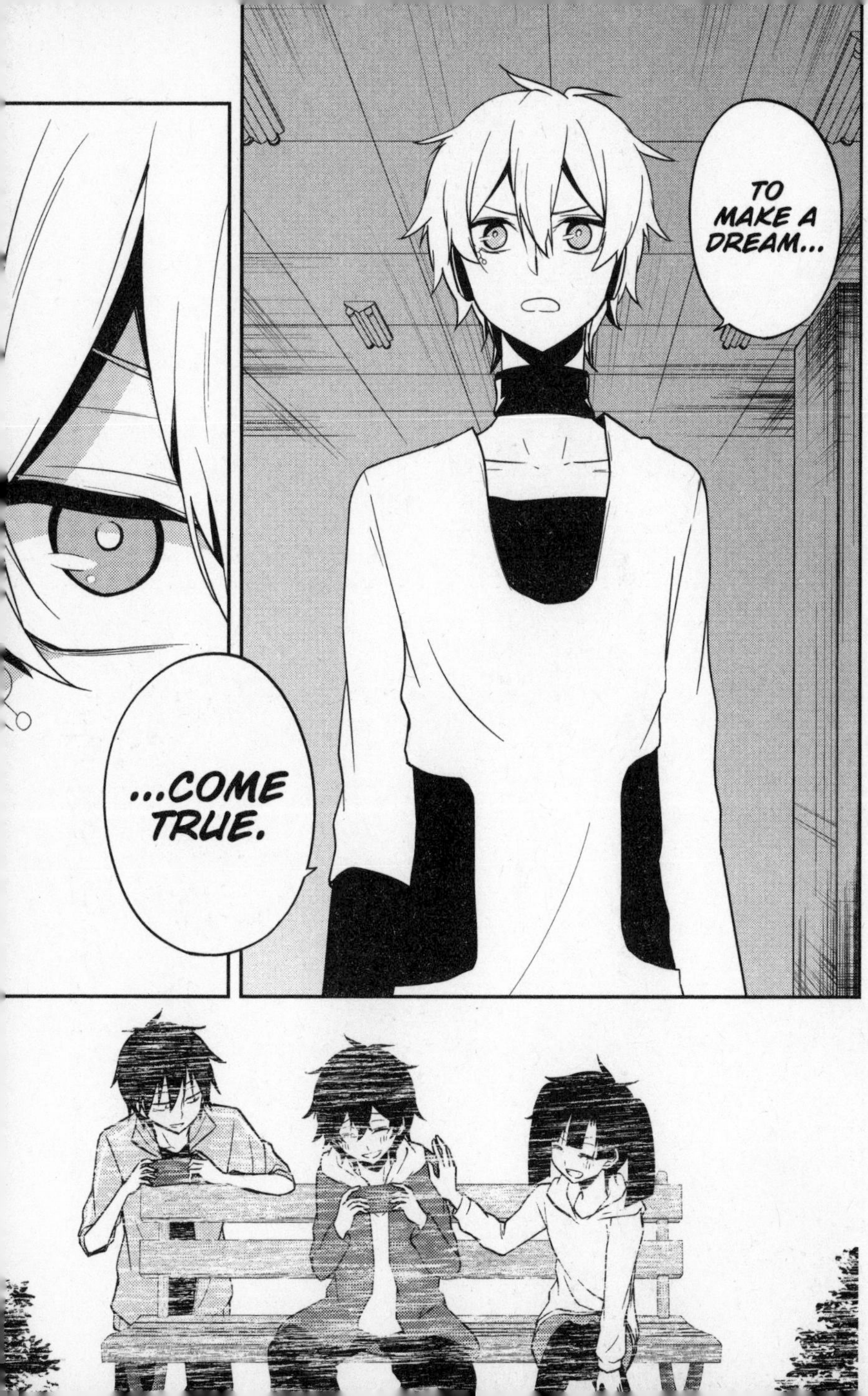
TO MAKE A DREAM...
...COME TRUE.

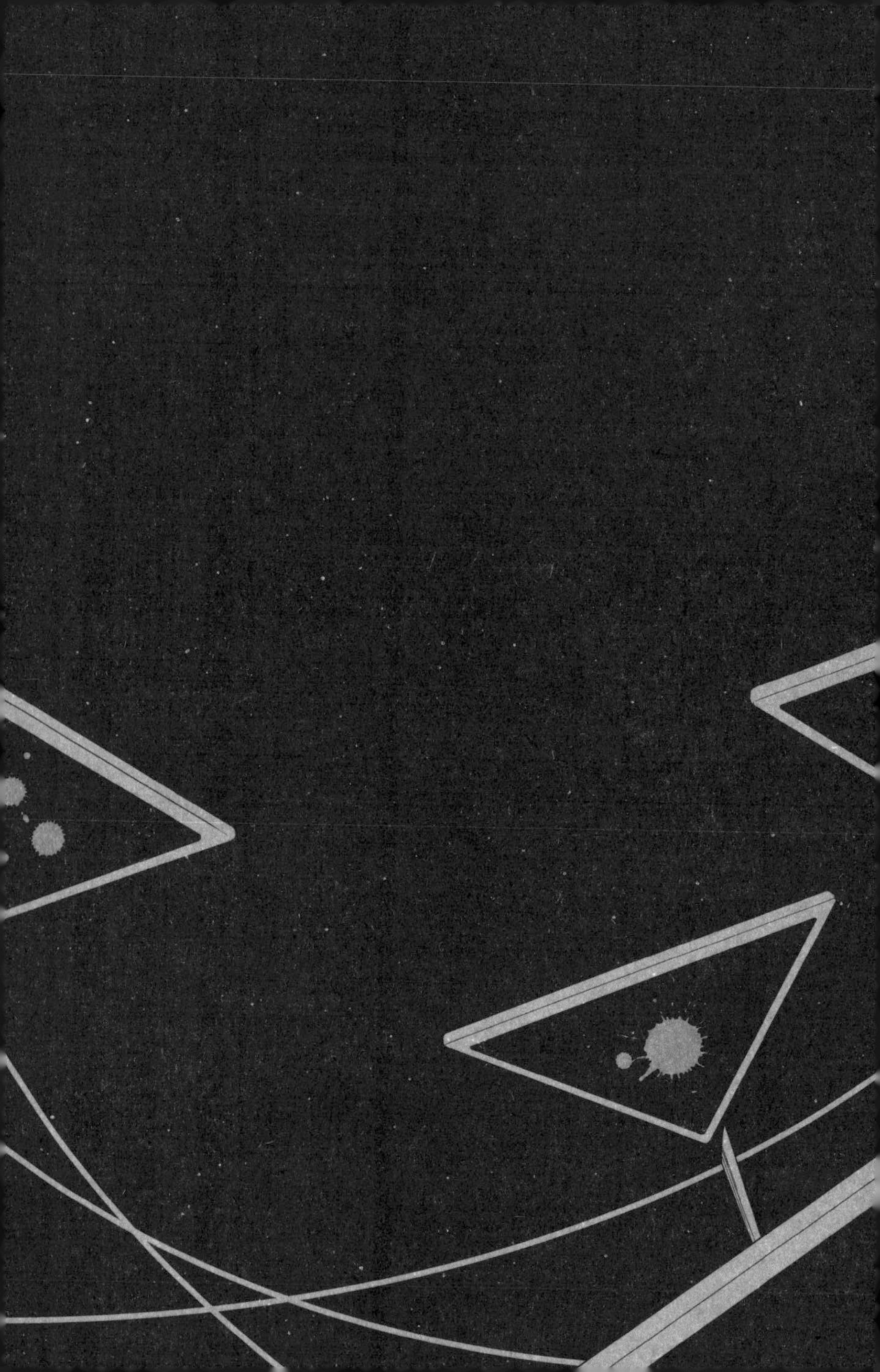

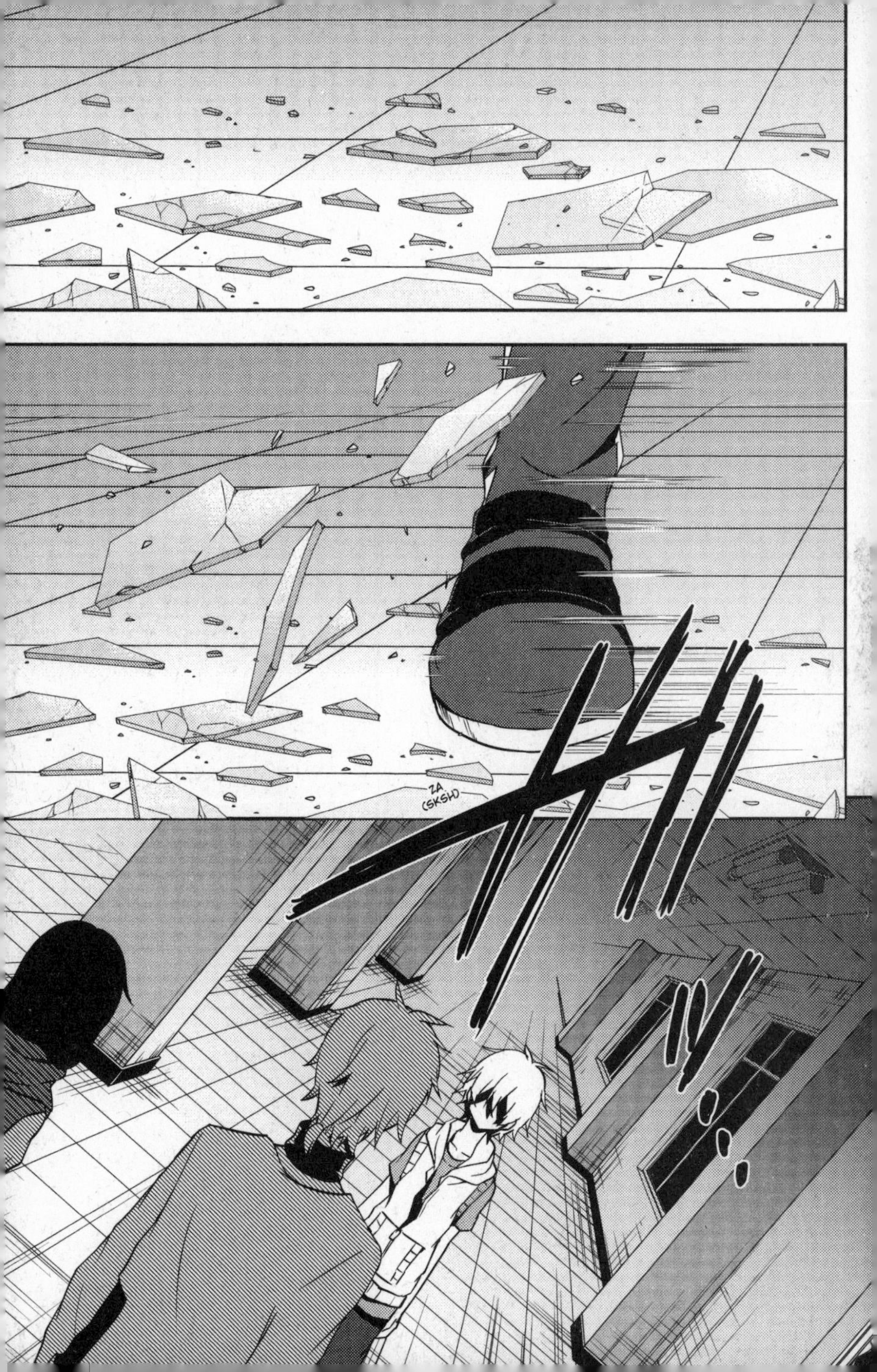
ZA
(SKSH)

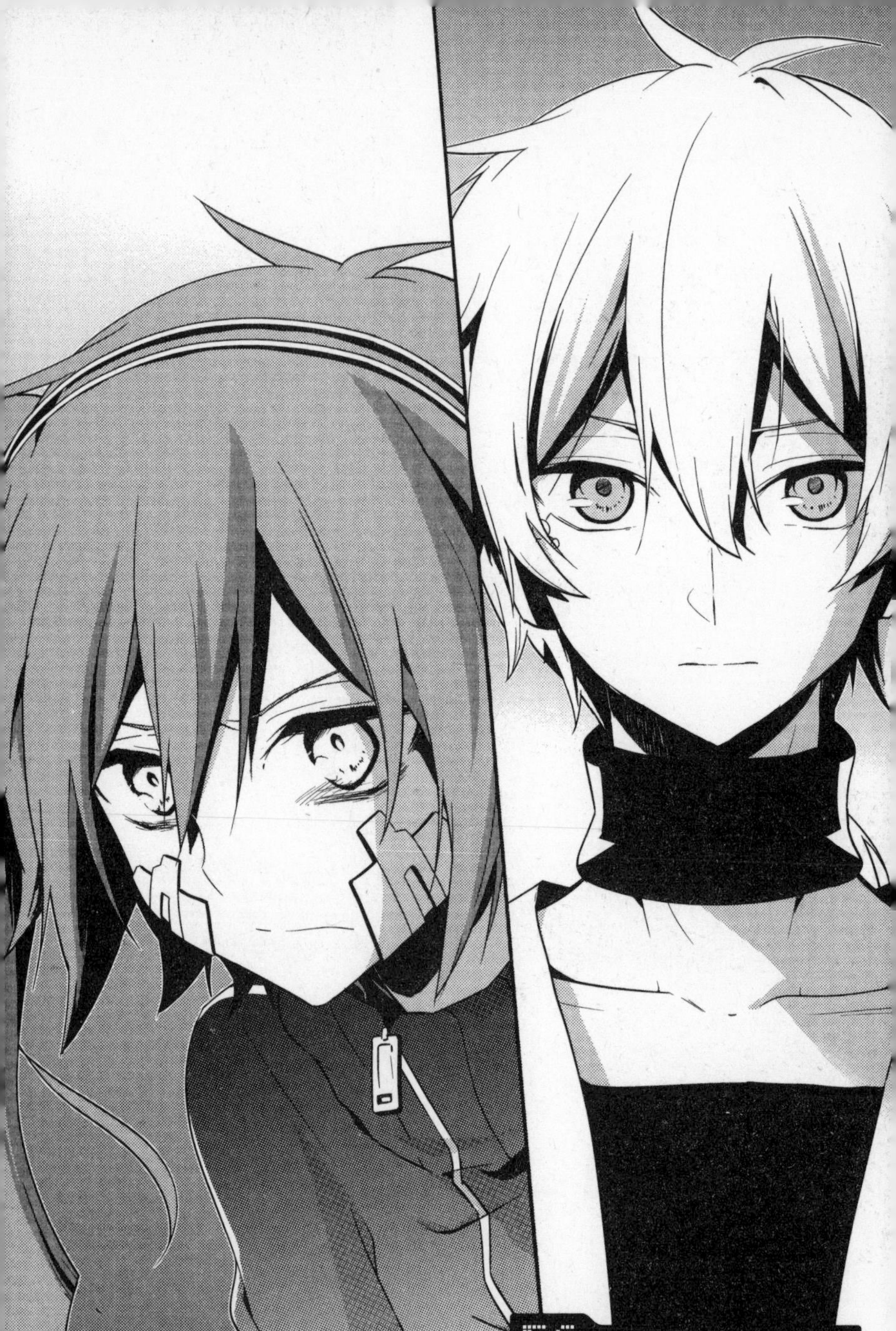

56 >> ADDITIONAL MEMORY II

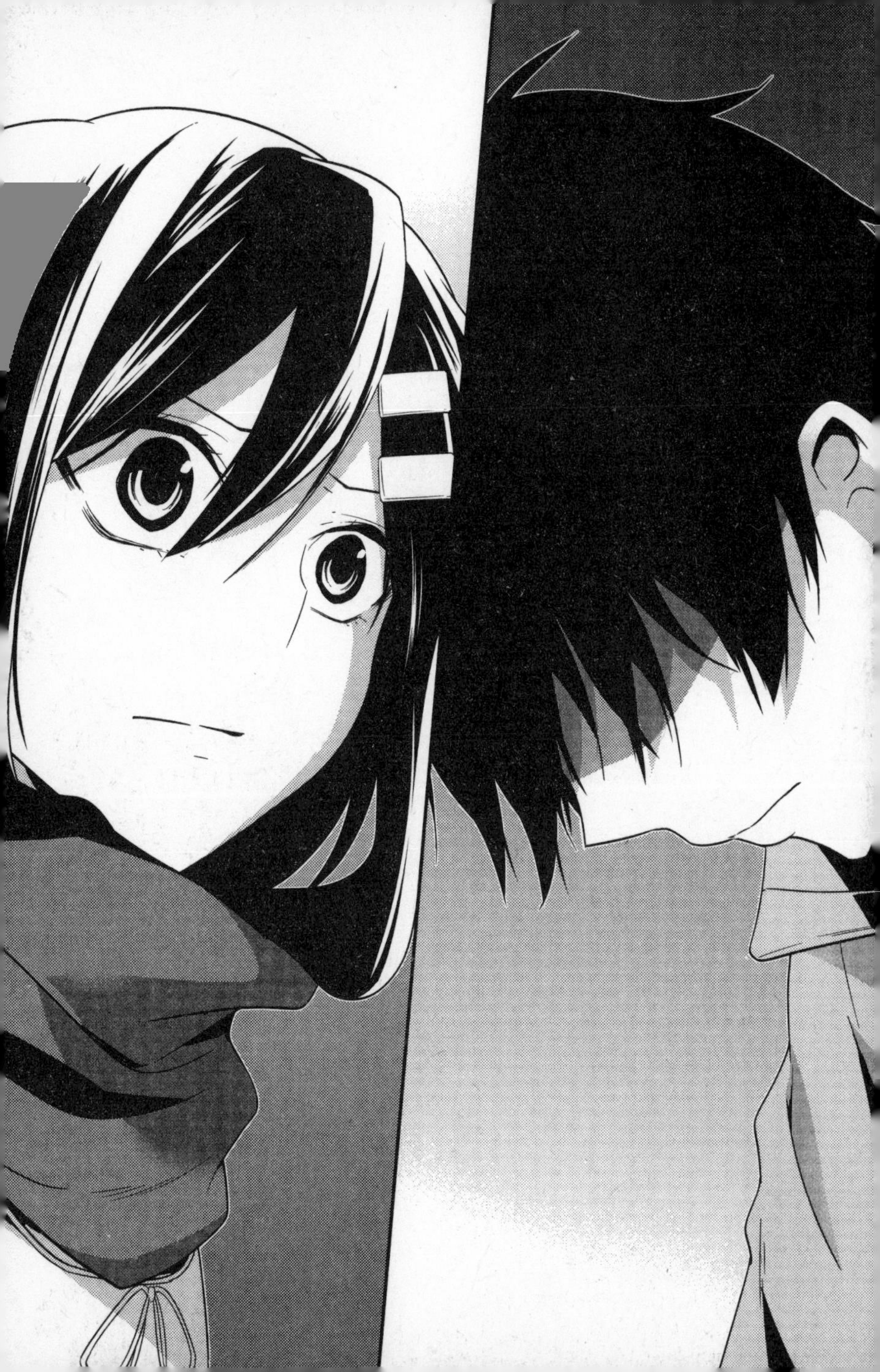

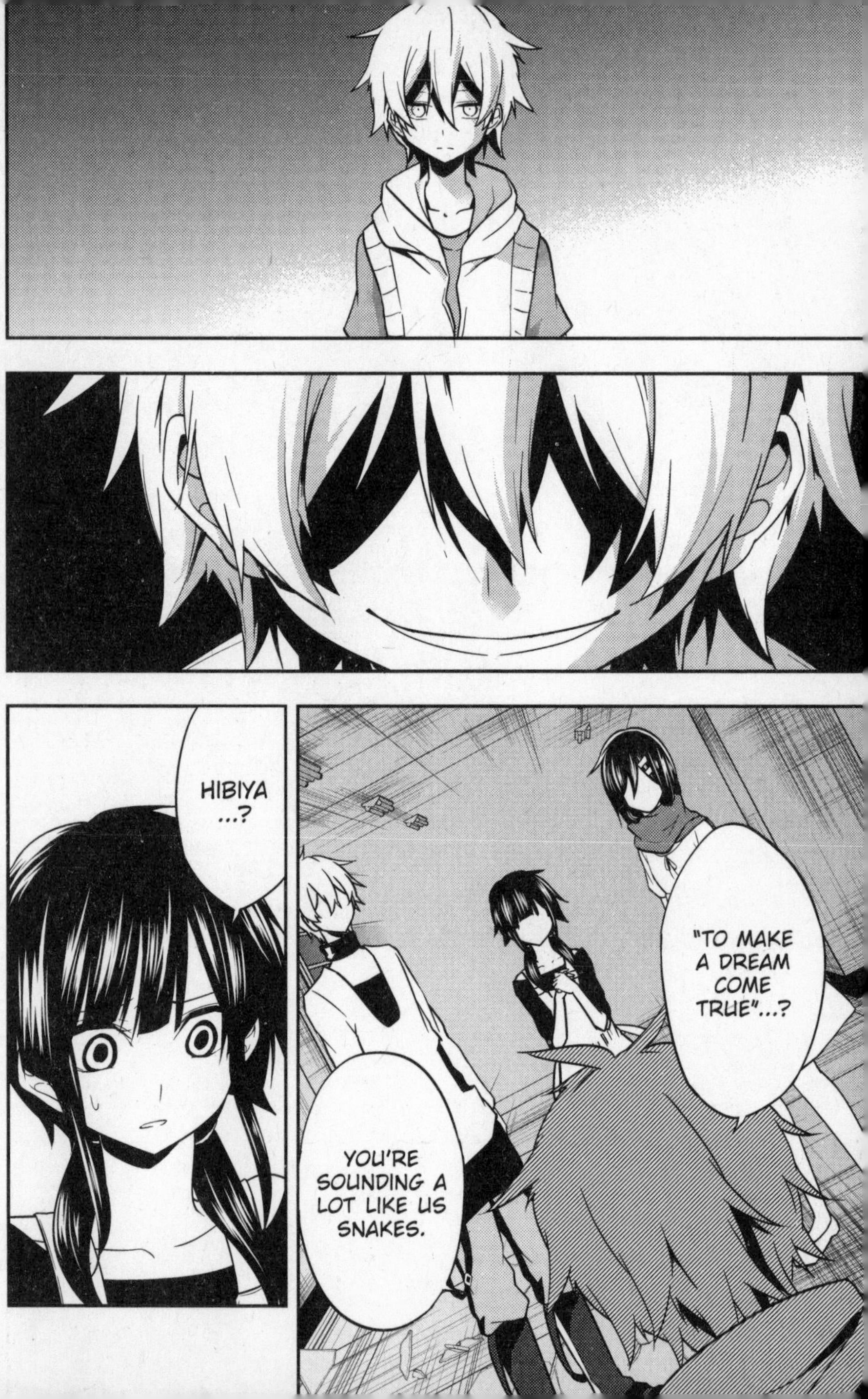
"TO MAKE A DREAM COME TRUE"...?
YOU'RE SOUNDING A LOT LIKE US SNAKES.
HIBIYA ...?

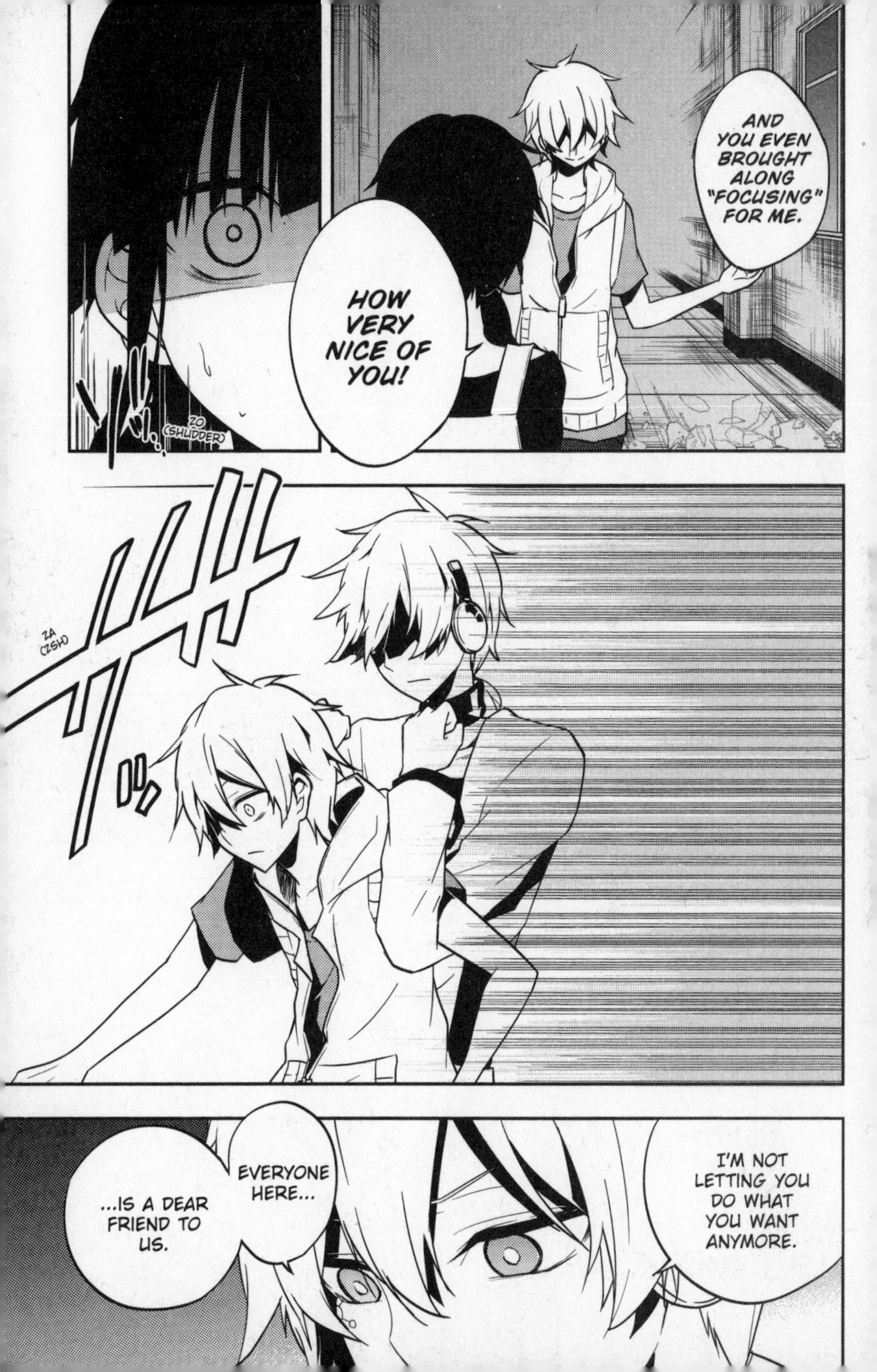
AND YOU EVEN BROUGHT ALONG "FOCUSING" FOR ME.
HOW VERY NICE OF YOU!
ZO (SHUDDER)
ZA (ZSH)
I'M NOT LETTING YOU DO WHAT YOU WANT ANYMORE.
EVERYONE HERE...
...IS A DEAR FRIEND TO US.

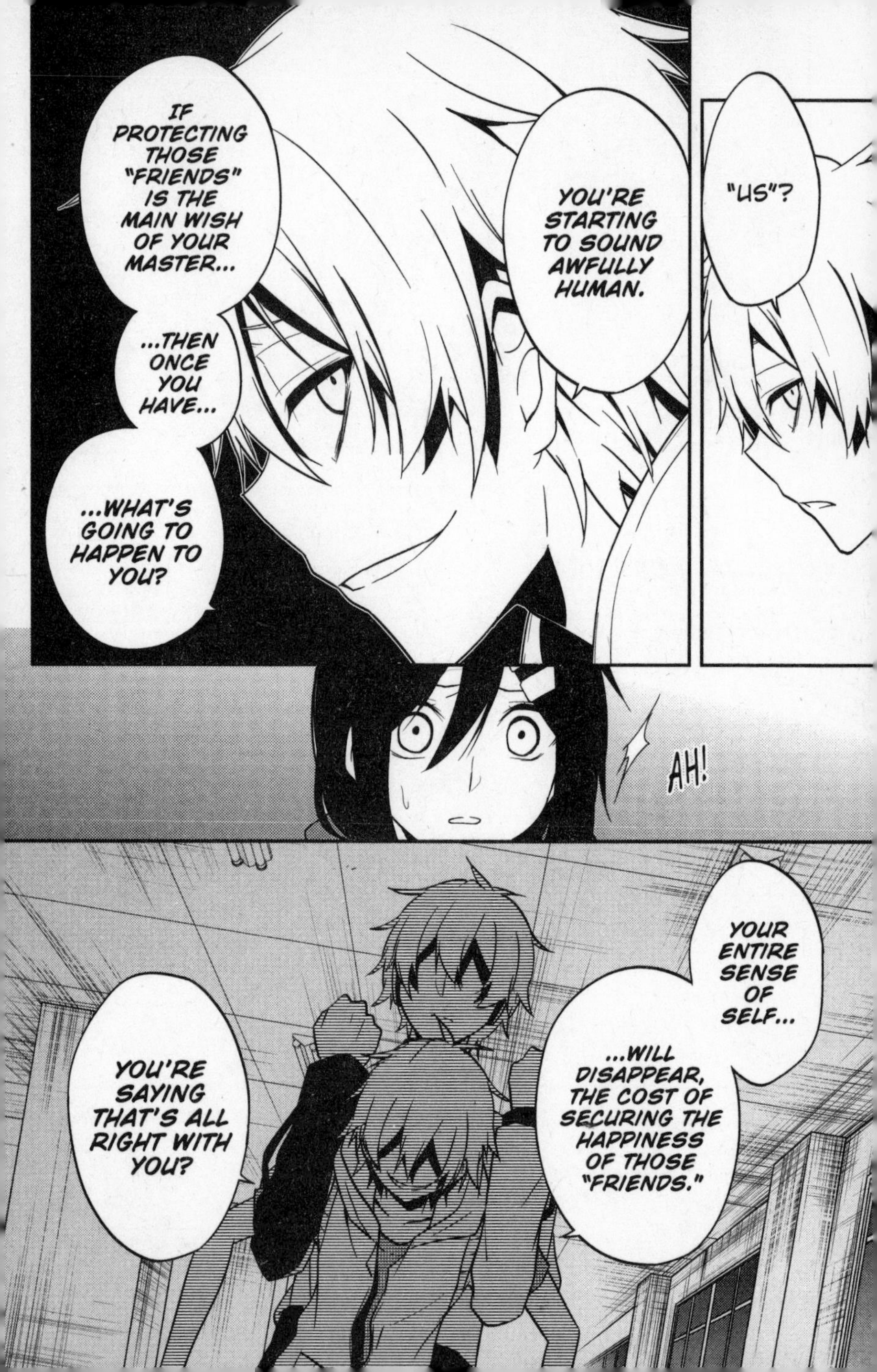
"US"?
YOU'RE STARTING TO SOUND AWFULLY HUMAN.
IF PROTECTING THOSE "FRIENDS" IS THE MAIN WISH OF YOUR MASTER...
...THEN ONCE YOU HAVE...
...WHAT'S GOING TO HAPPEN TO YOU?
AH!
YOUR ENTIRE SENSE OF SELF...
...WILL DISAPPEAR, THE COST OF SECURING THE HAPPINESS OF THOSE "FRIENDS."
YOU'RE SAYING THAT'S ALL RIGHT WITH YOU?

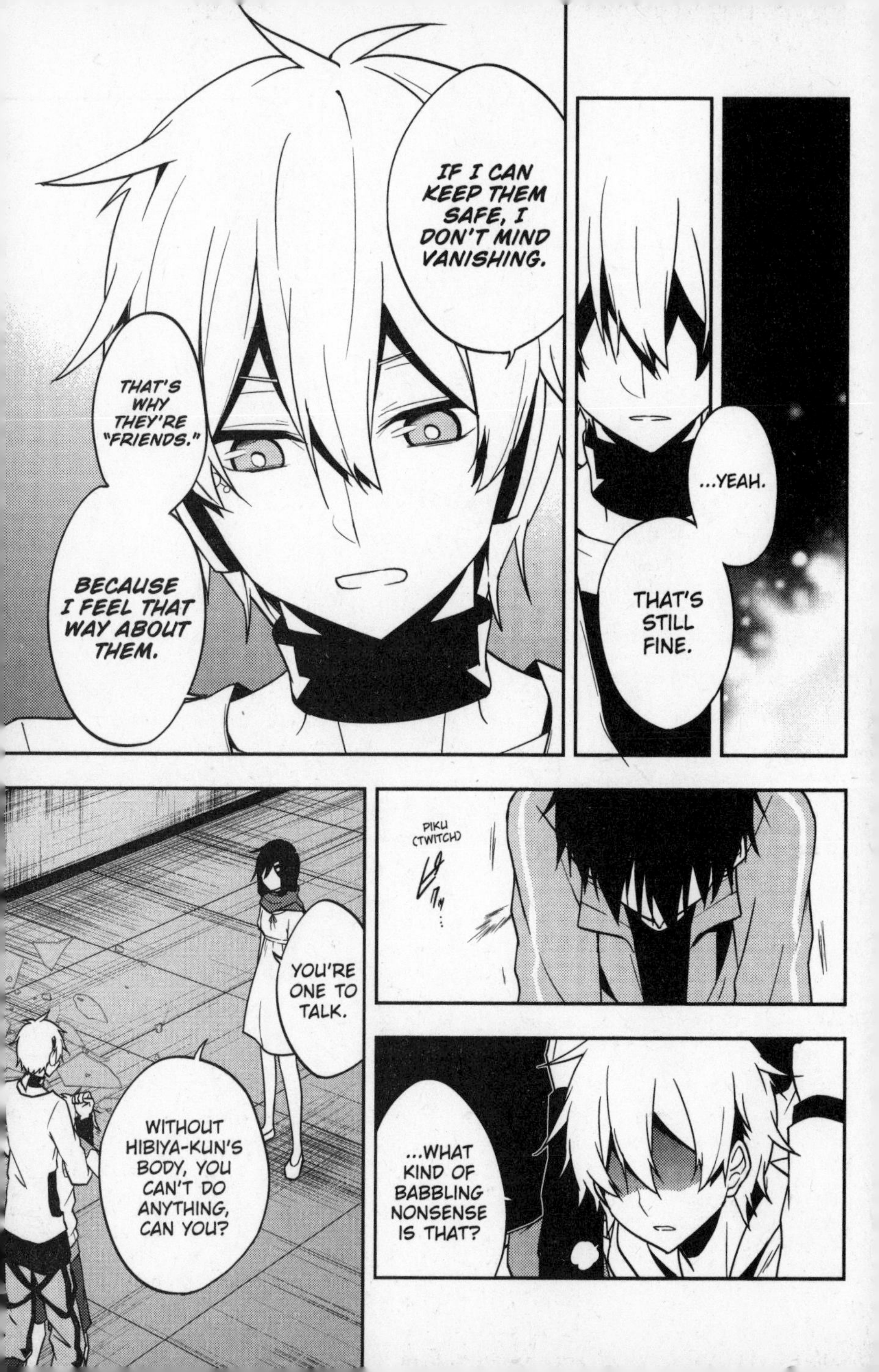
...YEAH.
THAT'S STILL FINE.
IF I CAN KEEP THEM SAFE, I DON'T MIND VANISHING.
THAT'S WHY THEY'RE "FRIENDS."
BECAUSE I FEEL THAT WAY ABOUT THEM.
PIKU (TWITCH)
...WHAT KIND OF BABBLING NONSENSE IS THAT?
YOU'RE ONE TO TALK.
WITHOUT HIBIYA-KUN'S BODY, YOU CAN'T DO ANYTHING, CAN YOU?

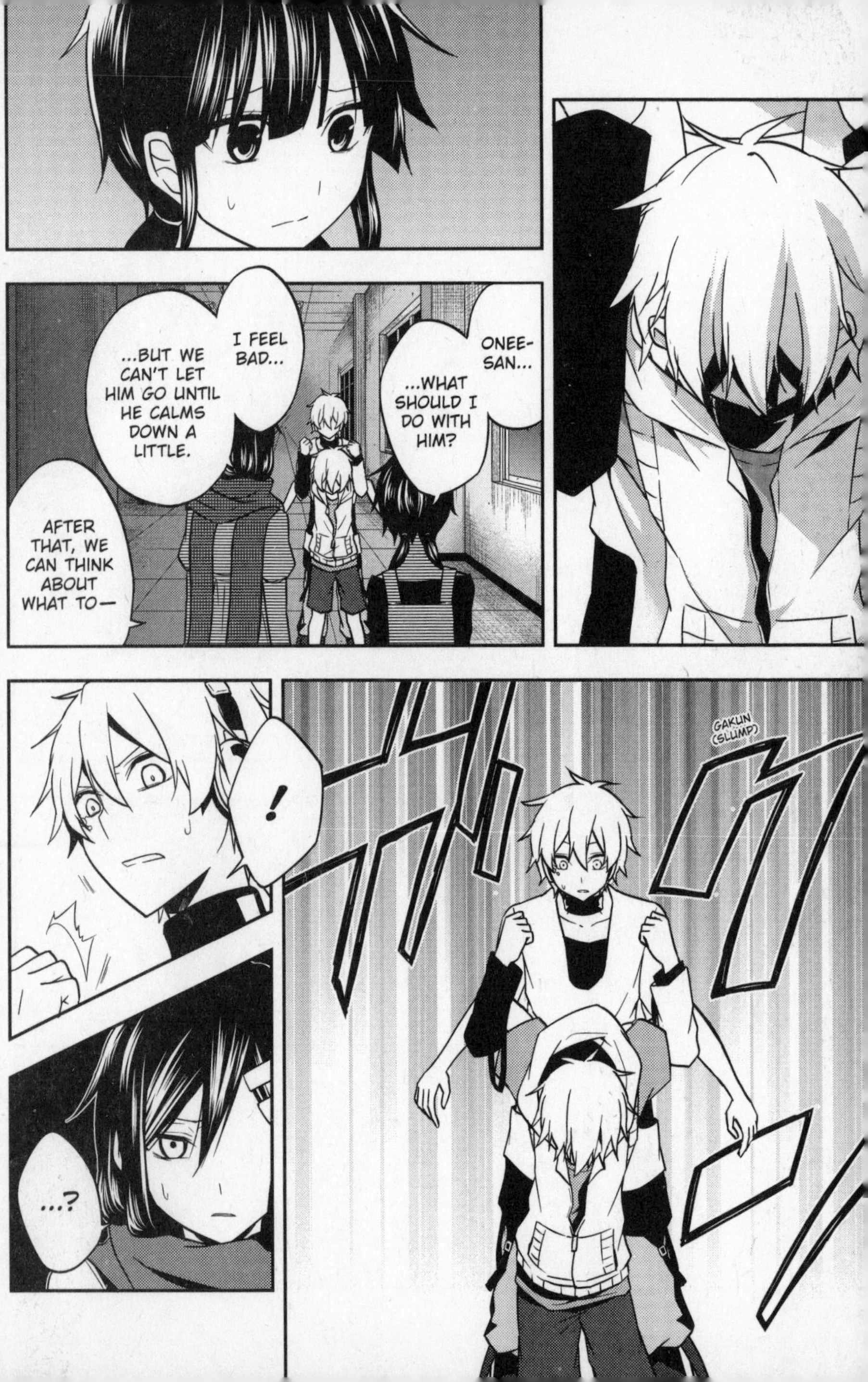
ONEE-SAN...
...WHAT SHOULD I DO WITH HIM?
I FEEL BAD...
...BUT WE CAN'T LET HIM GO UNTIL HE CALMS DOWN A LITTLE.
AFTER THAT, WE CAN THINK ABOUT WHAT TO—
GAKUN (SLUMP)
!
...?

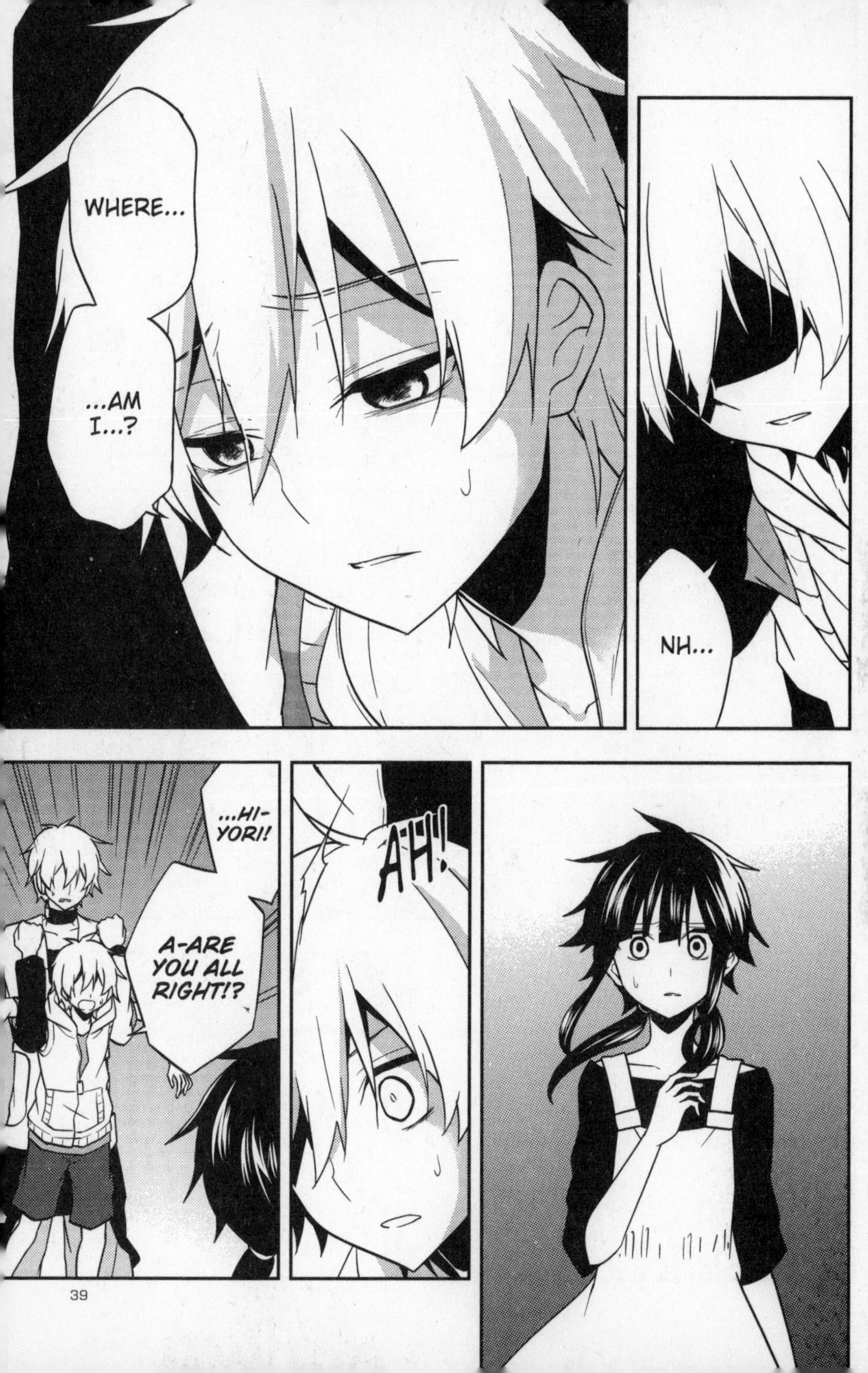
NH...
WHERE...
...AM I...?
AH!
...HI-YORI!
A-ARE YOU ALL RIGHT!?

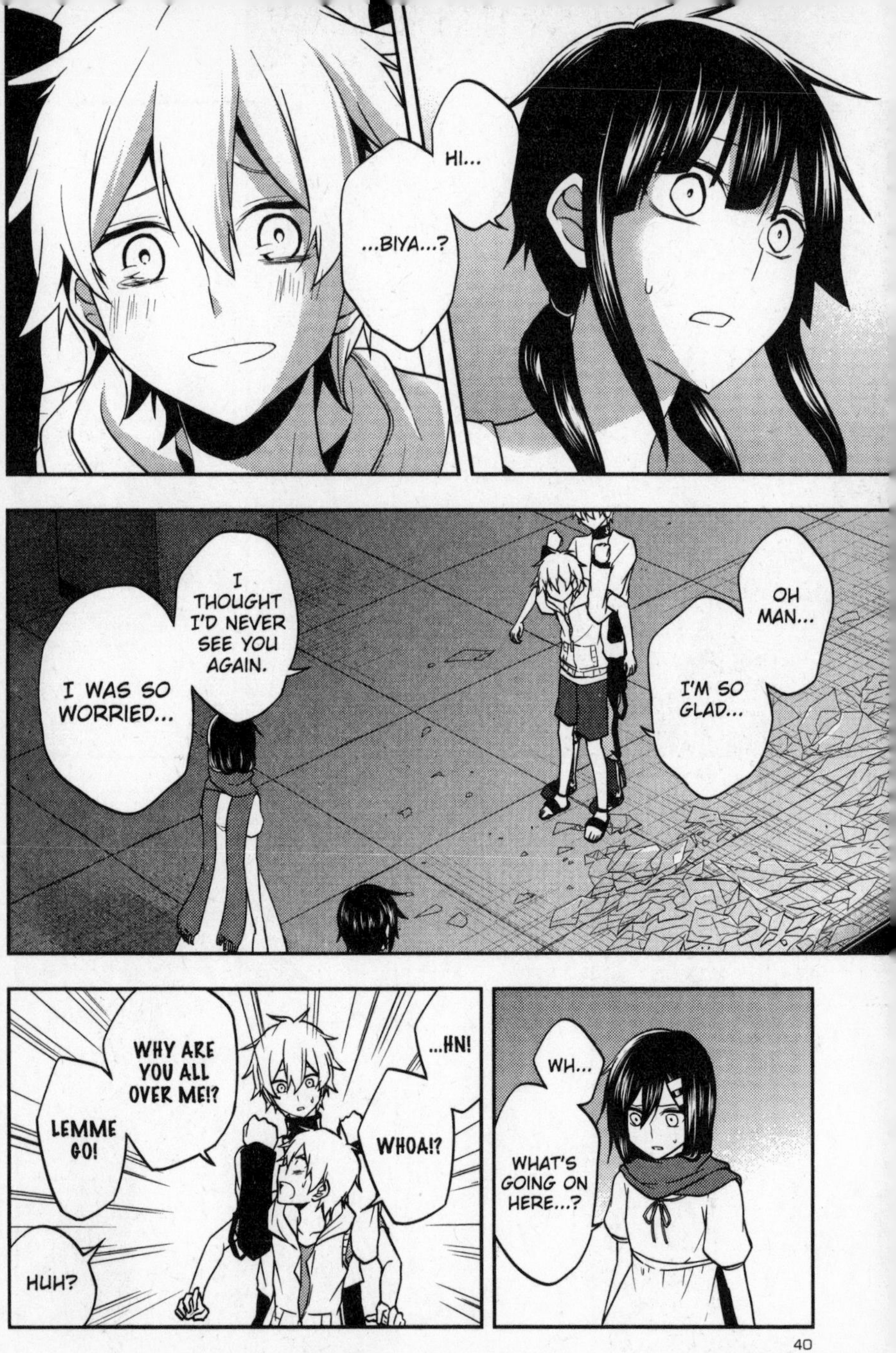
HI...
...BIYA...?
OH MAN...
I'M SO GLAD...
I THOUGHT I'D NEVER SEE YOU AGAIN.
I WAS SO WORRIED...
WH...
WHAT'S GOING ON HERE...?
...HN!
WHOA!?
WHY ARE YOU ALL OVER ME!?
LEMME GO!
HUH?

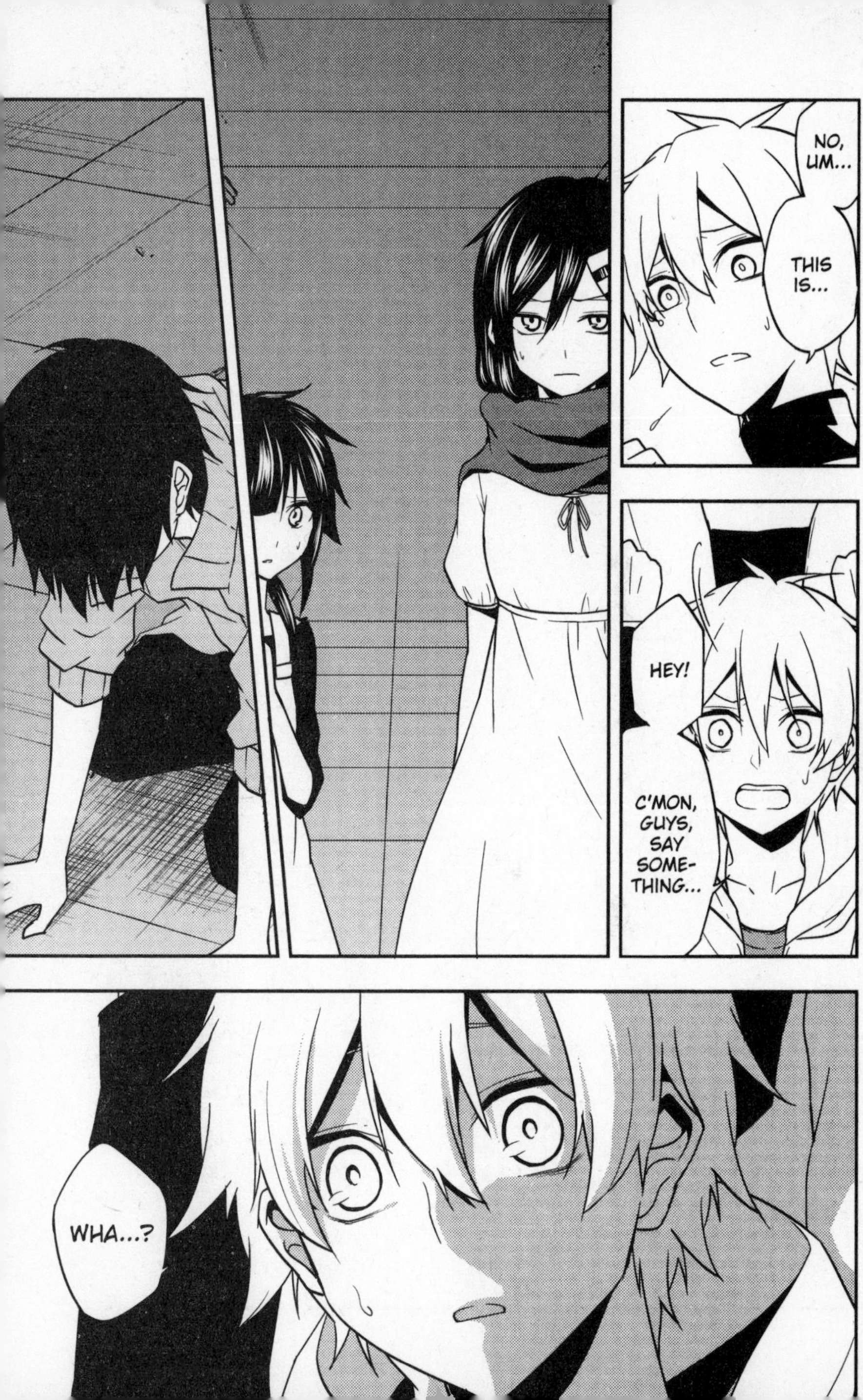
NO, UM...
THIS IS...
HEY!
C'MON, GUYS, SAY SOME-THING...
WHA...?

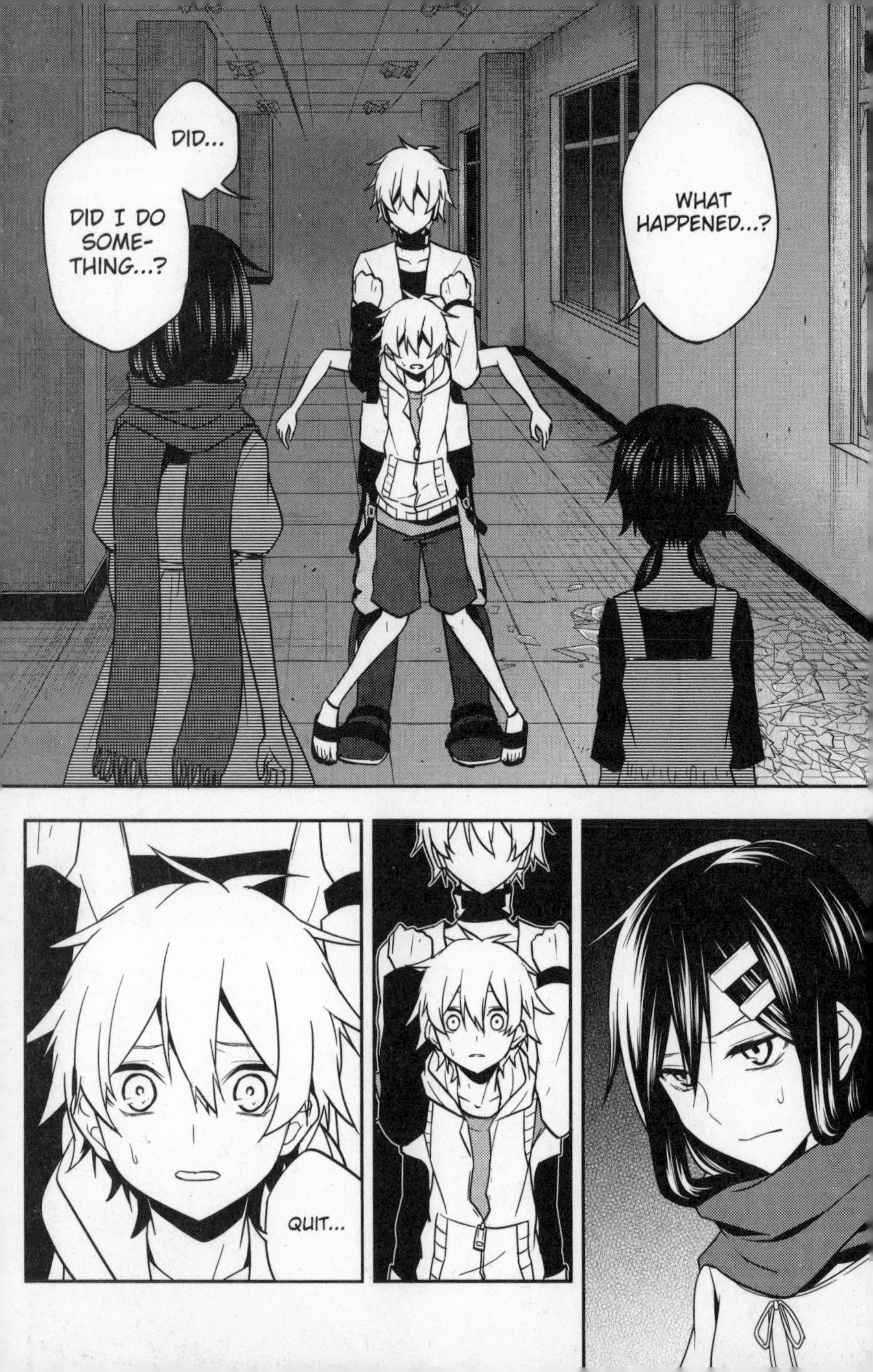
WHAT HAPPENED...?
DID...
DID I DO SOMETHING...?
QUIT...

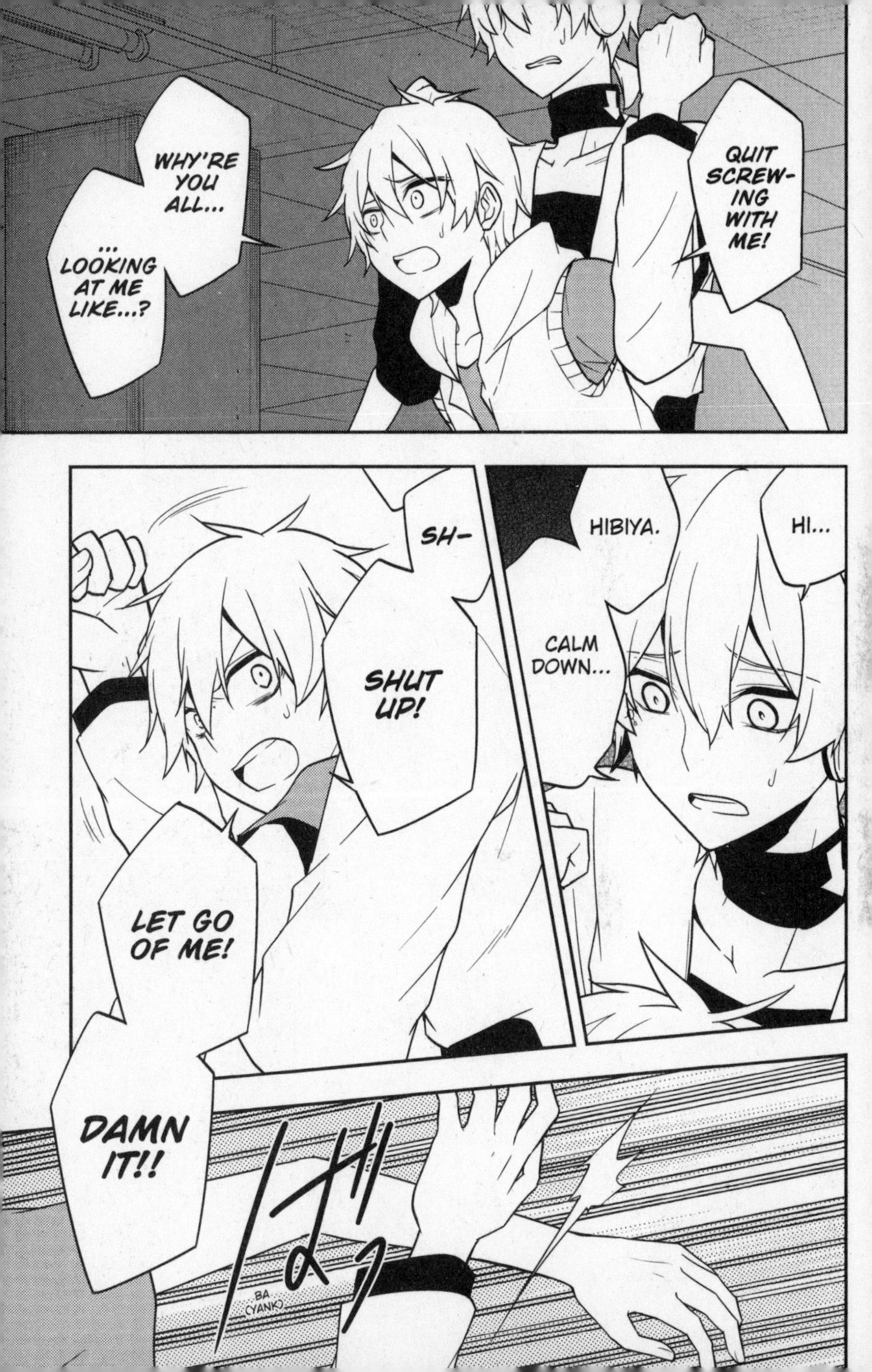
QUIT SCREWING WITH ME!
WHY'RE YOU ALL...
...LOOKING AT ME LIKE...?
HI...
HIBIYA.
CALM DOWN...
SH-
SHUT UP!
LET GO OF ME!
DAMN IT!!
BA (YANK)

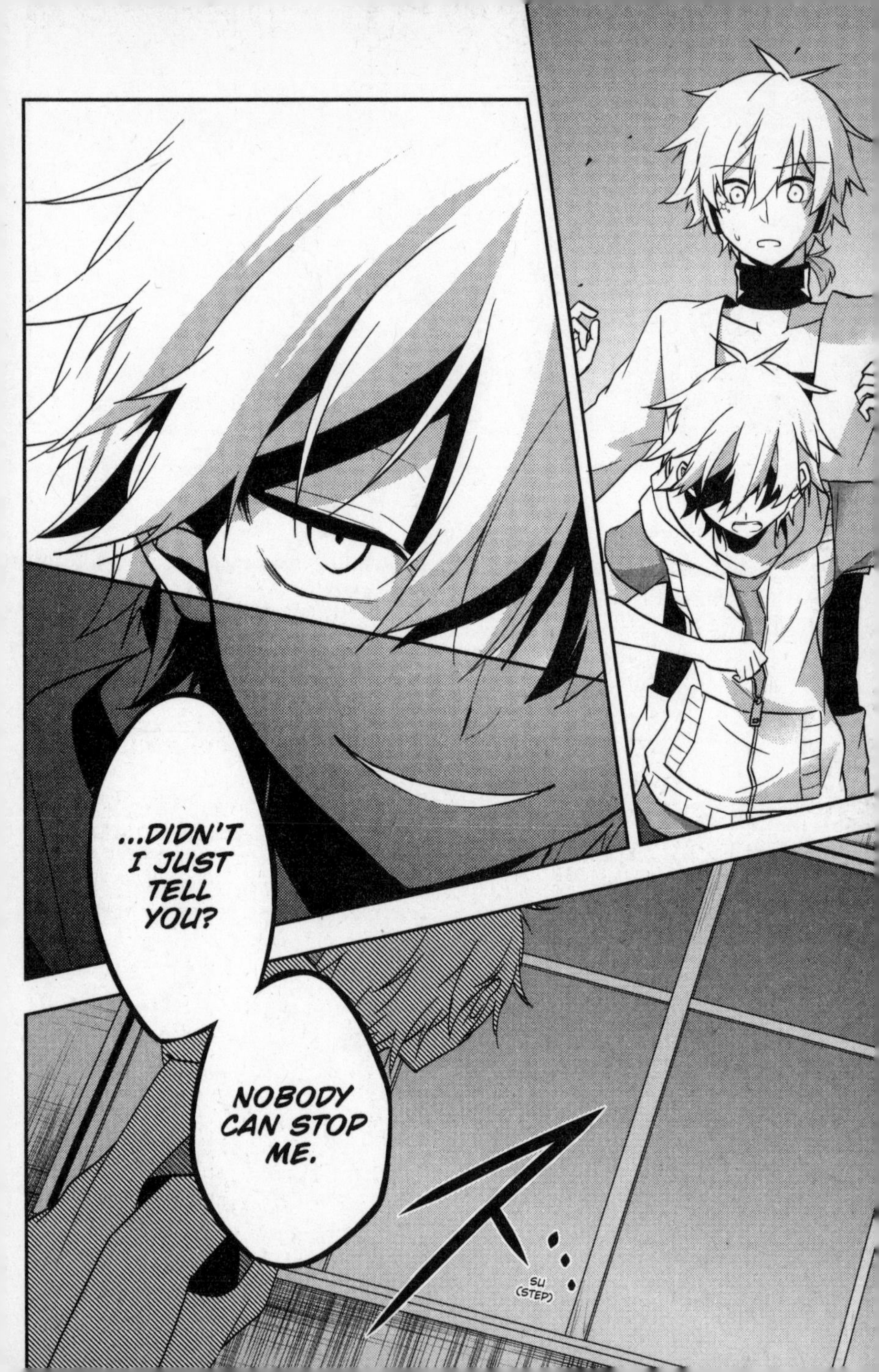
...DIDN'T I JUST TELL YOU?
NOBODY CAN STOP ME.
SU (STEP)

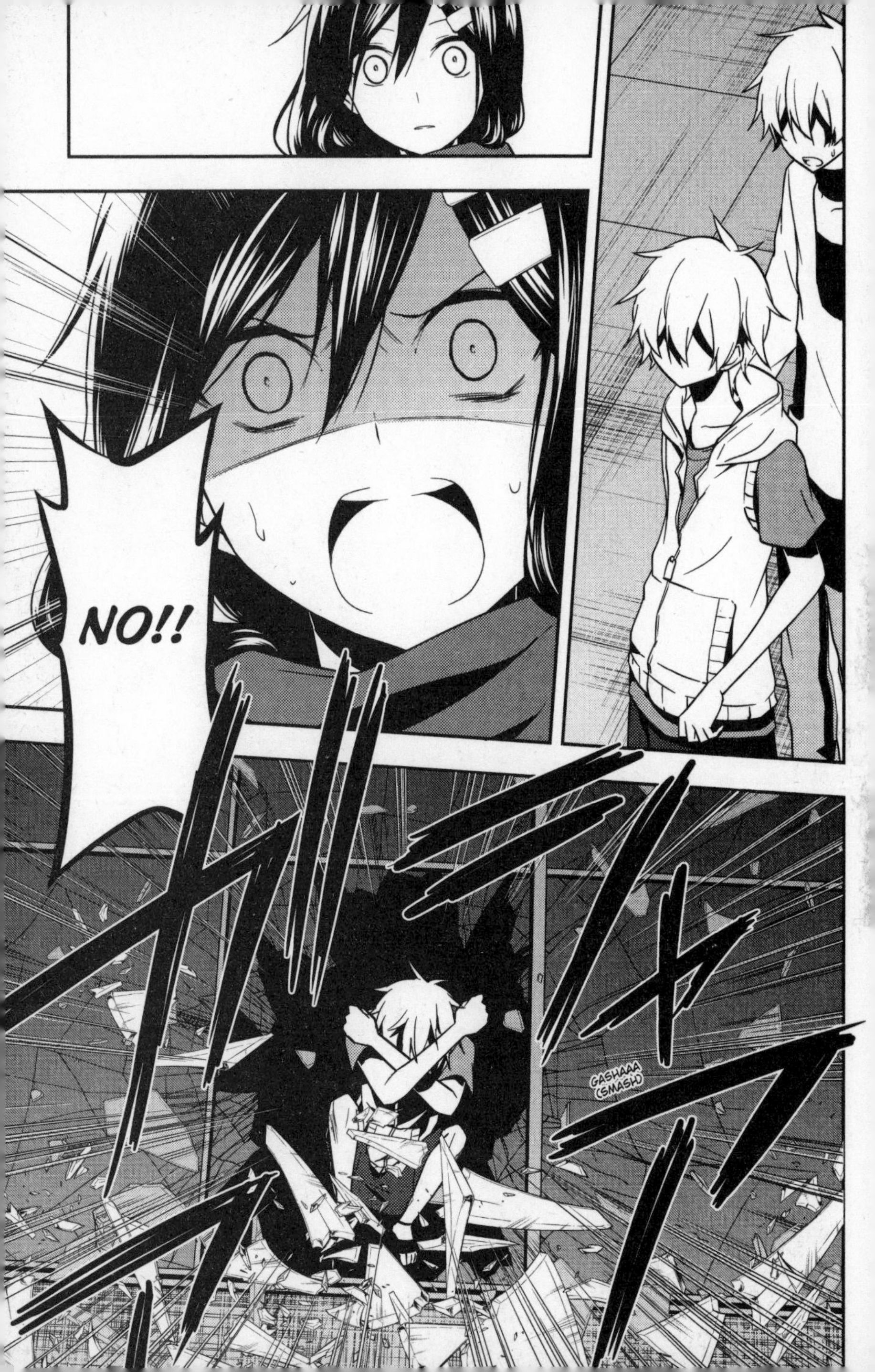
NO!!
GASHAAA (SMASH)

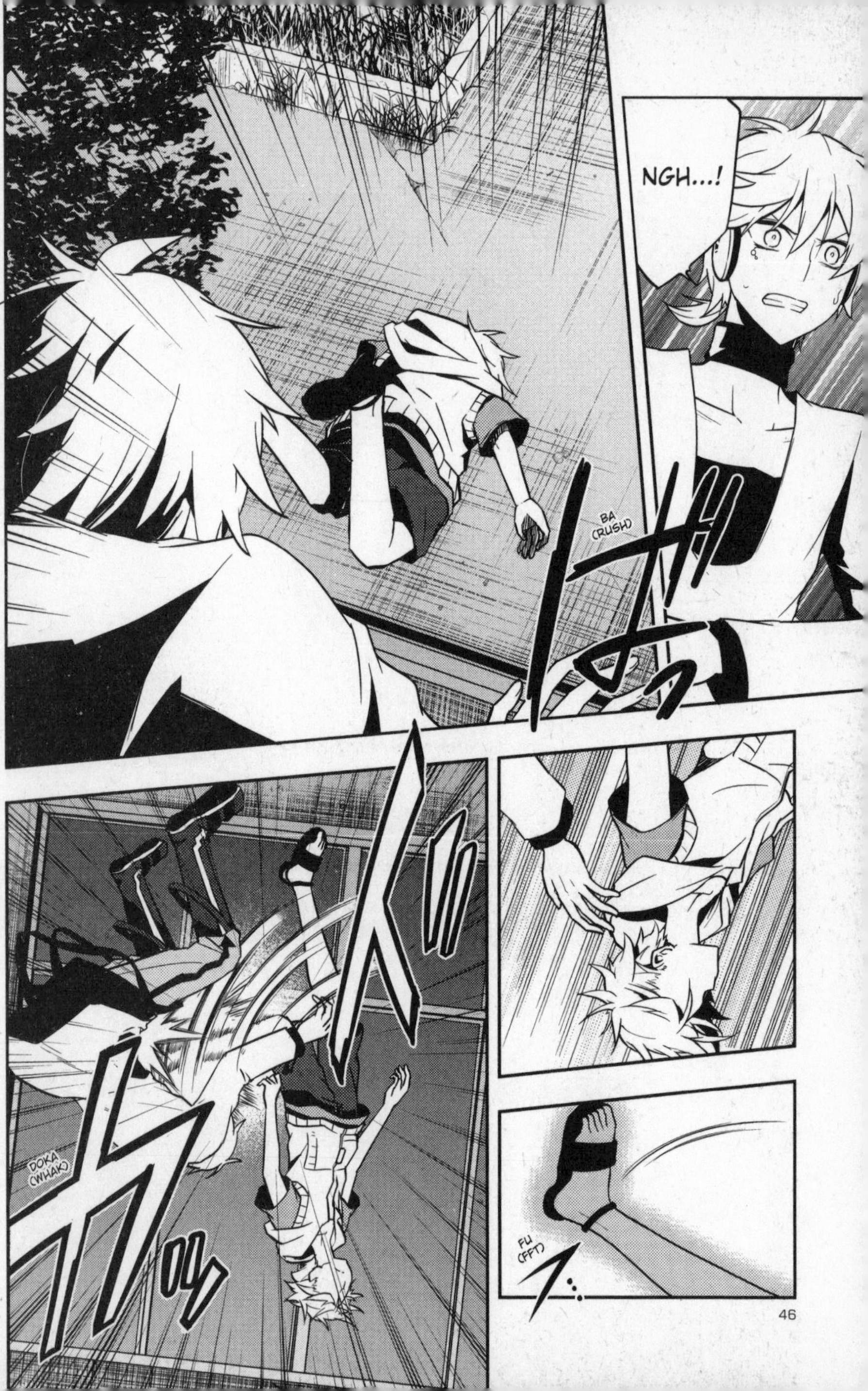
NGH...!
BA (RUSH)
FU (FFT)
DOKA (WHAK)

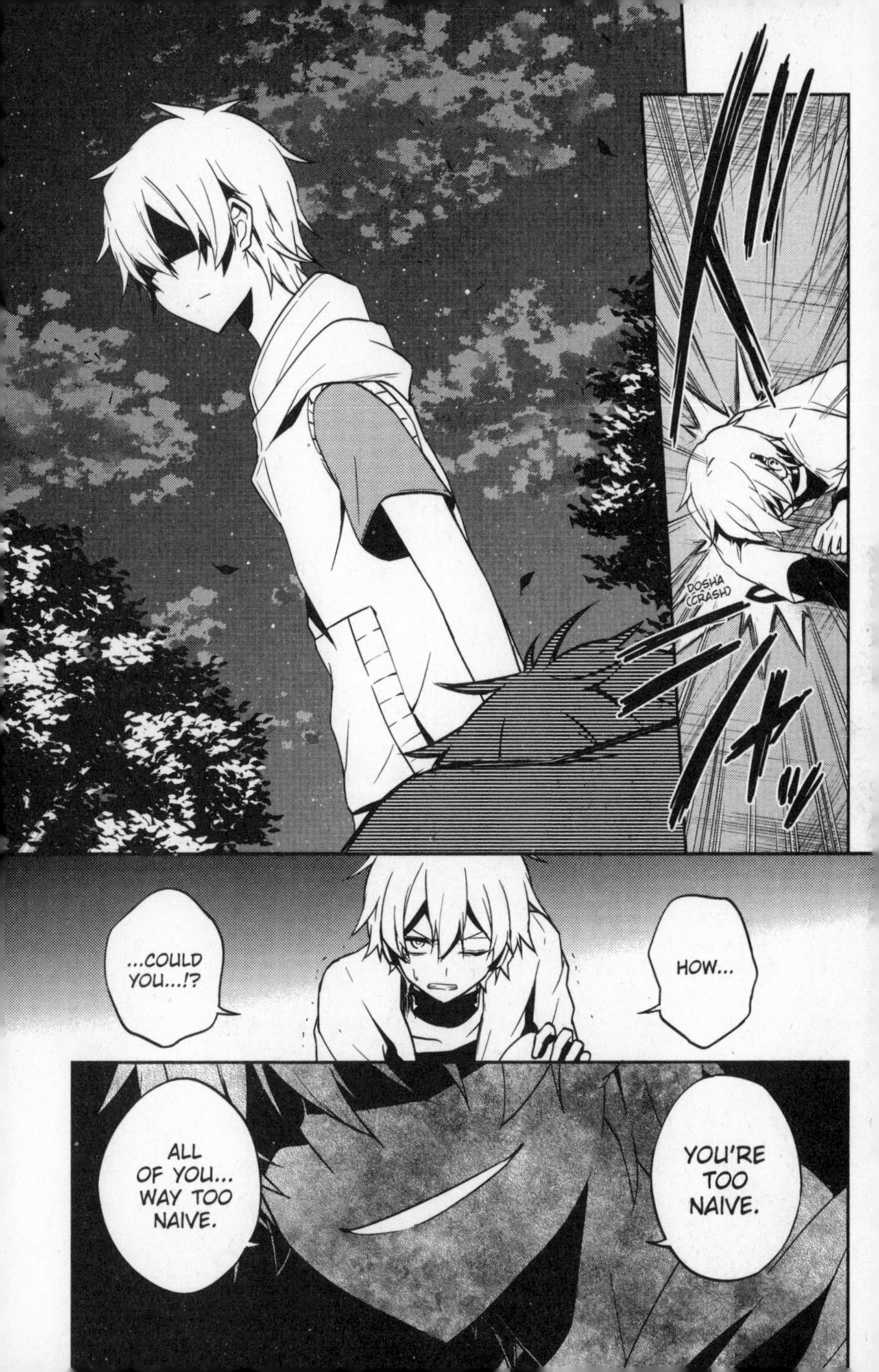
DOSHA (CRASH)
HOW...
...COULD YOU...!?
YOU'RE TOO NAIVE.
ALL OF YOU... WAY TOO NAIVE.

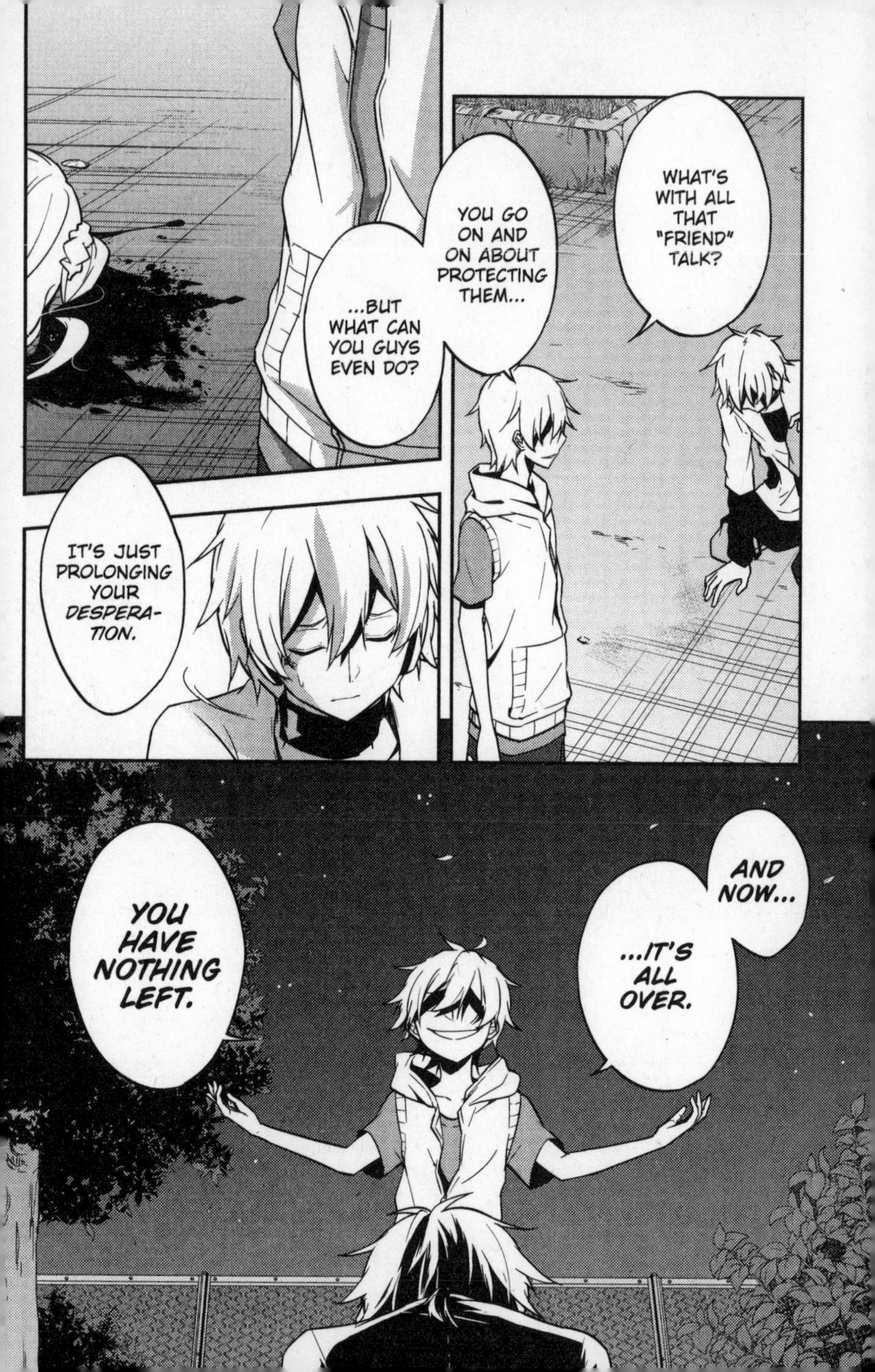
WHAT'S WITH ALL THAT "FRIEND" TALK?
YOU GO ON AND ON ABOUT PROTECTING THEM...
...BUT WHAT CAN YOU GUYS EVEN DO?
IT'S JUST PROLONGING YOUR *DESPERATION.*
AND NOW...
...IT'S ALL OVER.
YOU HAVE NOTHING LEFT.

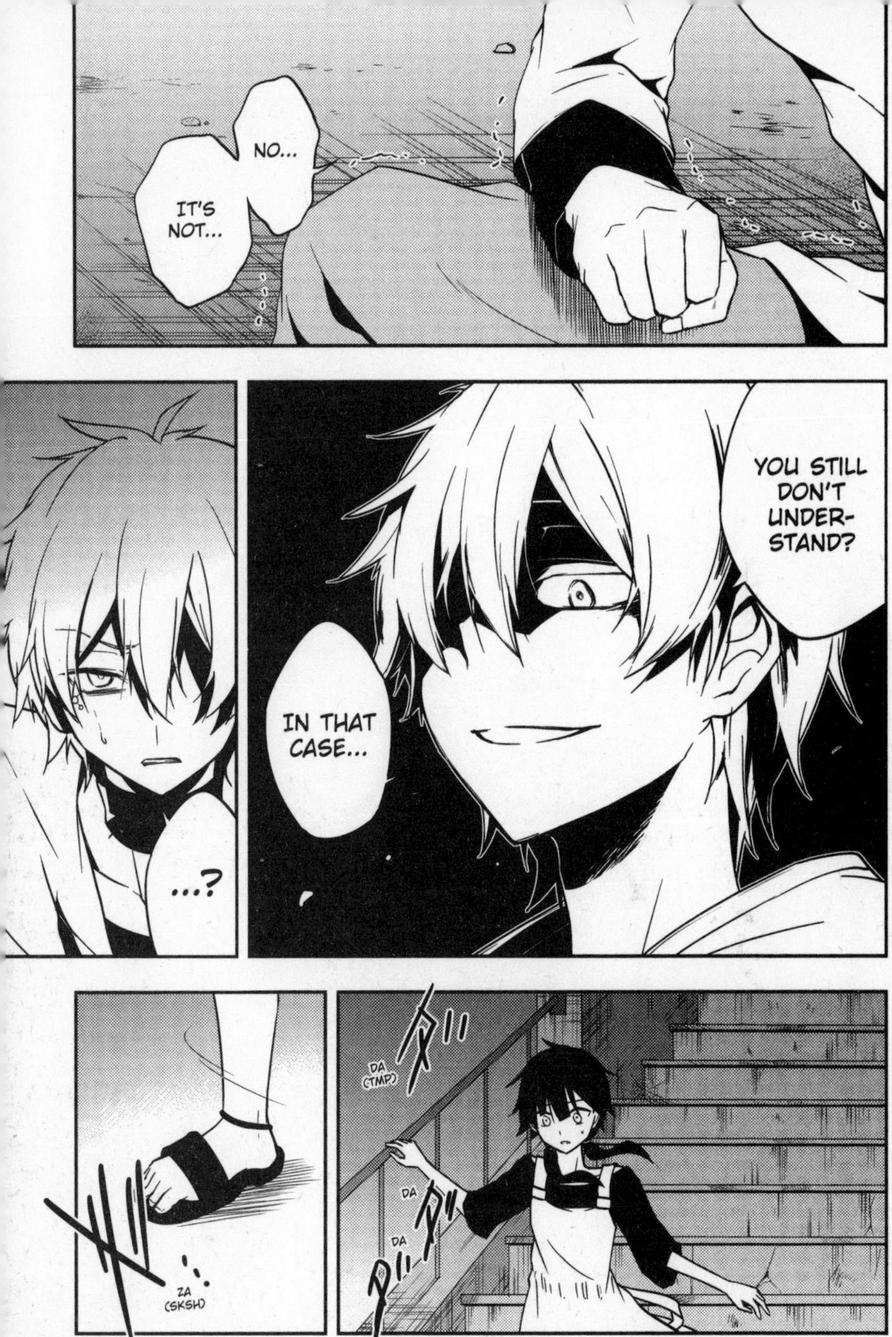
NO...
IT'S NOT...
YOU STILL DON'T UNDER-STAND?
IN THAT CASE...
...?
DA (TMP)
DA
DA
ZA (SKSH)

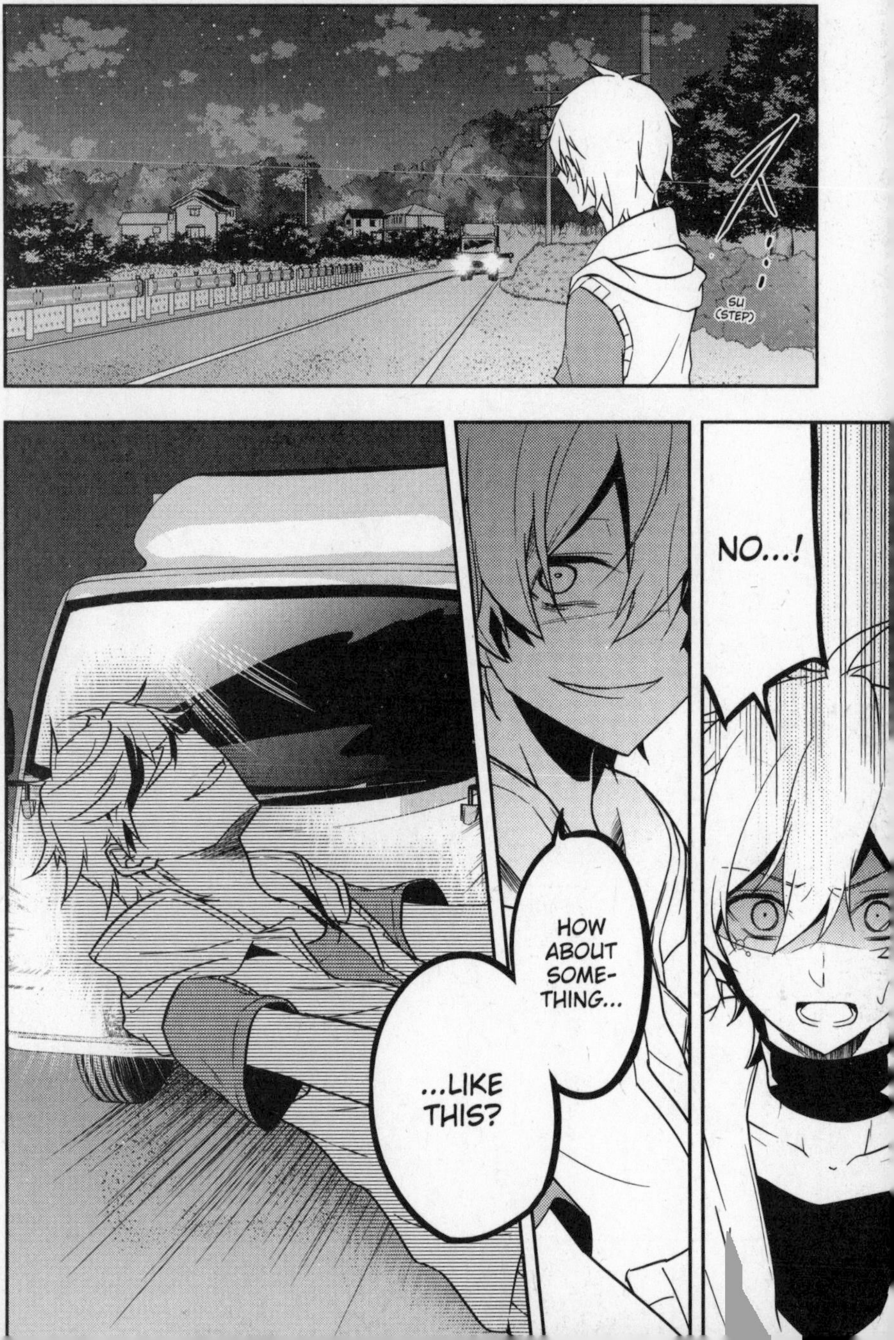
SU (STEP)
NO...!
HOW ABOUT SOME-THING...
...LIKE THIS?

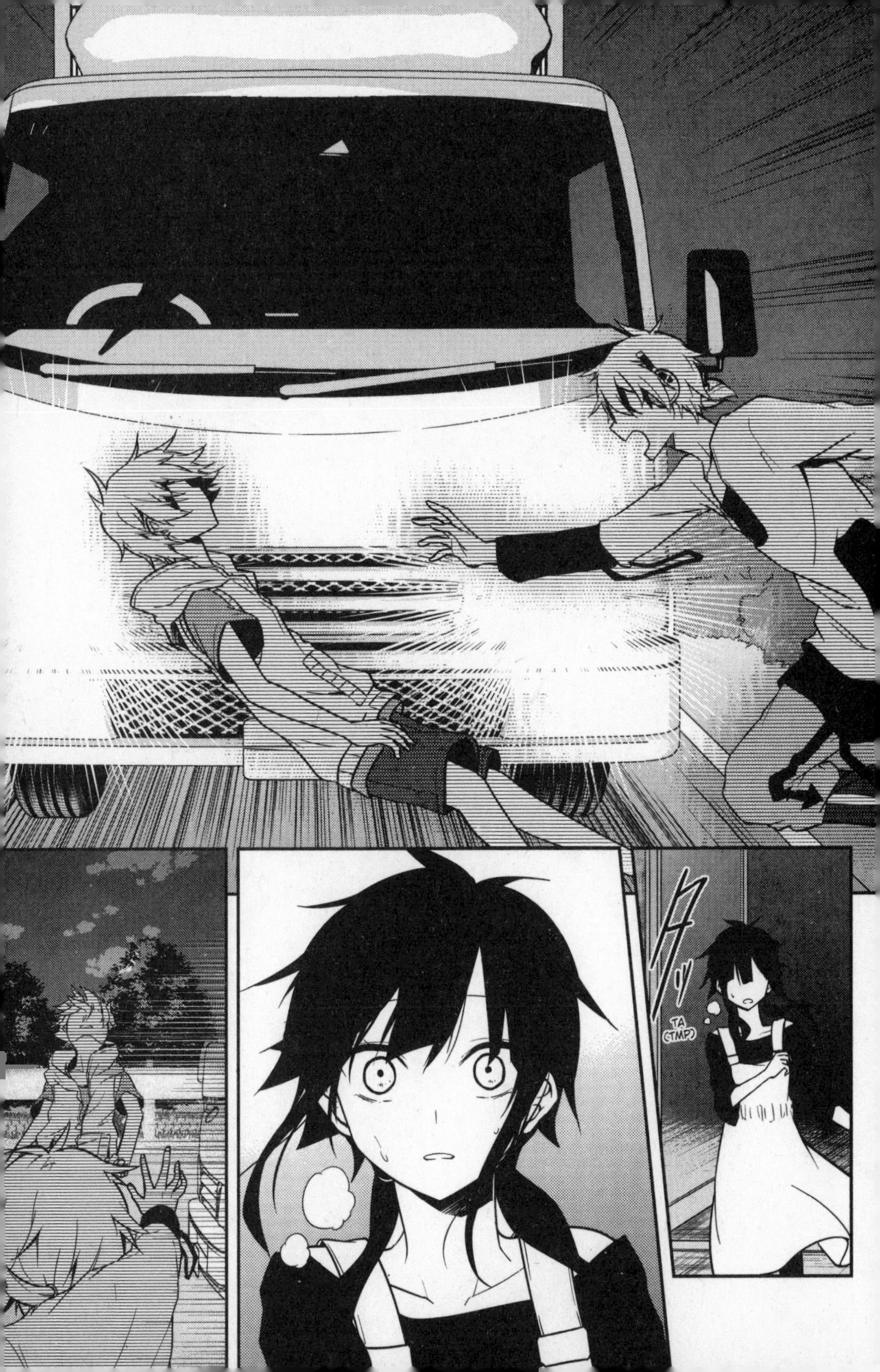
TA
(TMP)

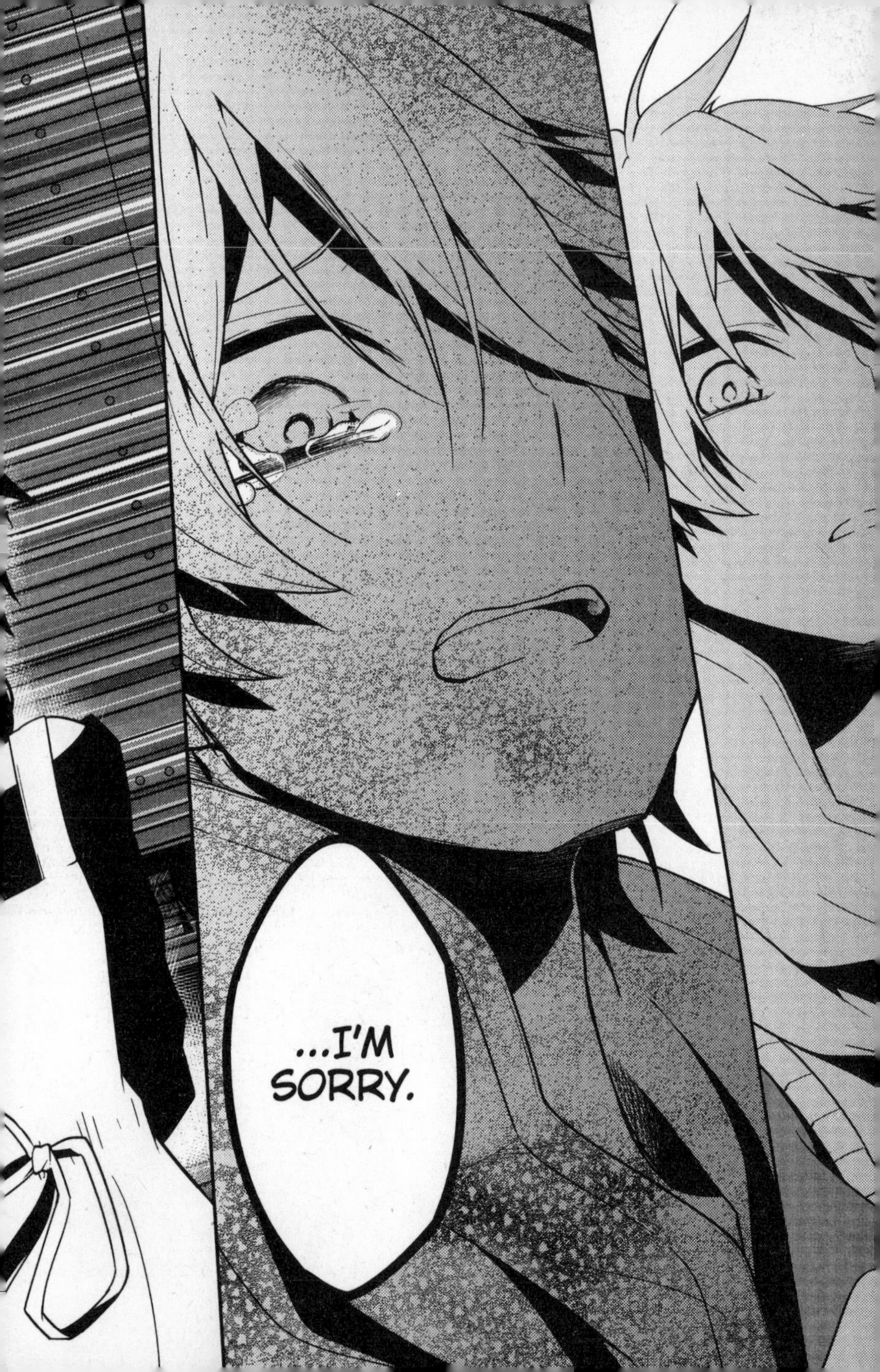
...I'M SORRY.

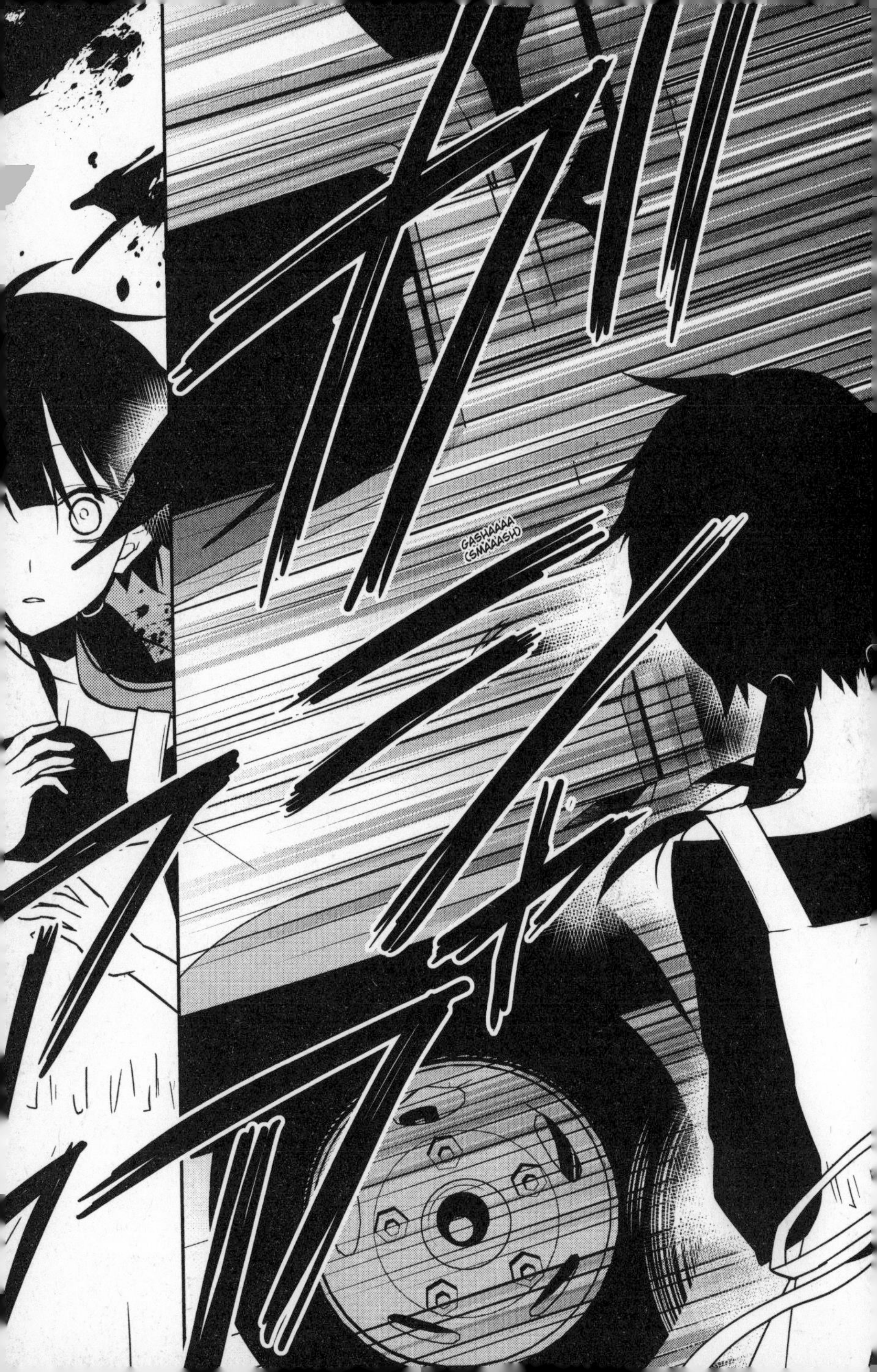
GASHAAAA
(SMAAASH)

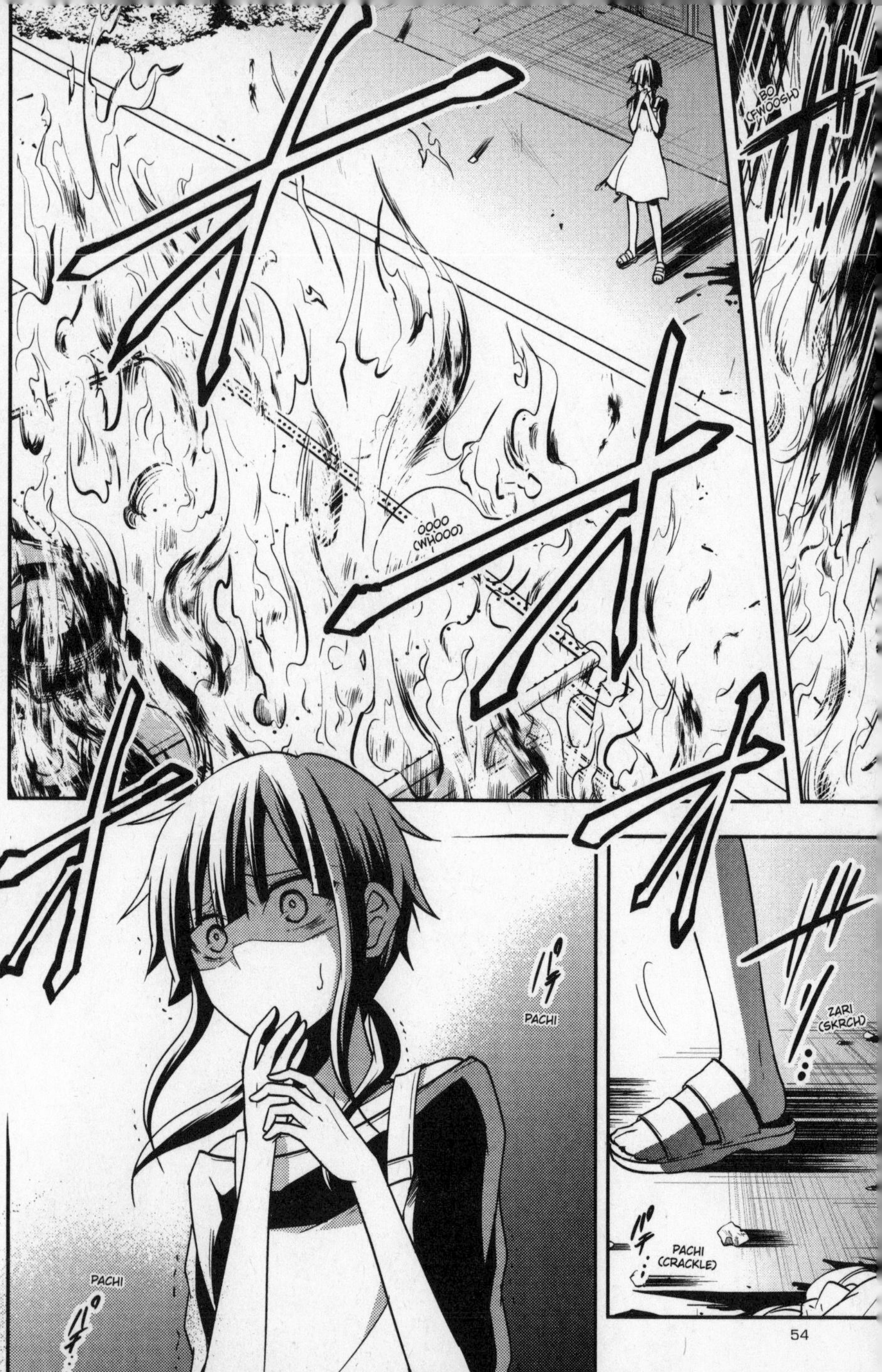
BO (FWOOSH)
OOOO (WHOOO)
ZARI (SKRCH)
PACHI (CRACKLE)
PACHI
PACHI

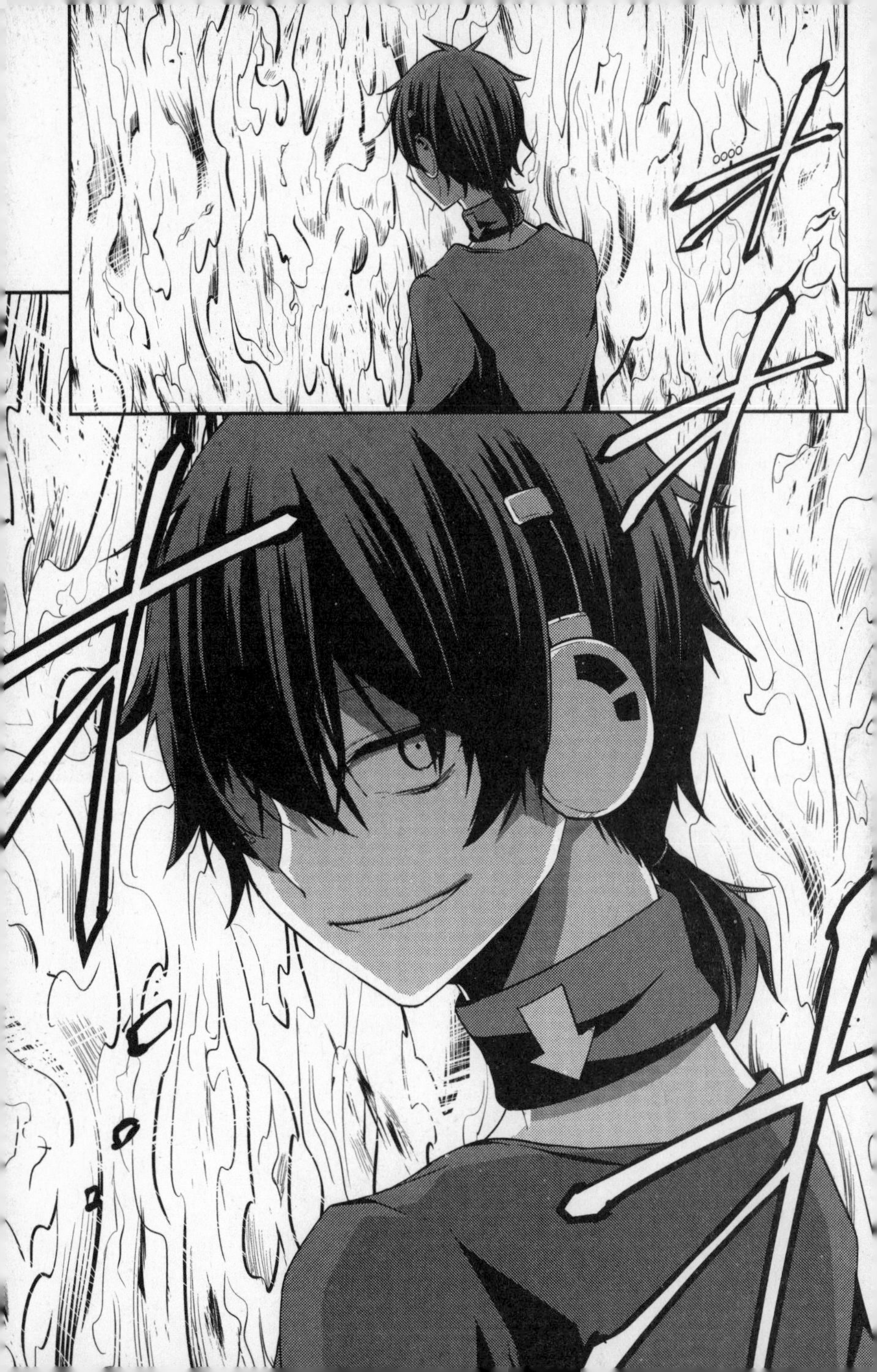

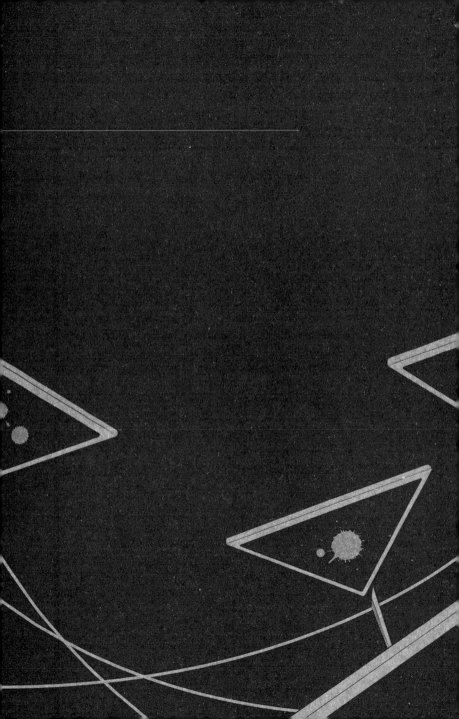

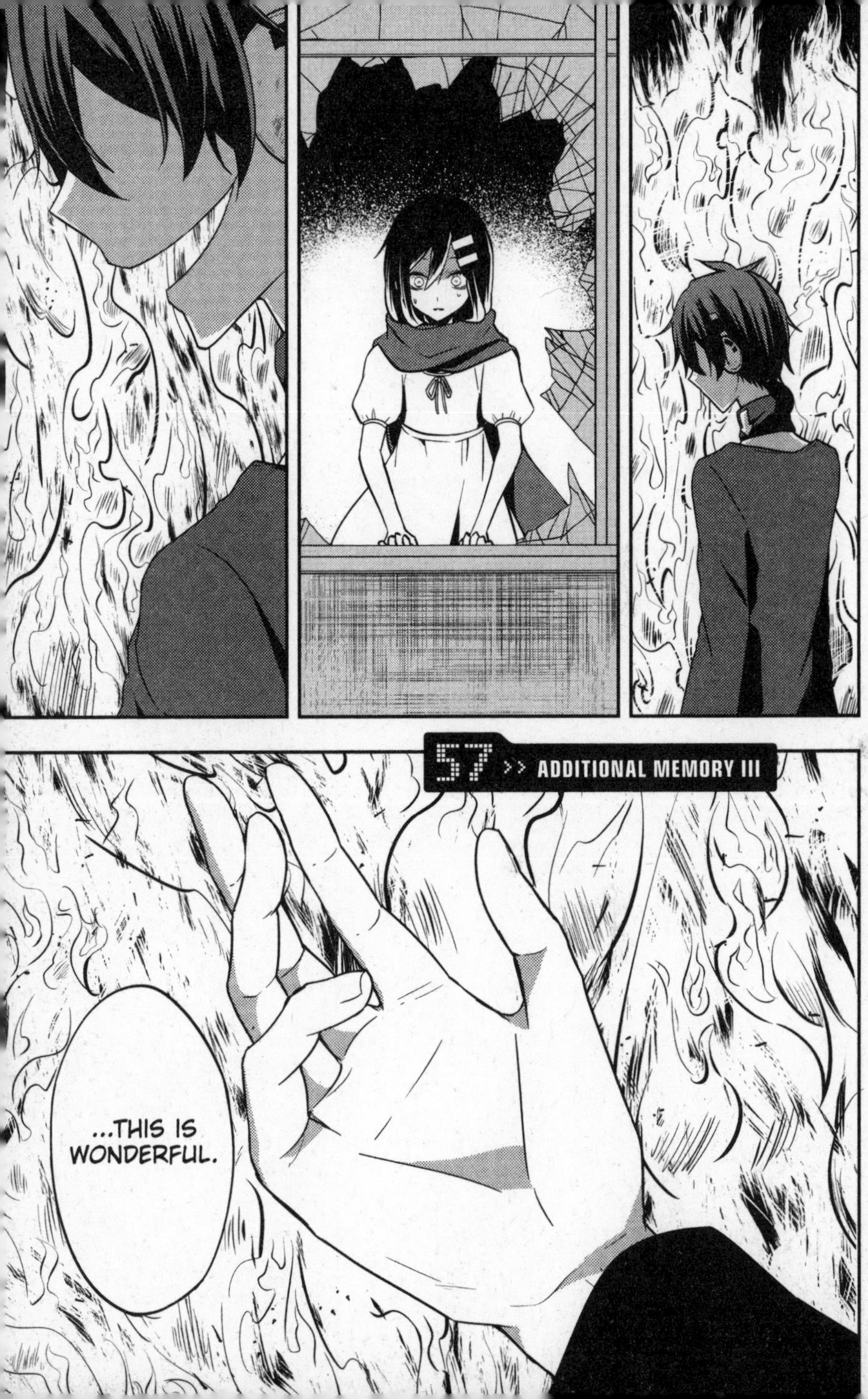
57 >> ADDITIONAL MEMORY III
...THIS IS WONDERFUL.

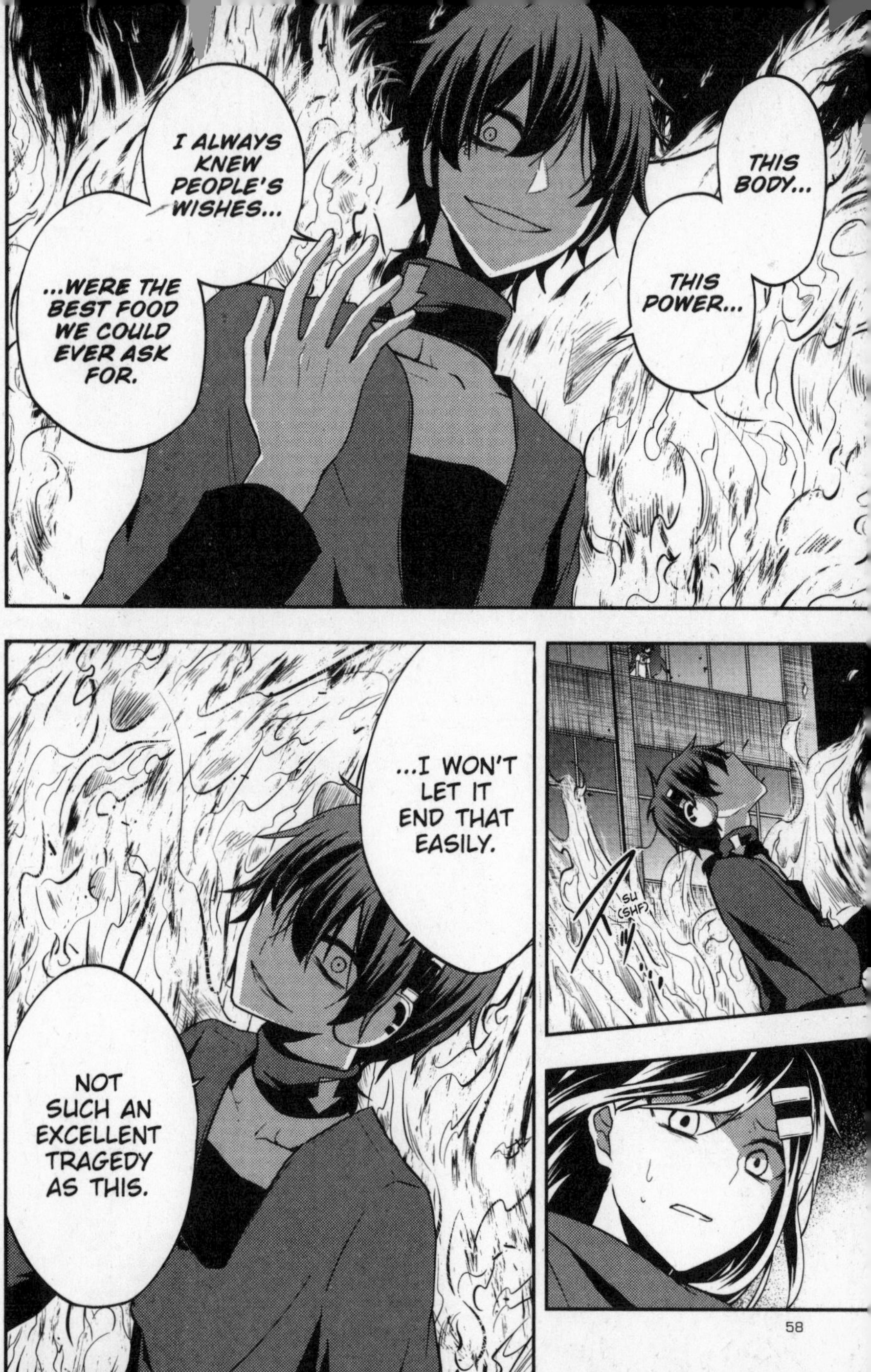
THIS BODY...
THIS POWER...
I ALWAYS KNEW PEOPLE'S WISHES...
...WERE THE BEST FOOD WE COULD EVER ASK FOR.
SU (SHF)
...I WON'T LET IT END THAT EASILY.
NOT SUCH AN EXCELLENT TRAGEDY AS THIS.

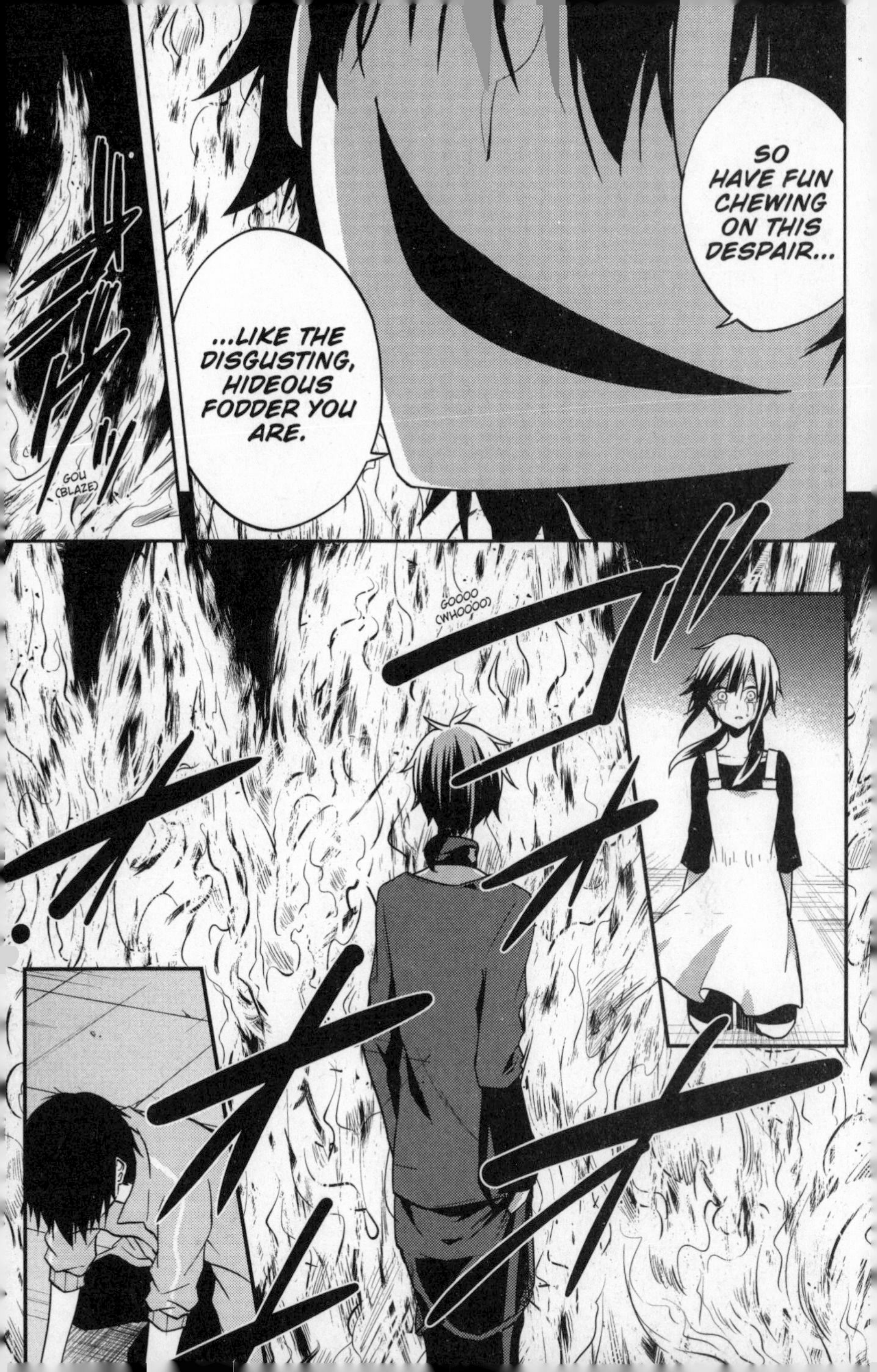
SO HAVE FUN CHEWING ON THIS DESPAIR...
...LIKE THE DISGUSTING, HIDEOUS FODDER YOU ARE.
GOU (BLAZE)
GOOOO (WHOOOO)

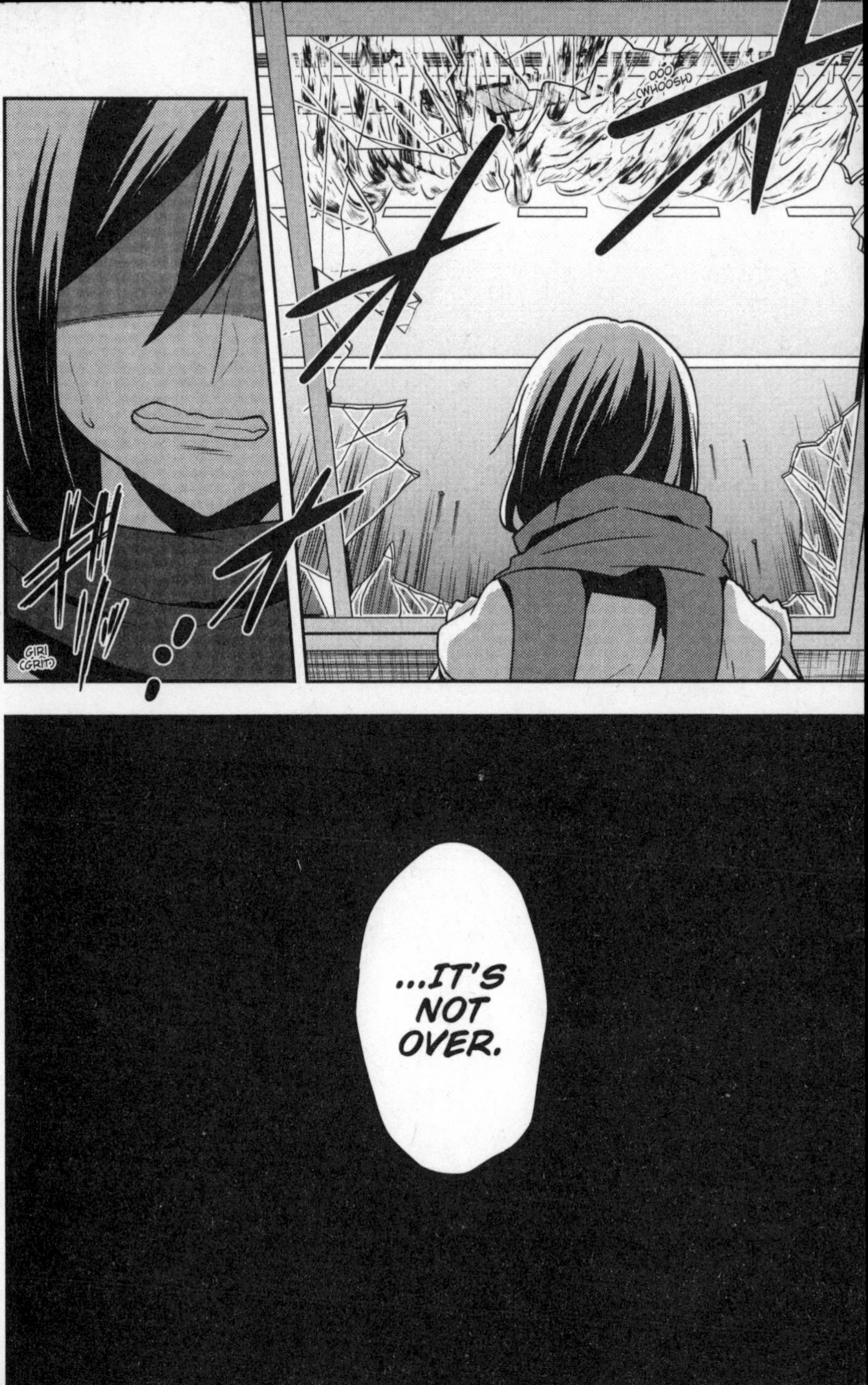
OOO (WHOOSH)
GIRI (GRIT)
...IT'S NOT OVER.

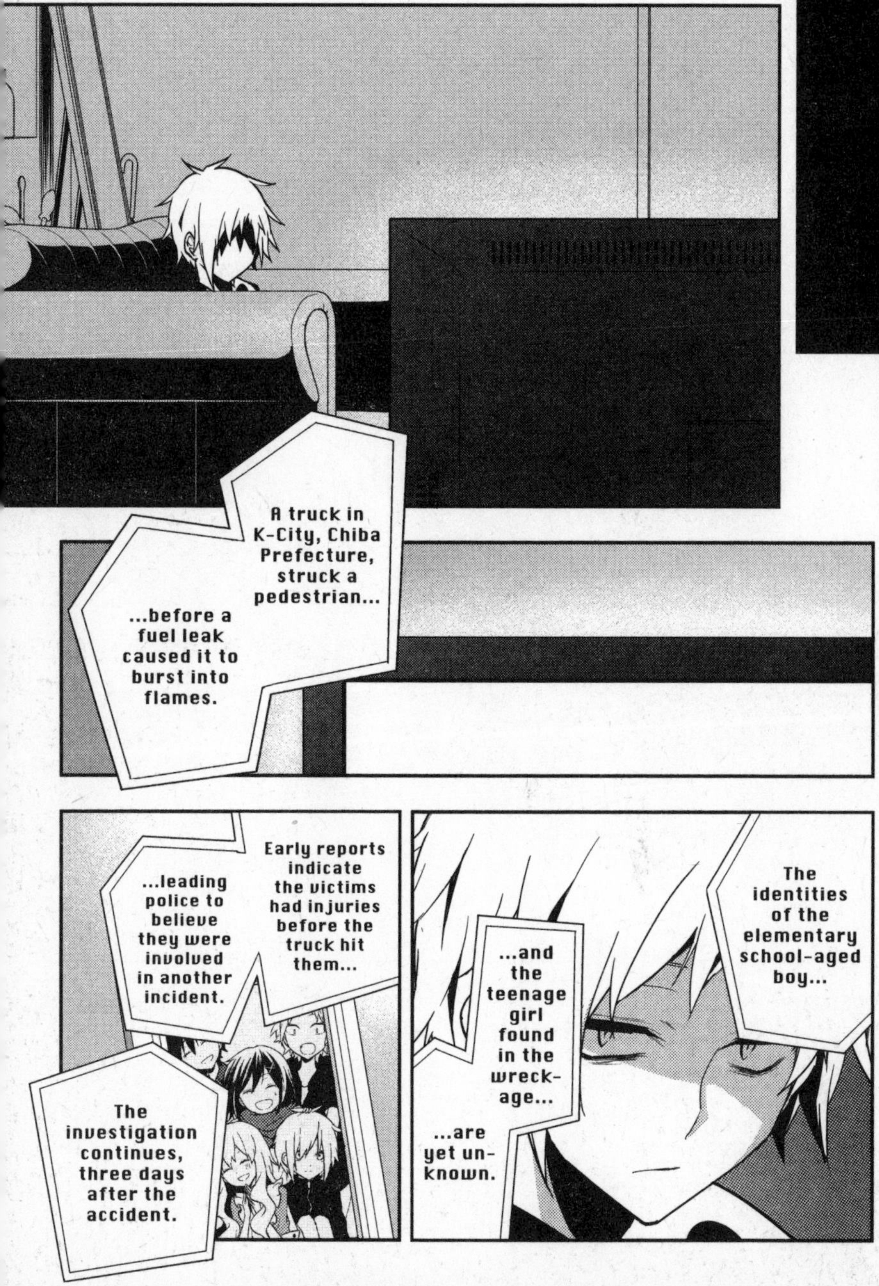
A truck in K-City, Chiba Prefecture, struck a pedestrian...
...before a fuel leak caused it to burst into flames.
The identities of the elementary school-aged boy...
...and the teenage girl found in the wreck-age...
...are yet un-known.
Early reports indicate the victims had injuries before the truck hit them...
...leading police to believe they were involved in another incident.
The investigation continues, three days after the accident.

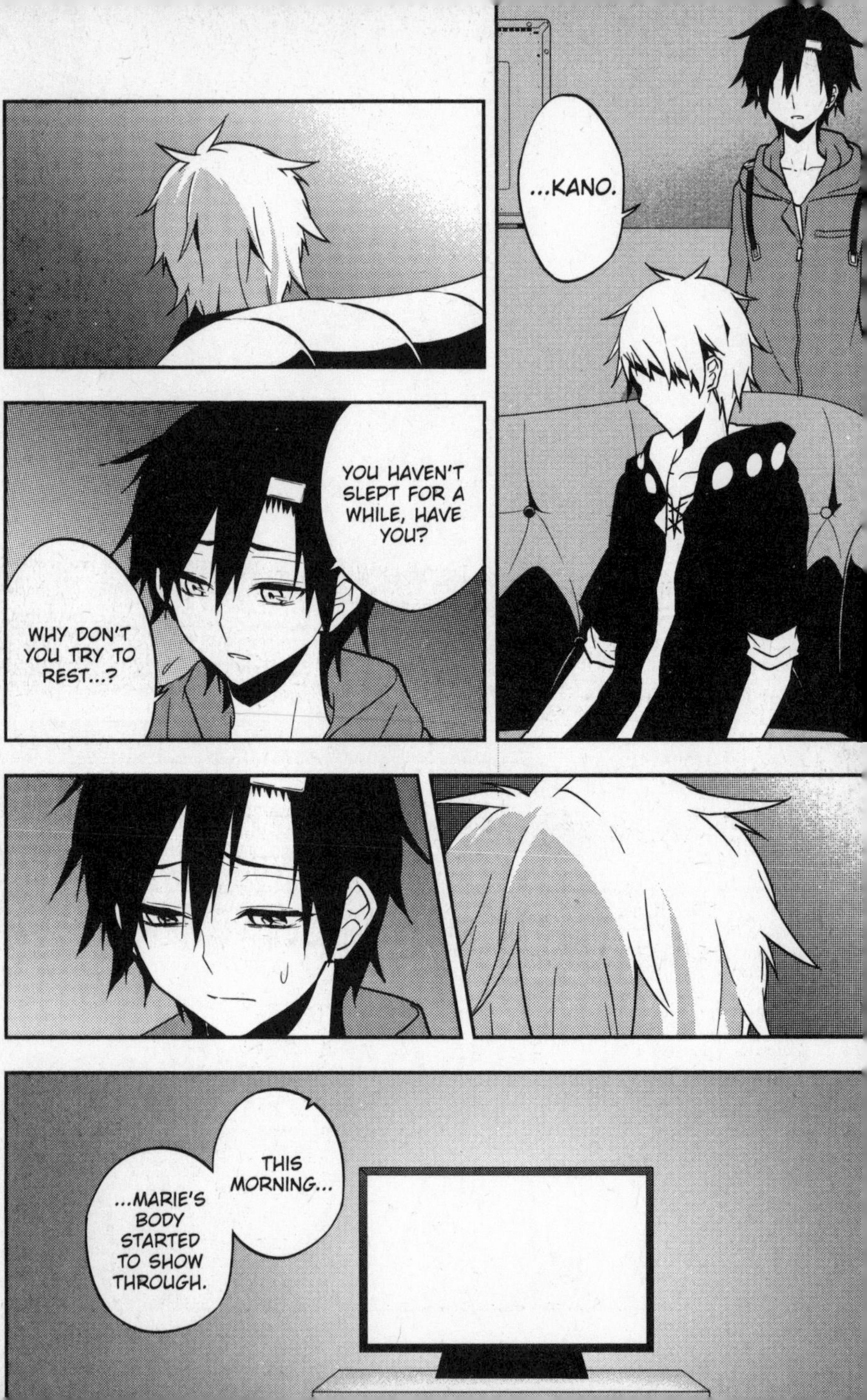
...KANO.
YOU HAVEN'T SLEPT FOR A WHILE, HAVE YOU?
WHY DON'T YOU TRY TO REST...?
THIS MORNING...
...MARIE'S BODY STARTED TO SHOW THROUGH.

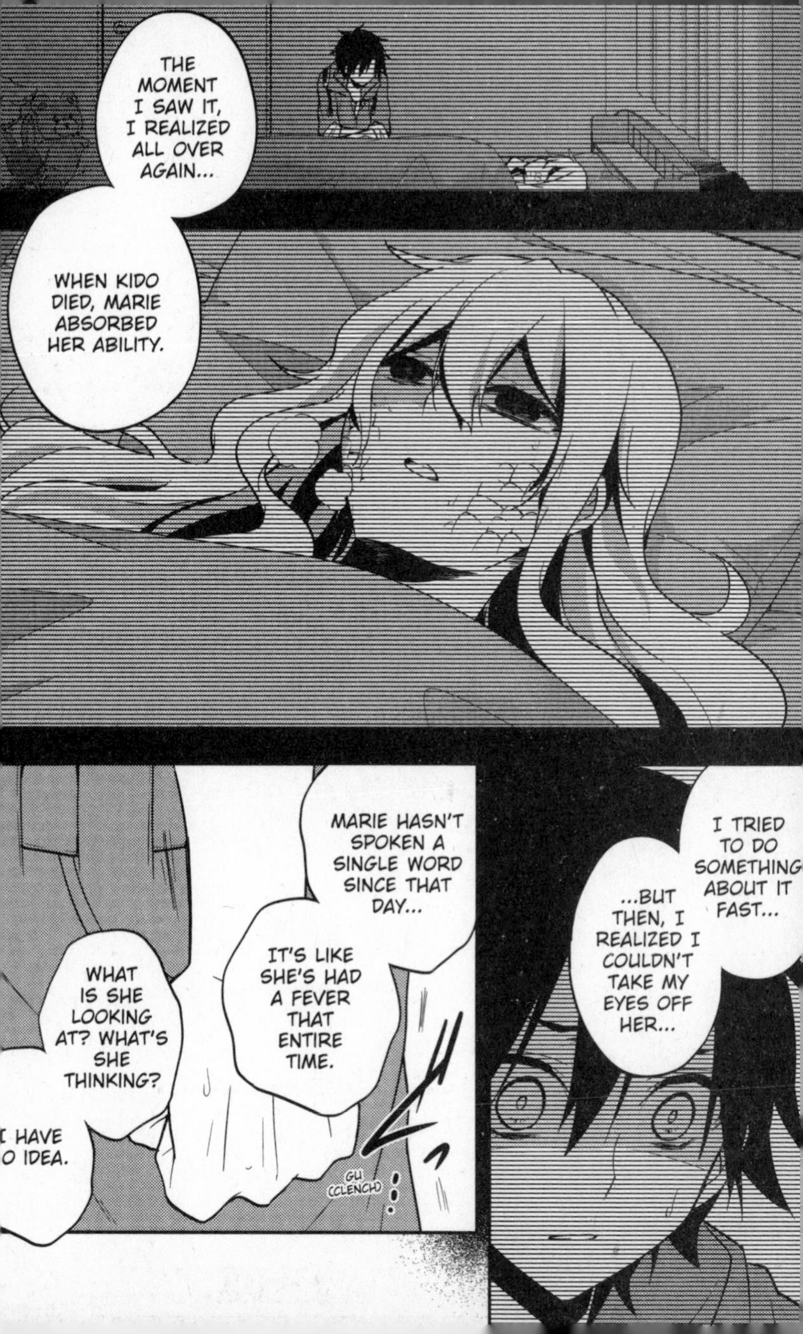
THE MOMENT I SAW IT, I REALIZED ALL OVER AGAIN...
WHEN KIDO DIED, MARIE ABSORBED HER ABILITY.
I TRIED TO DO SOMETHING ABOUT IT FAST...
...BUT THEN, I REALIZED I COULDN'T TAKE MY EYES OFF HER...
MARIE HASN'T SPOKEN A SINGLE WORD SINCE THAT DAY...
IT'S LIKE SHE'S HAD A FEVER THAT ENTIRE TIME.
WHAT IS SHE LOOKING AT? WHAT'S SHE THINKING?
I HAVE
O IDEA.
GU (CLENCH)

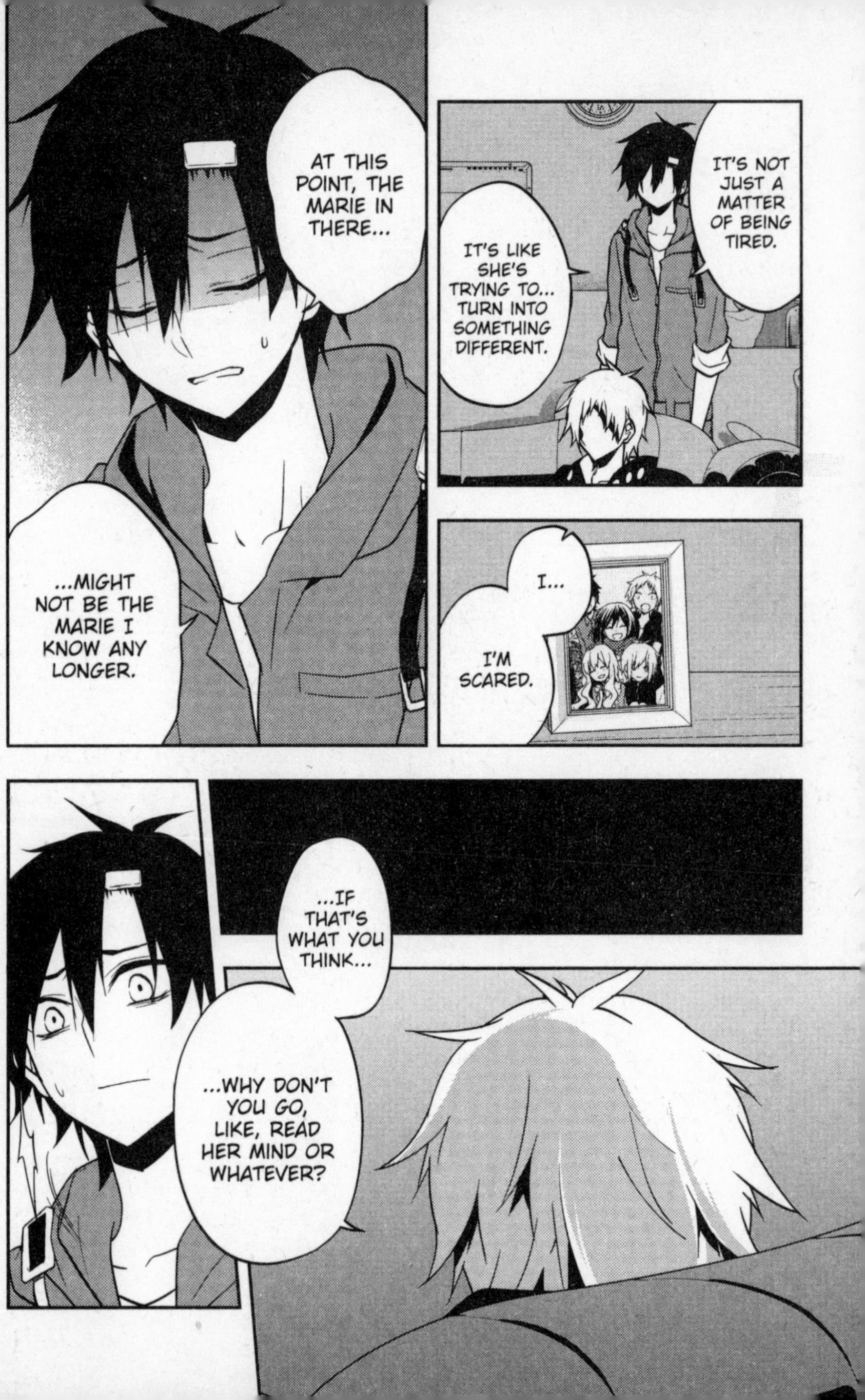
IT'S NOT JUST A MATTER OF BEING TIRED.
IT'S LIKE SHE'S TRYING TO... TURN INTO SOMETHING DIFFERENT.
I...
I'M SCARED.
AT THIS POINT, THE MARIE IN THERE...
...MIGHT NOT BE THE MARIE I KNOW ANY LONGER.
...IF THAT'S WHAT YOU THINK...
...WHY DON'T YOU GO, LIKE, READ HER MIND OR WHATEVER?

AT THIS POINT...

...THAT MIGHT BE GOOD, ACTUALLY.

...YEAH.

BUT...

...I...

...IF IT'S NOT SOMETHING WE CAN DO ANYTHING ABOUT...

...I WANT TO HEAR FROM HER...

...IN HER OWN VOICE.

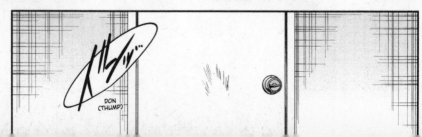

DON (THUMP)

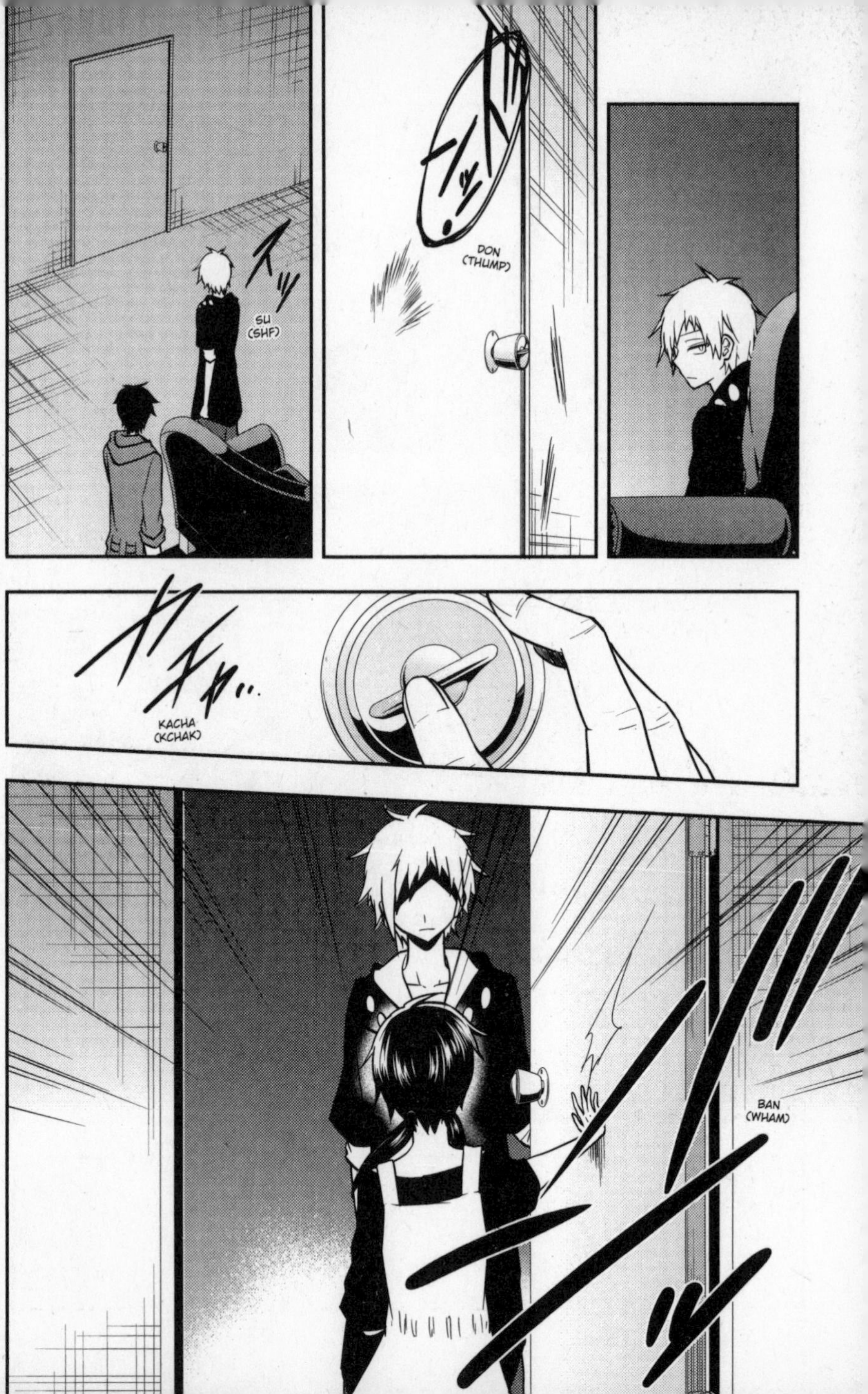
DON (THUMP)
SU (SHF)
KACHA (KCHAK)
BAN (WHAM)

...FOUND YOU.

...WHADDAYA WANT?

CHIRA
(GLANCE)

...IS THAT "MARIE" BEYOND THAT DOOR?

LOOKS LIKE SHE'S IN PAIN...

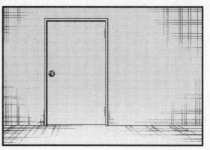

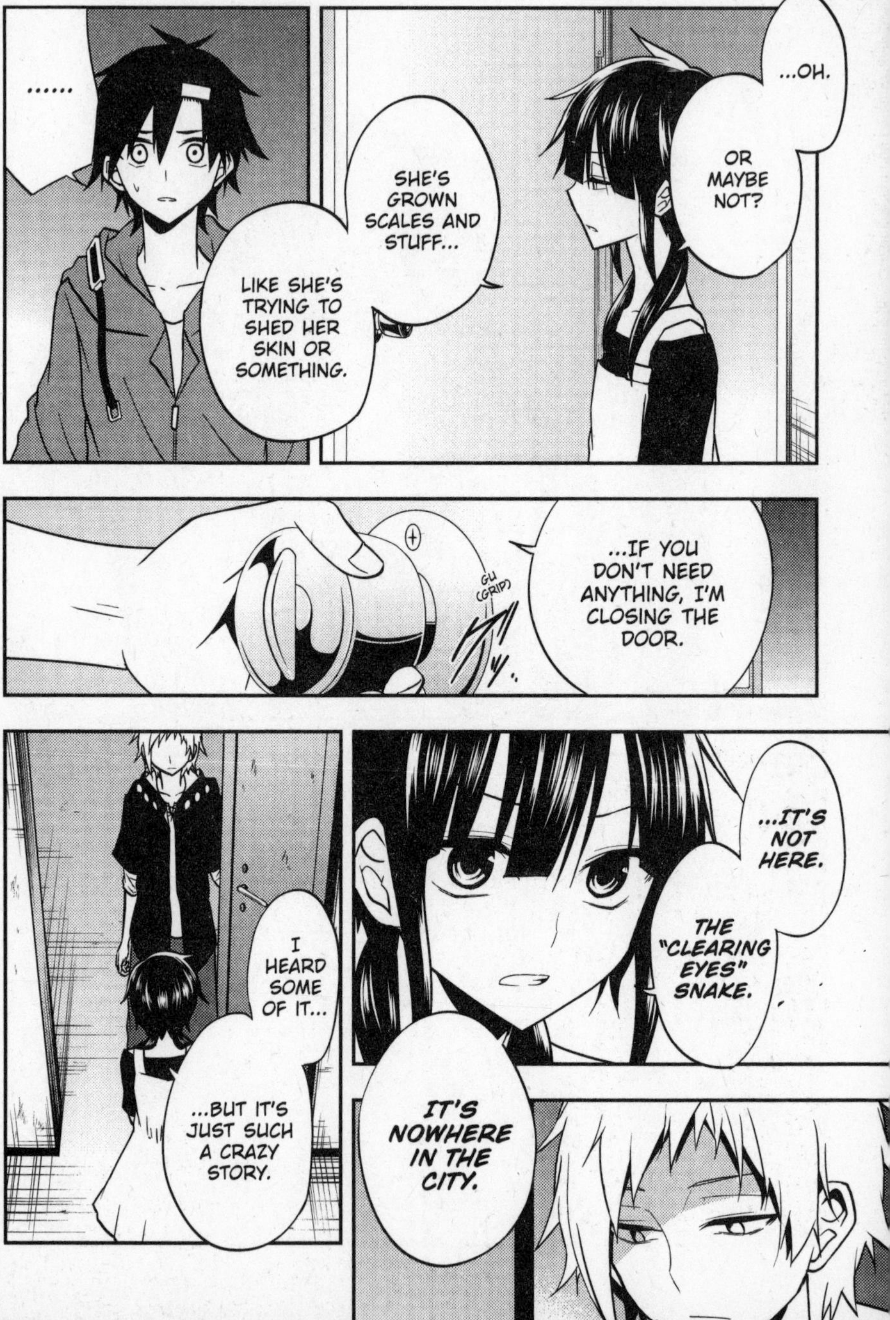
...OH.
OR MAYBE NOT?
SHE'S GROWN SCALES AND STUFF...
LIKE SHE'S TRYING TO SHED HER SKIN OR SOMETHING.
......
GU (GRIP)
...IF YOU DON'T NEED ANYTHING, I'M CLOSING THE DOOR.
...IT'S NOT HERE.
THE "CLEARING EYES" SNAKE.
IT'S NOWHERE IN THE CITY.
I HEARD SOME OF IT...
...BUT IT'S JUST SUCH A CRAZY STORY.

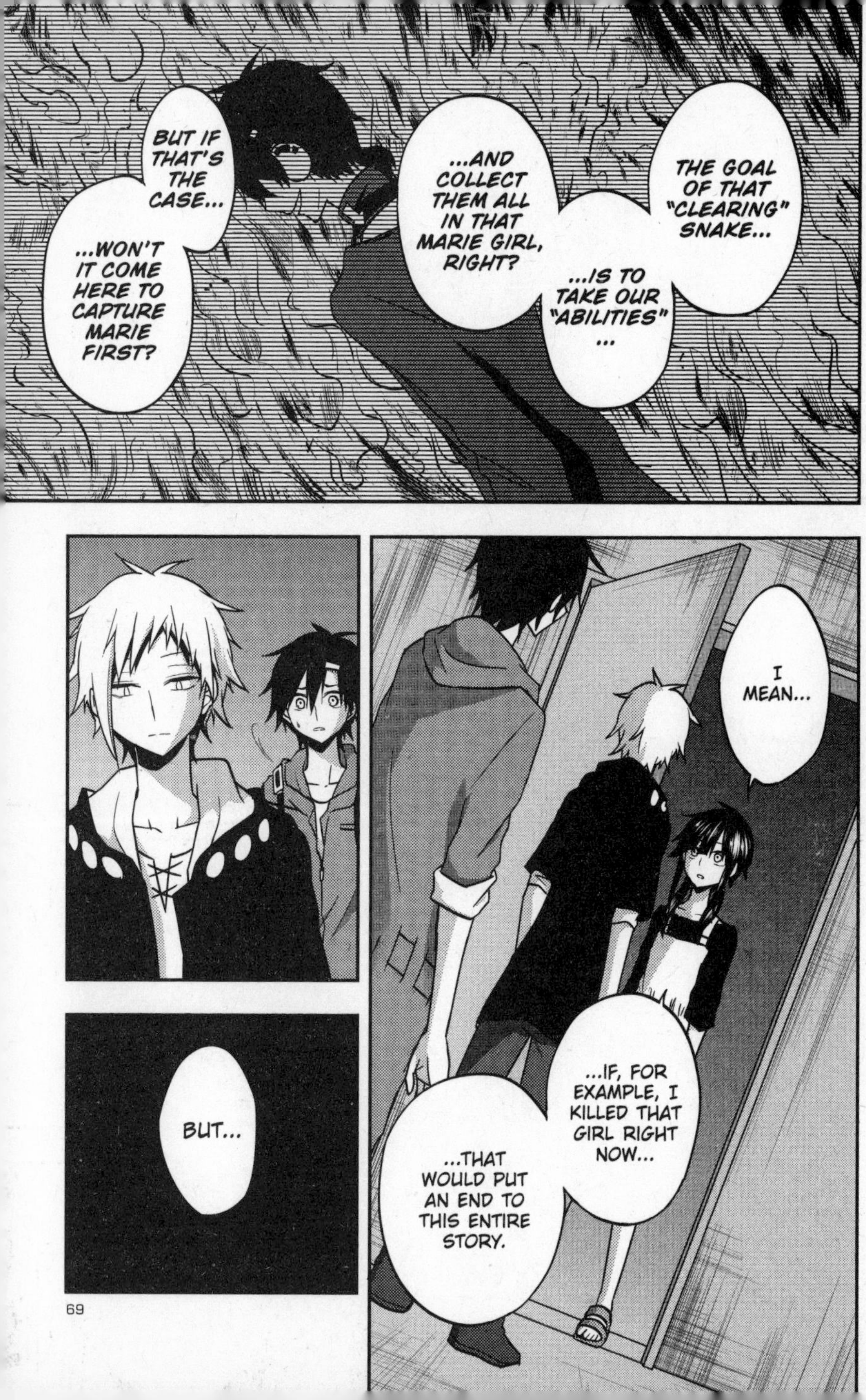
THE GOAL OF THAT "CLEARING" SNAKE...
...IS TO TAKE OUR "ABILITIES"...
...AND COLLECT THEM ALL IN THAT MARIE GIRL, RIGHT?
BUT IF THAT'S THE CASE...
...WON'T IT COME HERE TO CAPTURE MARIE FIRST?
I MEAN...
...IF, FOR EXAMPLE, I KILLED THAT GIRL RIGHT NOW...
...THAT WOULD PUT AN END TO THIS ENTIRE STORY.
BUT...

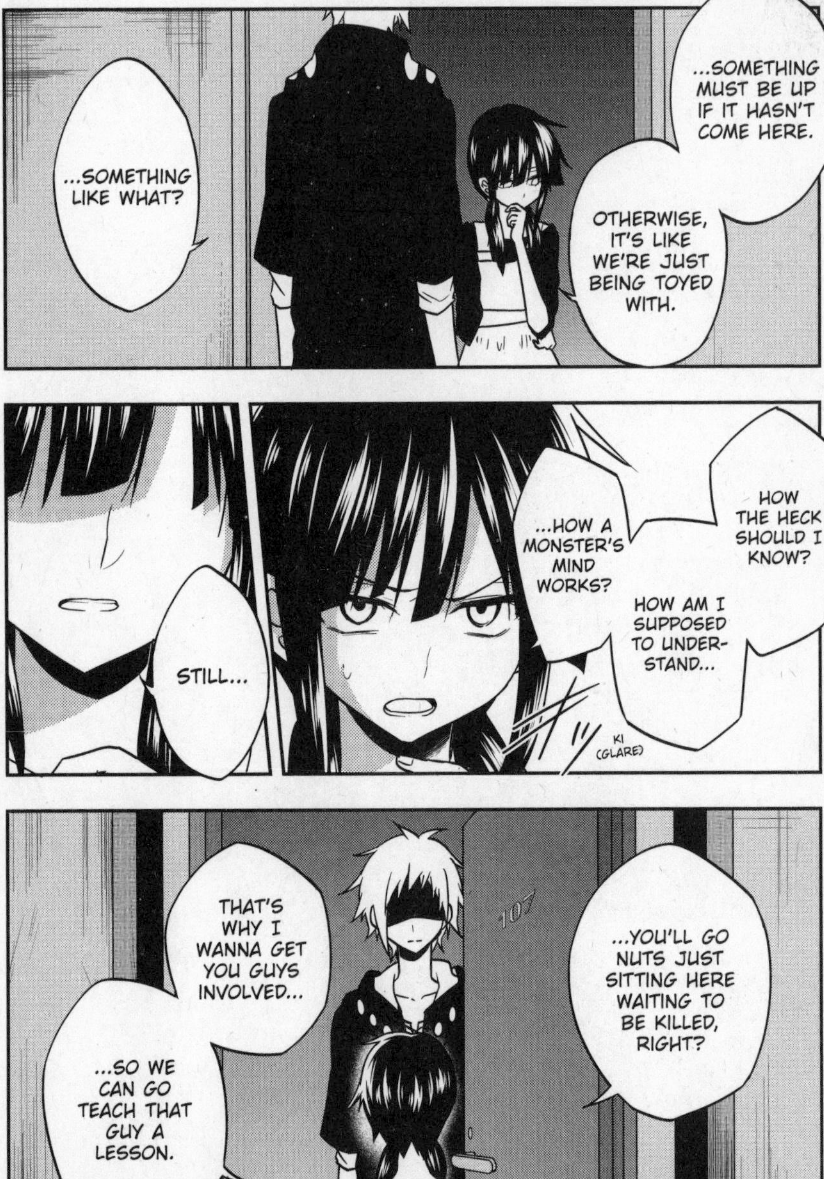
...SOMETHING MUST BE UP IF IT HASN'T COME HERE.
OTHERWISE, IT'S LIKE WE'RE JUST BEING TOYED WITH.
...SOMETHING LIKE WHAT?
HOW THE HECK SHOULD I KNOW?
HOW AM I SUPPOSED TO UNDER-STAND...
...HOW A MONSTER'S MIND WORKS?
KI (GLARE)
STILL...
...YOU'LL GO NUTS JUST SITTING HERE WAITING TO BE KILLED, RIGHT?
107
THAT'S WHY I WANNA GET YOU GUYS INVOLVED...
...SO WE CAN GO TEACH THAT GUY A LESSON.

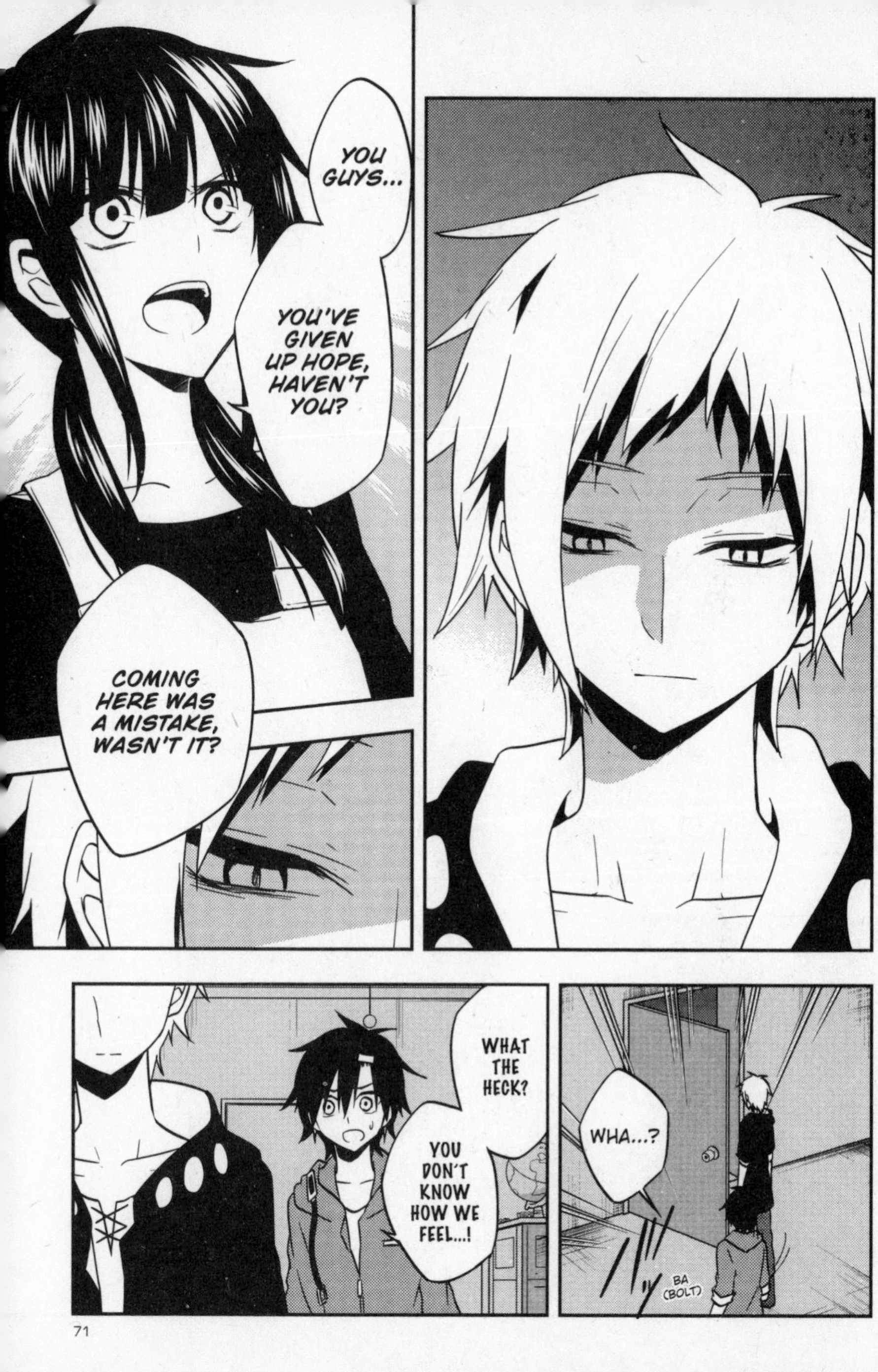
YOU GUYS...
YOU'VE GIVEN UP HOPE, HAVEN'T YOU?
COMING HERE WAS A MISTAKE, WASN'T IT?
WHA...?
BA (BOLT)
WHAT THE HECK?
YOU DON'T KNOW HOW WE FEEL...!

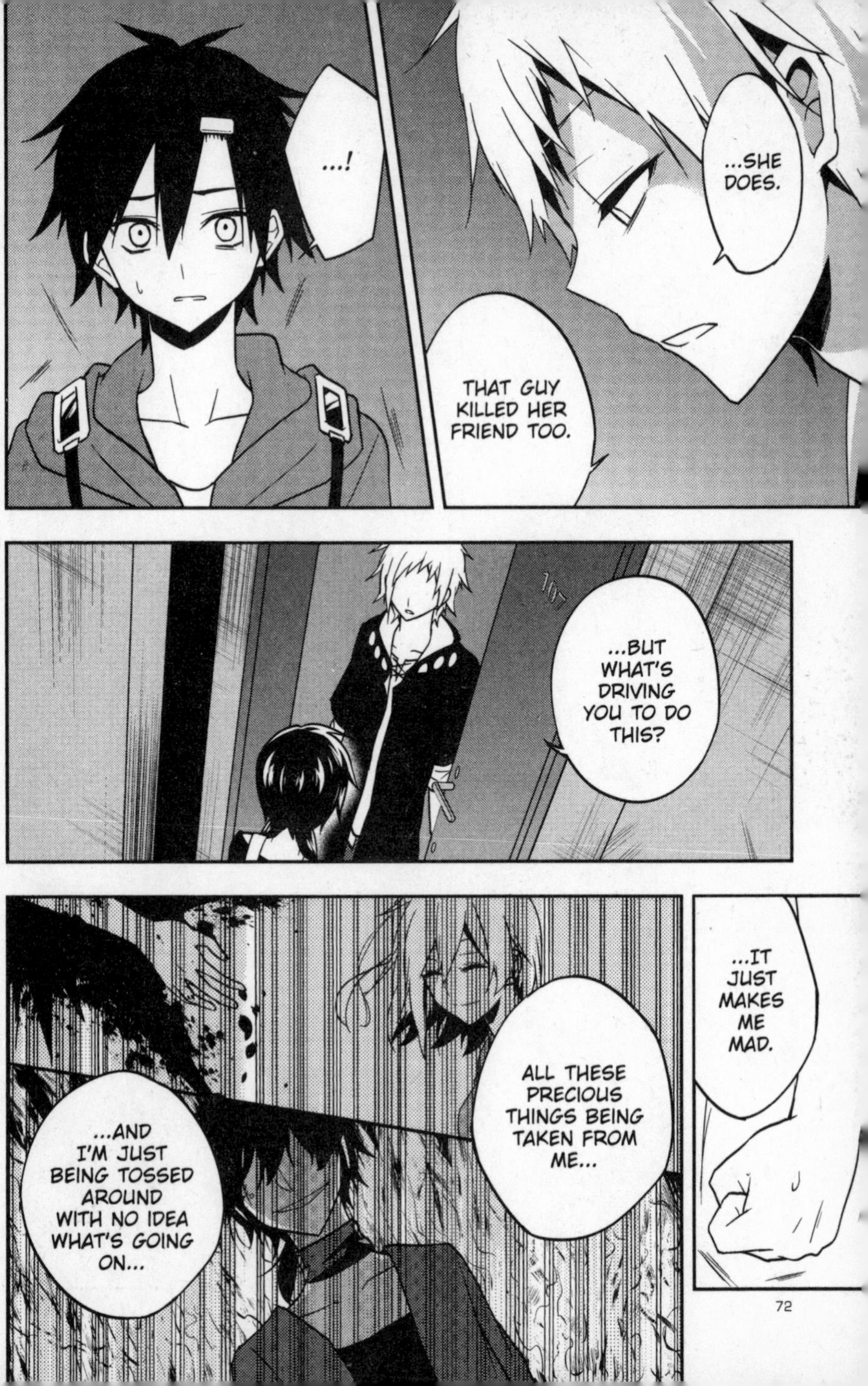
...SHE DOES.
THAT GUY KILLED HER FRIEND TOO.
...!
...BUT WHAT'S DRIVING YOU TO DO THIS?
...IT JUST MAKES ME MAD.
ALL THESE PRECIOUS THINGS BEING TAKEN FROM ME...
...AND I'M JUST BEING TOSSED AROUND WITH NO IDEA WHAT'S GOING ON...

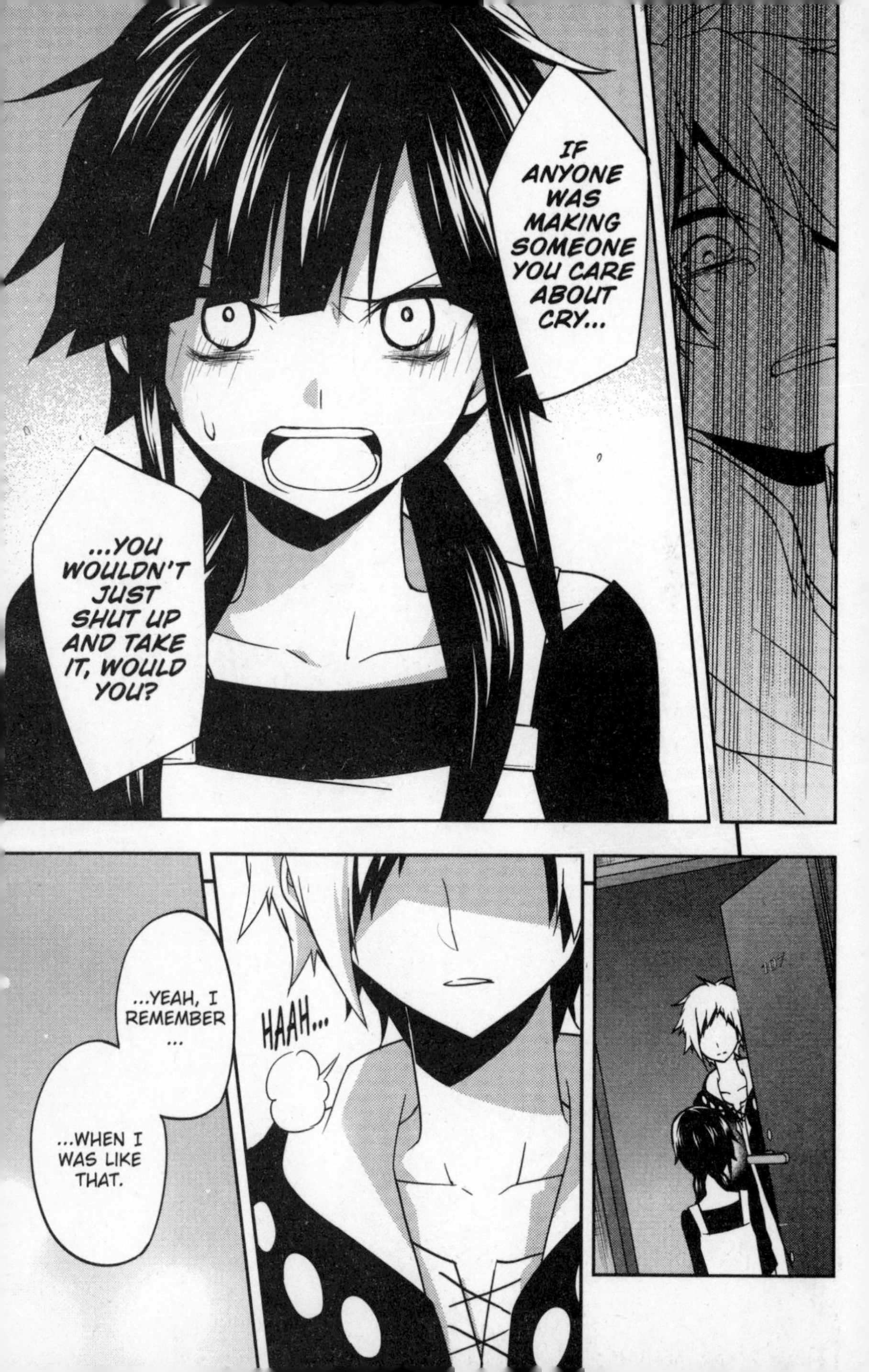
IF ANYONE WAS MAKING SOMEONE YOU CARE ABOUT CRY...
...YOU WOULDN'T JUST SHUT UP AND TAKE IT, WOULD YOU?
107
HAAH...
...YEAH, I REMEMBER...
...WHEN I WAS LIKE THAT.

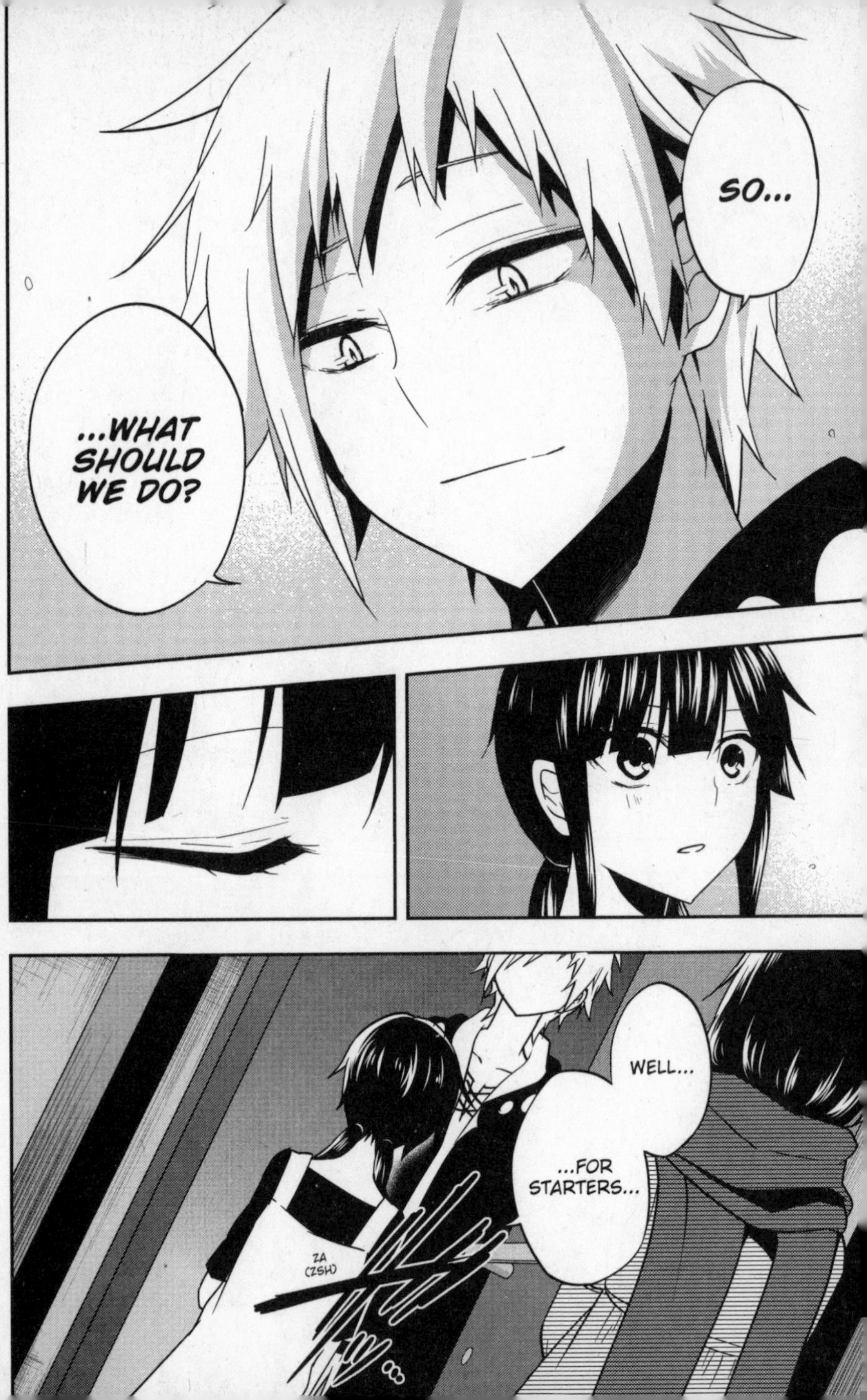
SO...
...WHAT SHOULD WE DO?
WELL...
...FOR STARTERS...
ZA (ZSH)

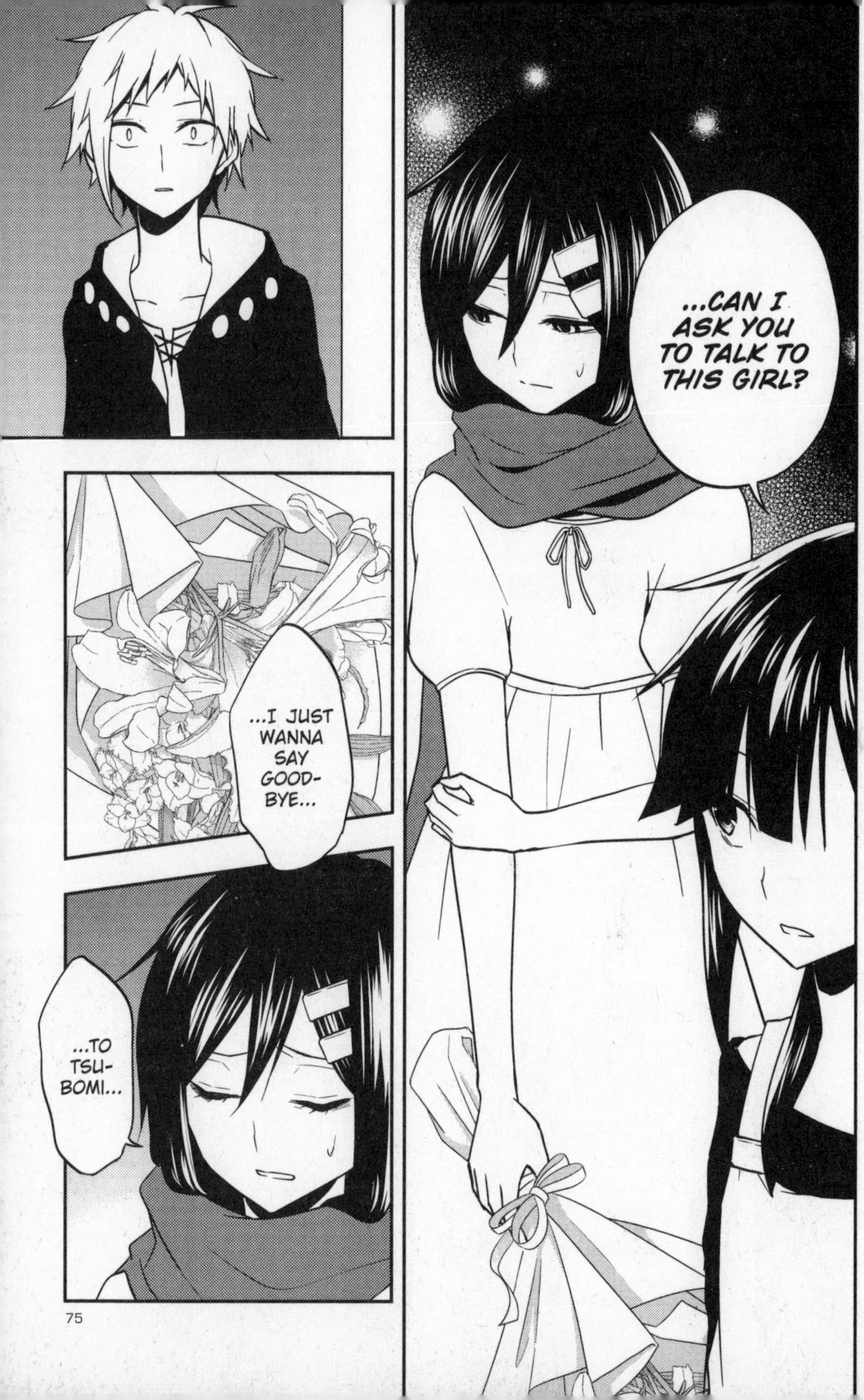
...CAN I ASK YOU TO TALK TO THIS GIRL?
...I JUST WANNA SAY GOOD-BYE...
...TO TSU-BOMI...

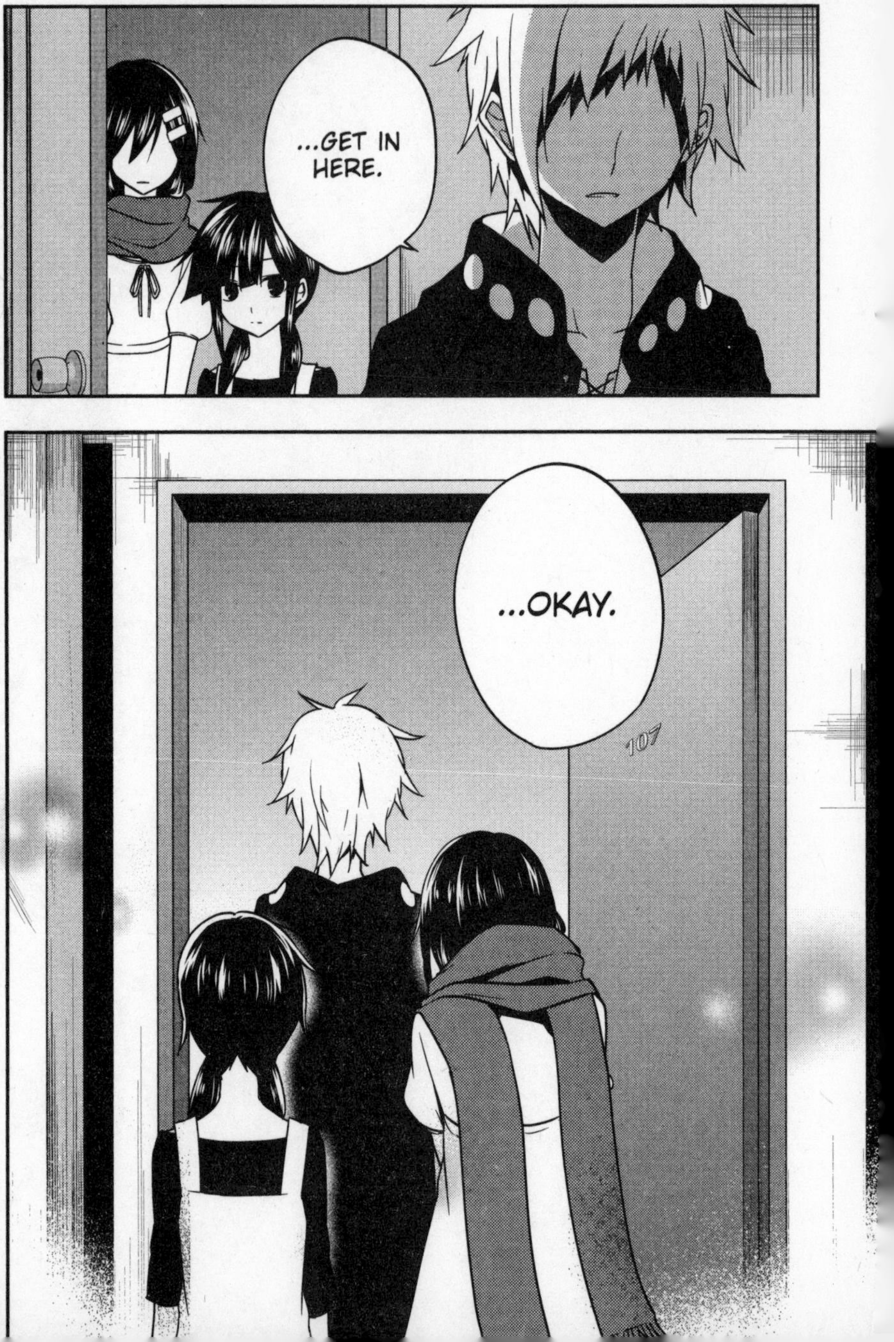
...GET IN HERE.
...OKAY.
107

KAGEROU DAZE

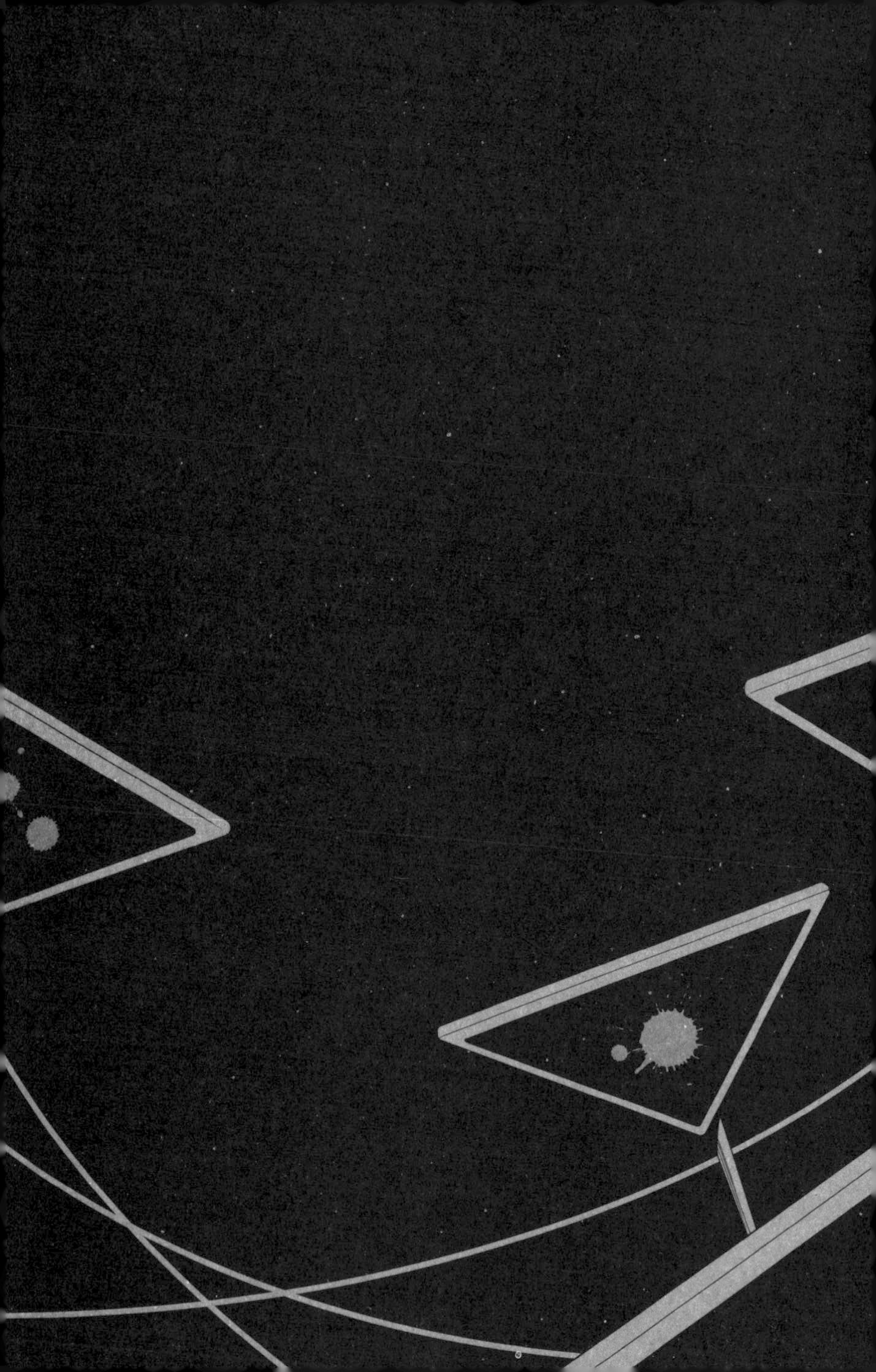

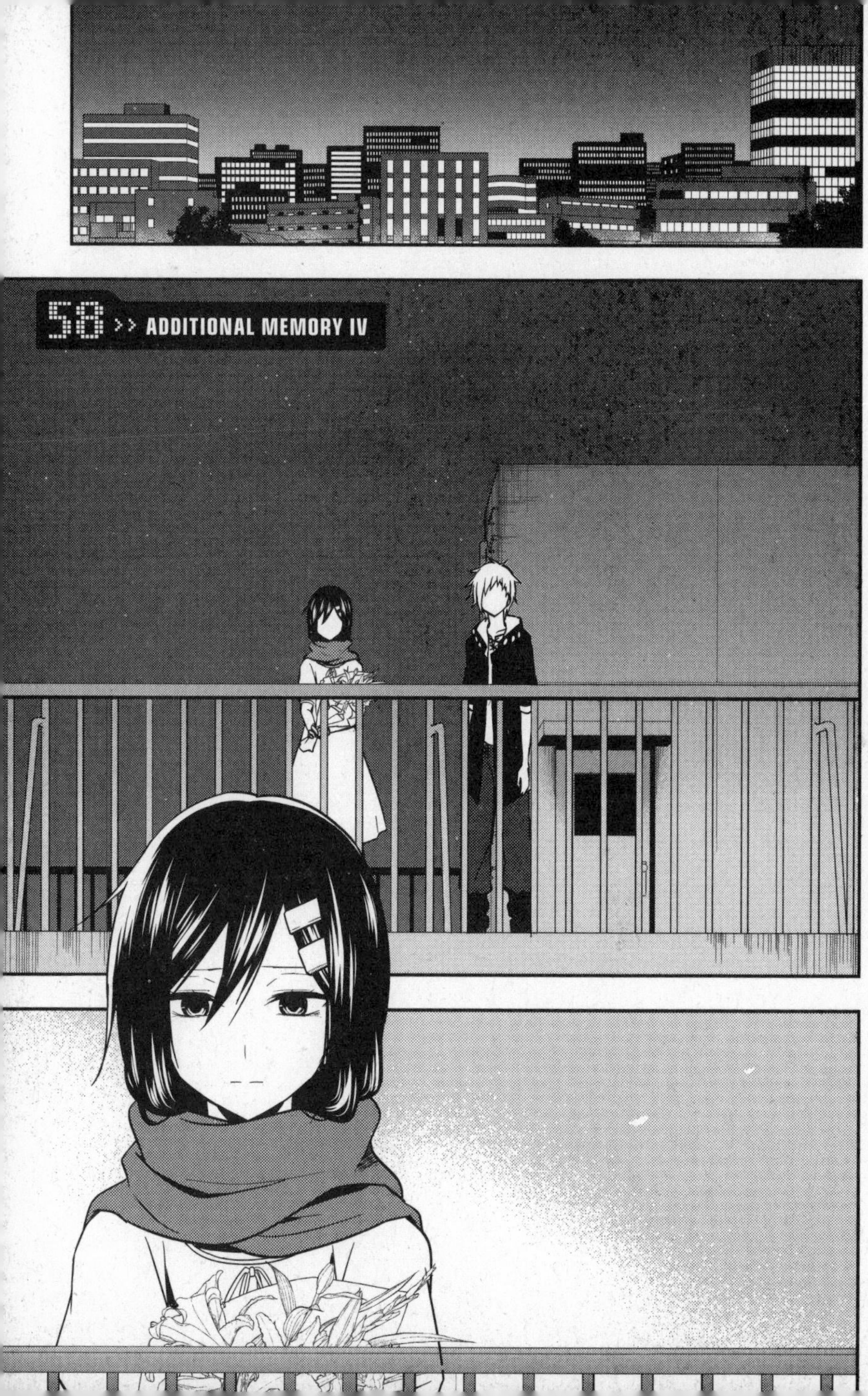
58 >> ADDITIONAL MEMORY IV

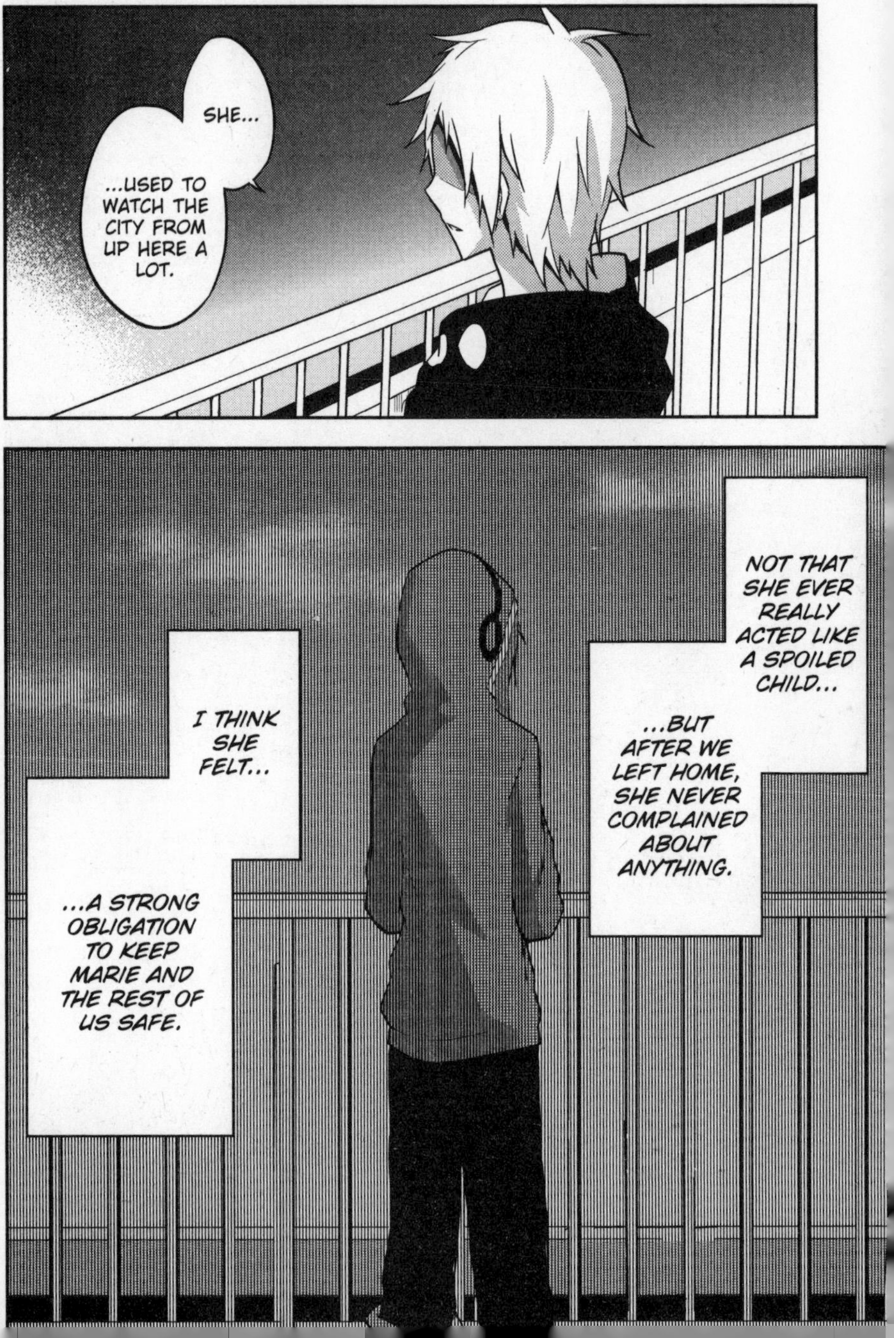
SHE...
...USED TO WATCH THE CITY FROM UP HERE A LOT.
NOT THAT SHE EVER REALLY ACTED LIKE A SPOILED CHILD...
...BUT AFTER WE LEFT HOME, SHE NEVER COMPLAINED ABOUT ANYTHING.
I THINK SHE FELT...
...A STRONG OBLIGATION TO KEEP MARIE AND THE REST OF US SAFE.

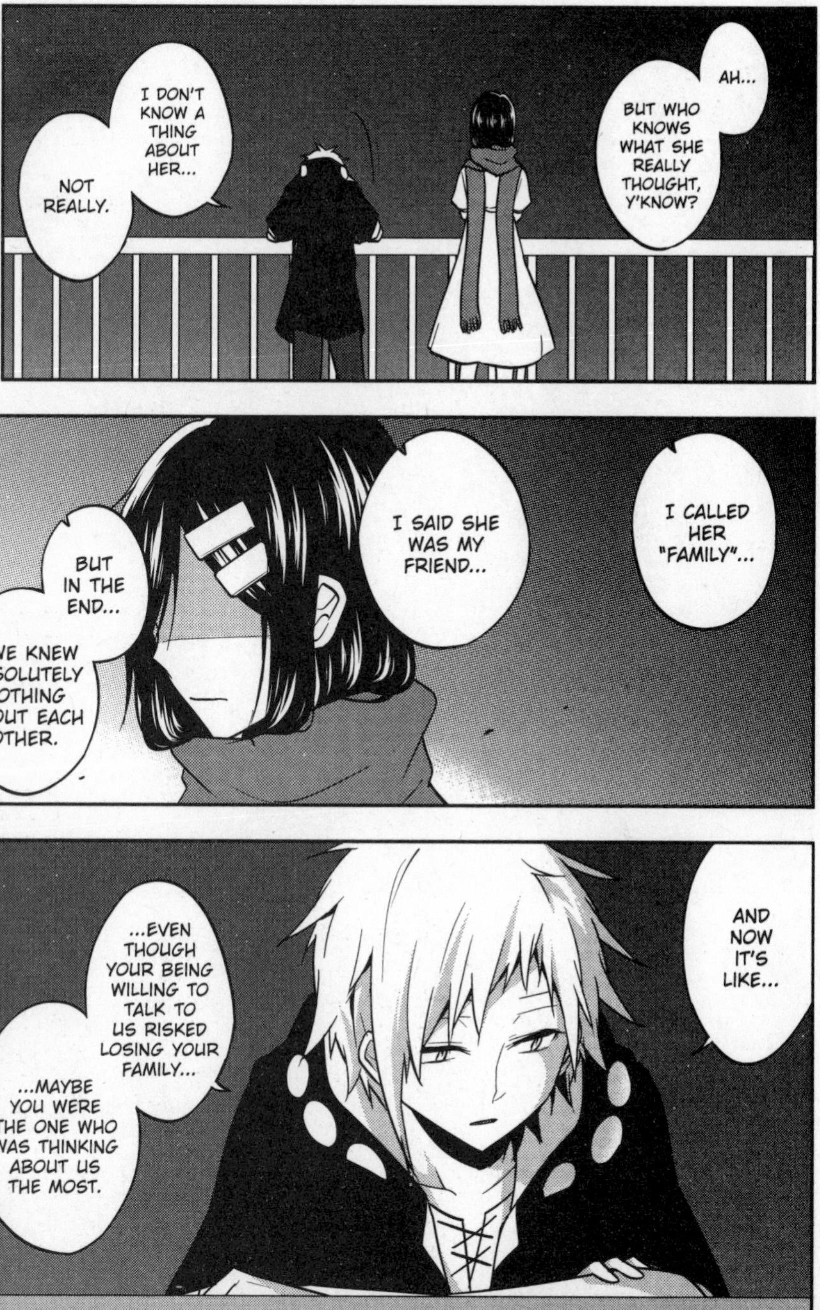
AH...
BUT WHO KNOWS WHAT SHE REALLY THOUGHT, Y'KNOW?
I DON'T KNOW A THING ABOUT HER...
NOT REALLY.
I CALLED HER "FAMILY"...
I SAID SHE WAS MY FRIEND...
BUT IN THE END...
...WE KNEW ABSOLUTELY NOTHING ABOUT EACH OTHER.
AND NOW IT'S LIKE...
...EVEN THOUGH YOUR BEING WILLING TO TALK TO US RISKED LOSING YOUR FAMILY...
...MAYBE YOU WERE THE ONE WHO WAS THINKING ABOUT US THE MOST.

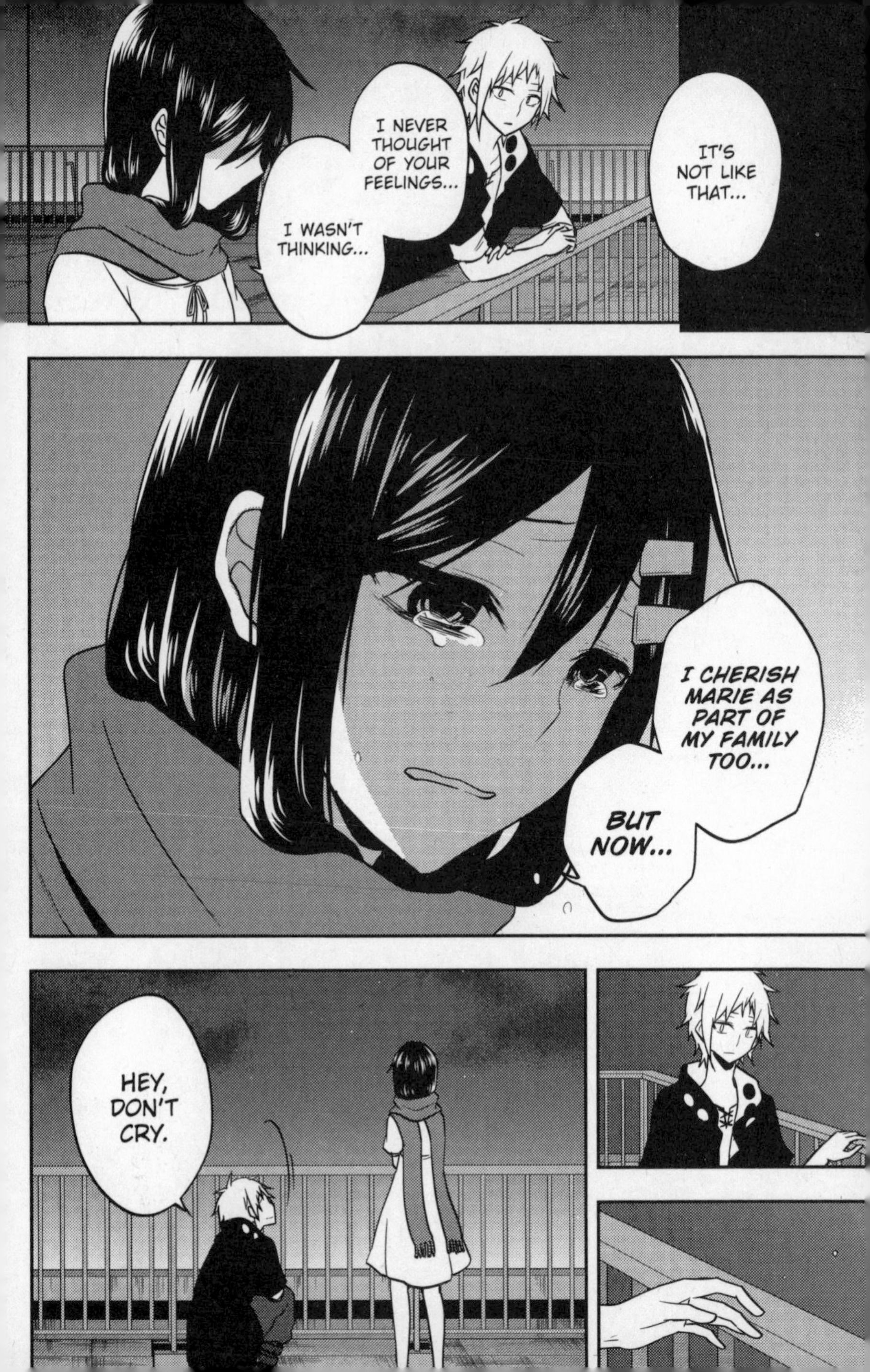
IT'S NOT LIKE THAT...
I NEVER THOUGHT OF YOUR FEELINGS...
I WASN'T THINKING...
I CHERISH MARIE AS PART OF MY FAMILY TOO...
BUT NOW...
HEY, DON'T CRY.

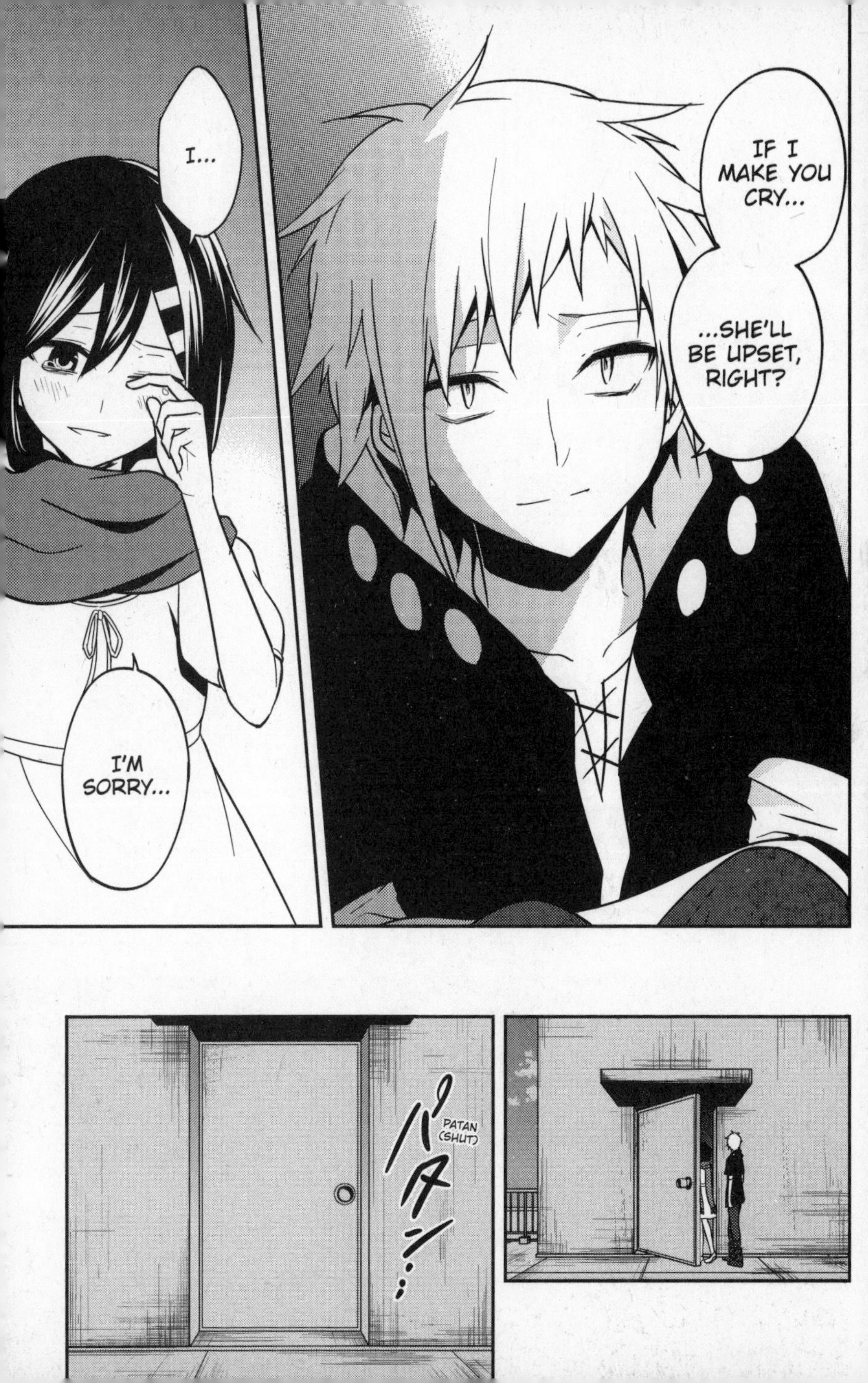
IF I MAKE YOU CRY...
...SHE'LL BE UPSET, RIGHT?
I...
I'M SORRY...
パタン…
PATAN (SHUT)

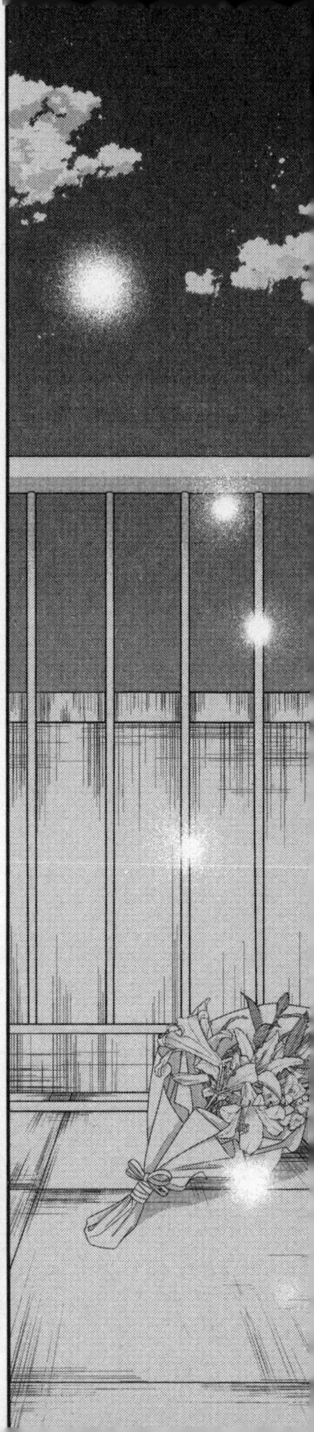

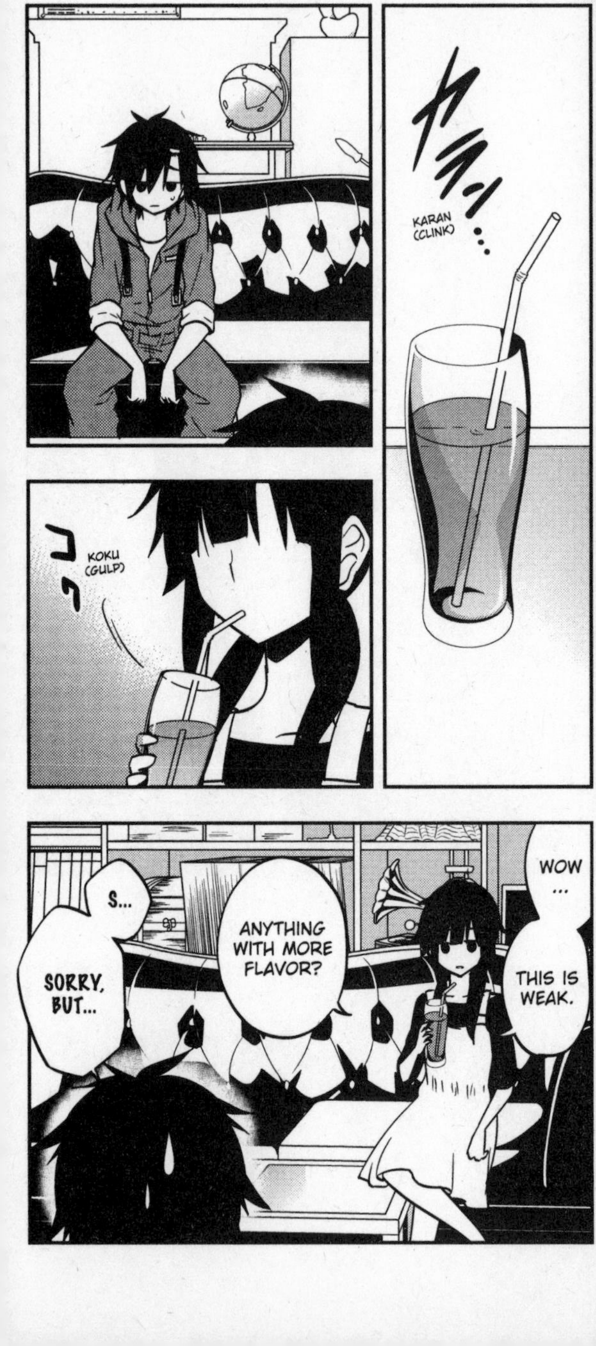
カラン…
KARAN (CLINK)
コク
KOKU (GULP)
WOW ...
THIS IS WEAK.
S...
SORRY, BUT...
ANYTHING WITH MORE FLAVOR?

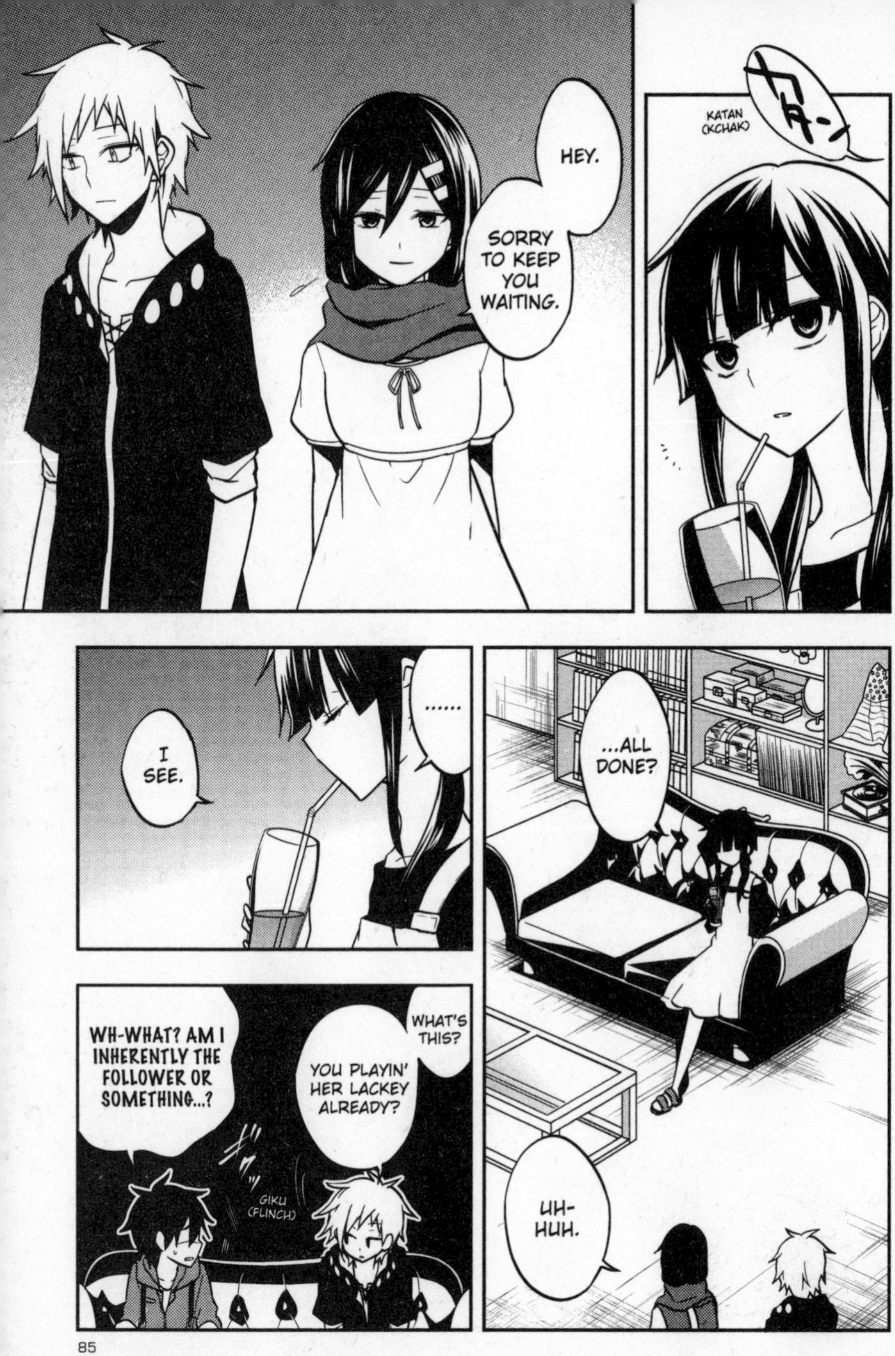
KATAN (KCHAK)
HEY.
SORRY TO KEEP YOU WAITING.
...ALL DONE?
UH-HUH.
......
I SEE.
WHAT'S THIS?
YOU PLAYIN' HER LACKEY ALREADY?
GIKU (FLINCH)
WH-WHAT? AM I INHERENTLY THE FOLLOWER OR SOMETHING...?

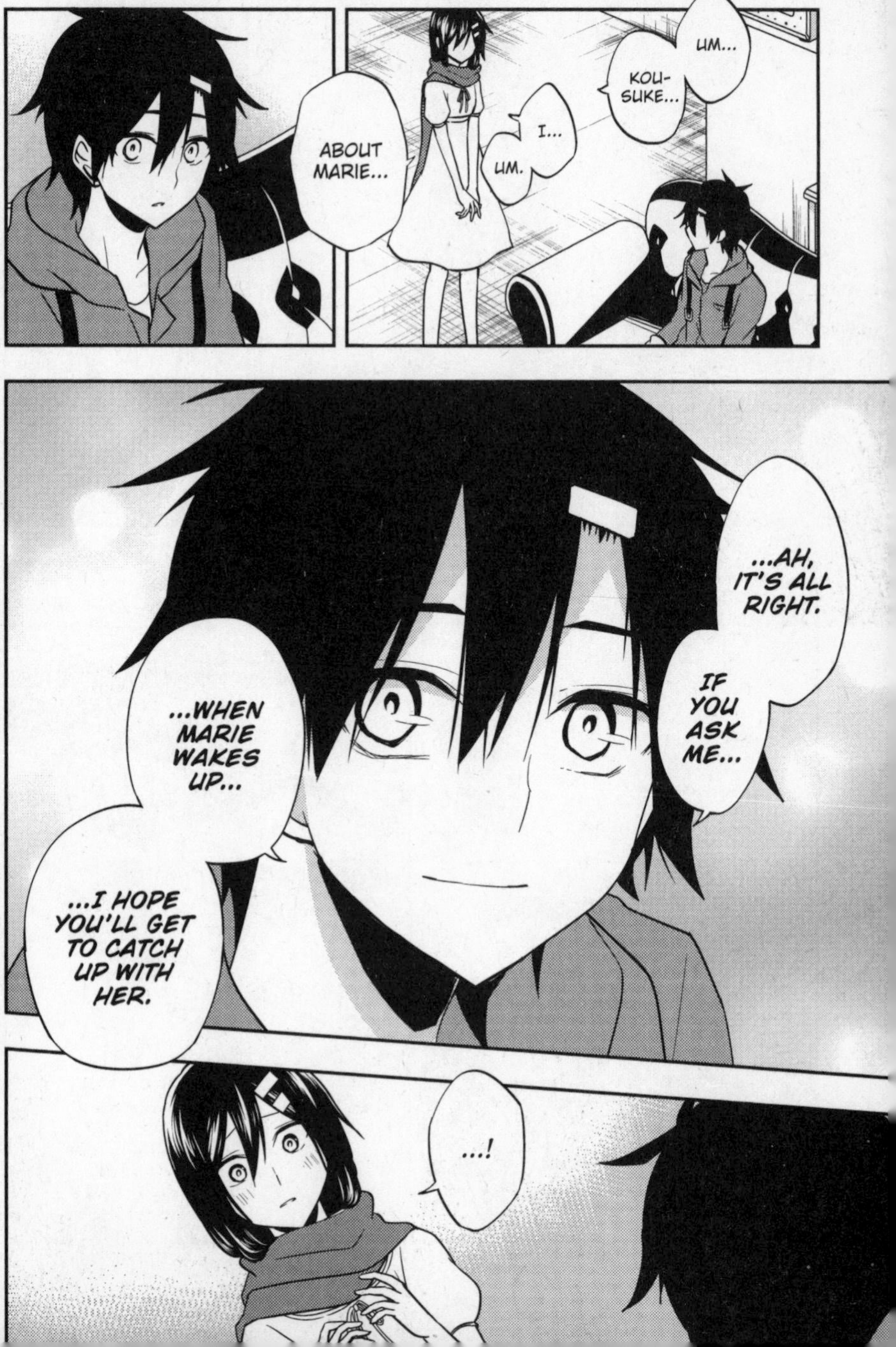
UM...
KOU-SUKE...
I...
UM.
ABOUT MARIE...
...AH, IT'S ALL RIGHT.
IF YOU ASK ME...
...WHEN MARIE WAKES UP...
...I HOPE YOU'LL GET TO CATCH UP WITH HER.
...!

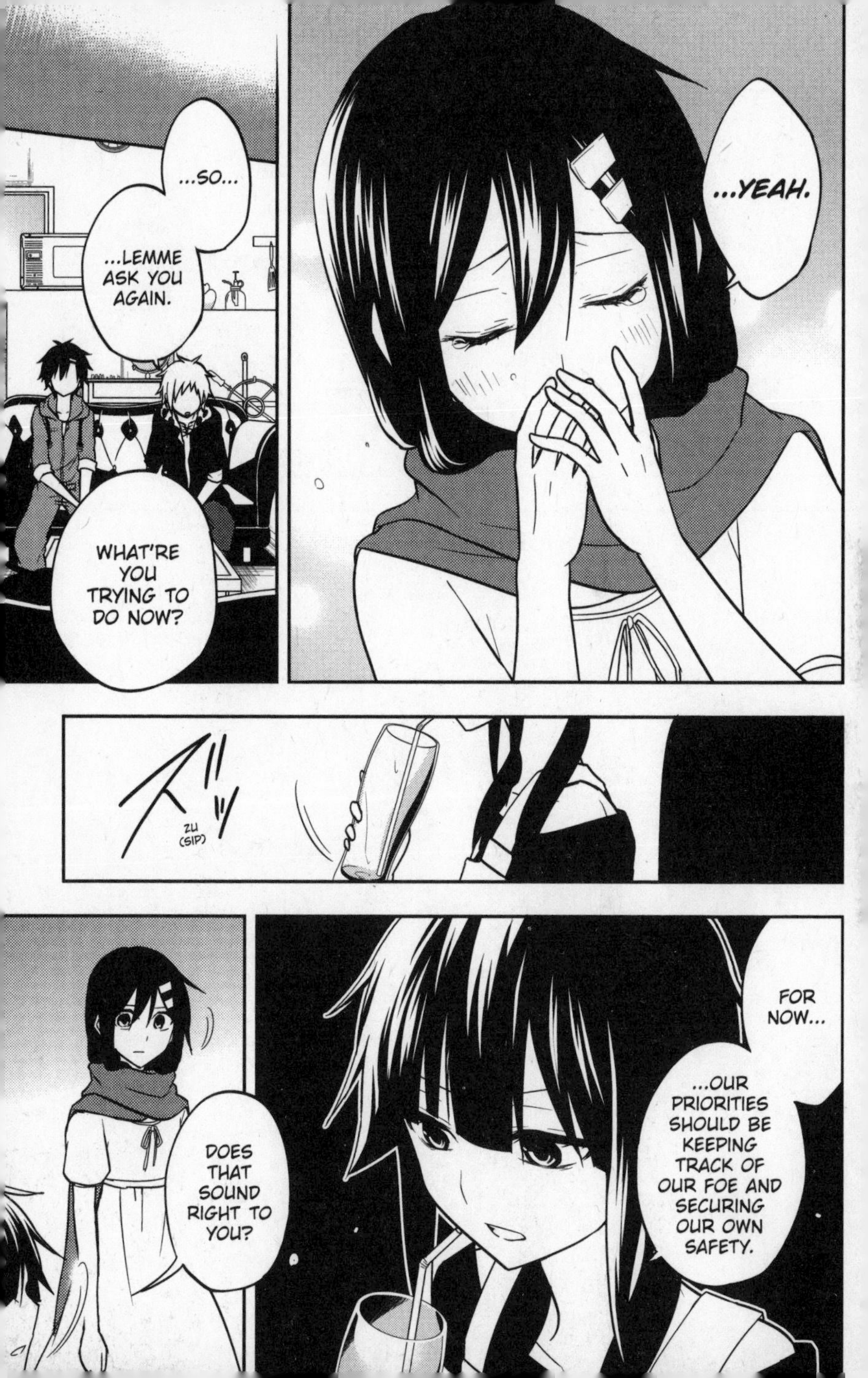
...YEAH.
...SO...
...LEMME ASK YOU AGAIN.
WHAT'RE YOU TRYING TO DO NOW?
ZU (SIP)
FOR NOW...
...OUR PRIORITIES SHOULD BE KEEPING TRACK OF OUR FOE AND SECURING OUR OWN SAFETY.
DOES THAT SOUND RIGHT TO YOU?

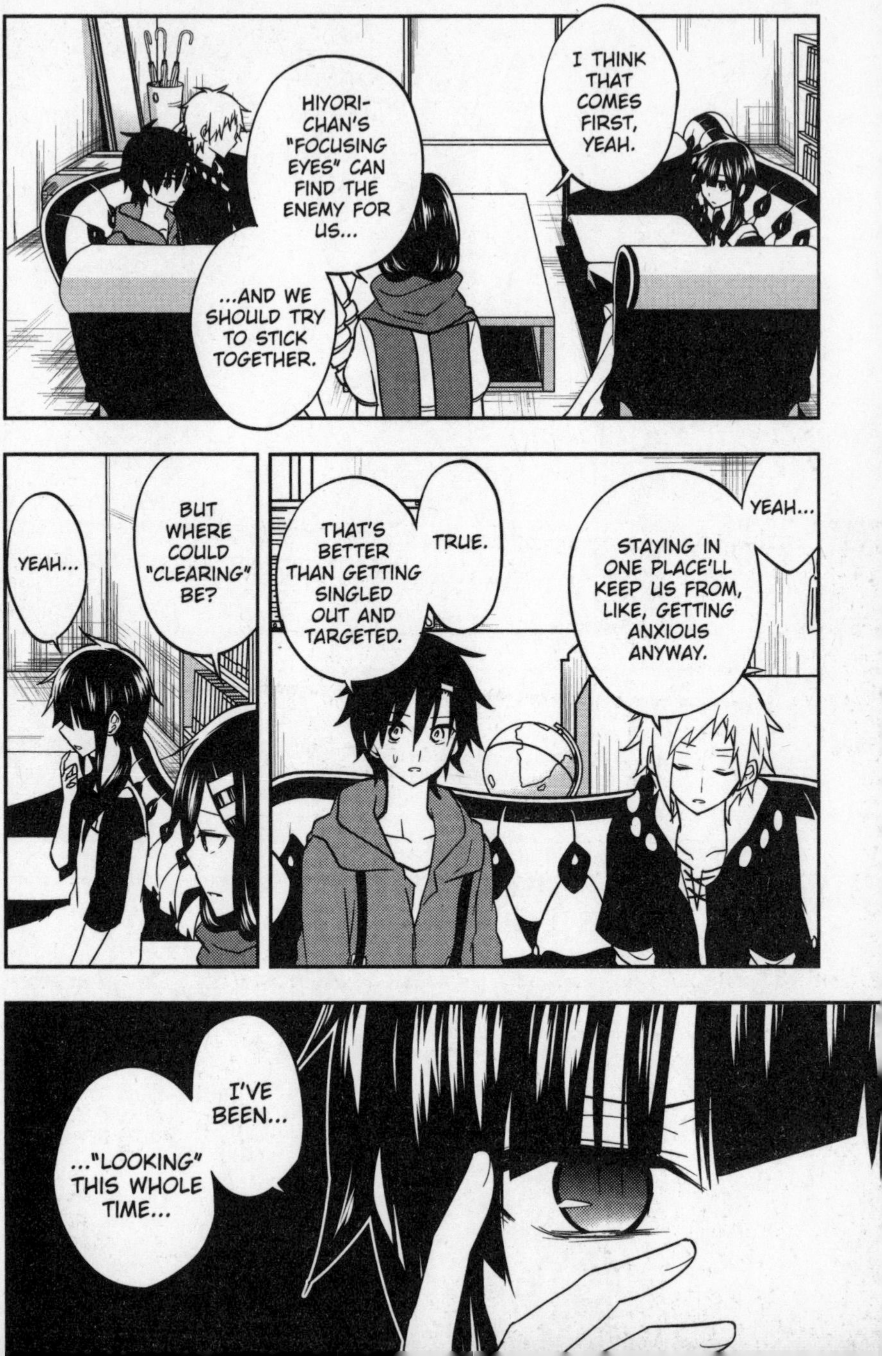
I THINK THAT COMES FIRST, YEAH.
HIYORI-CHAN'S "FOCUSING EYES" CAN FIND THE ENEMY FOR US...
...AND WE SHOULD TRY TO STICK TOGETHER.
YEAH...
STAYING IN ONE PLACE'LL KEEP US FROM, LIKE, GETTING ANXIOUS ANYWAY.
TRUE.
THAT'S BETTER THAN GETTING SINGLED OUT AND TARGETED.
BUT WHERE COULD "CLEARING" BE?
YEAH...
I'VE BEEN...
..."LOOKING" THIS WHOLE TIME...

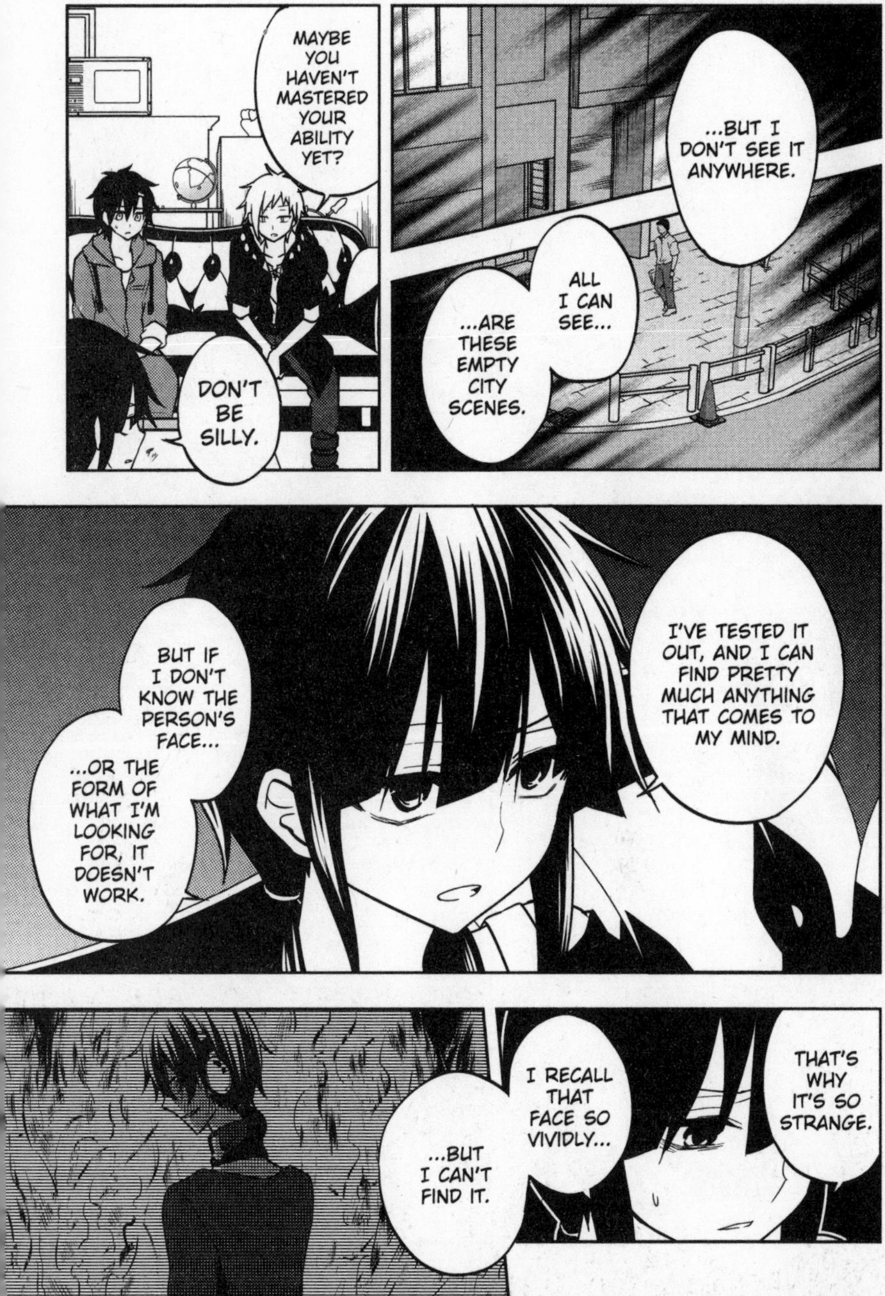
...BUT I DON'T SEE IT ANYWHERE.
ALL I CAN SEE...
...ARE THESE EMPTY CITY SCENES.
MAYBE YOU HAVEN'T MASTERED YOUR ABILITY YET?
DON'T BE SILLY.
I'VE TESTED IT OUT, AND I CAN FIND PRETTY MUCH ANYTHING THAT COMES TO MY MIND.
BUT IF I DON'T KNOW THE PERSON'S FACE...
...OR THE FORM OF WHAT I'M LOOKING FOR, IT DOESN'T WORK.
THAT'S WHY IT'S SO STRANGE.
I RECALL THAT FACE SO VIVIDLY...
...BUT I CAN'T FIND IT.

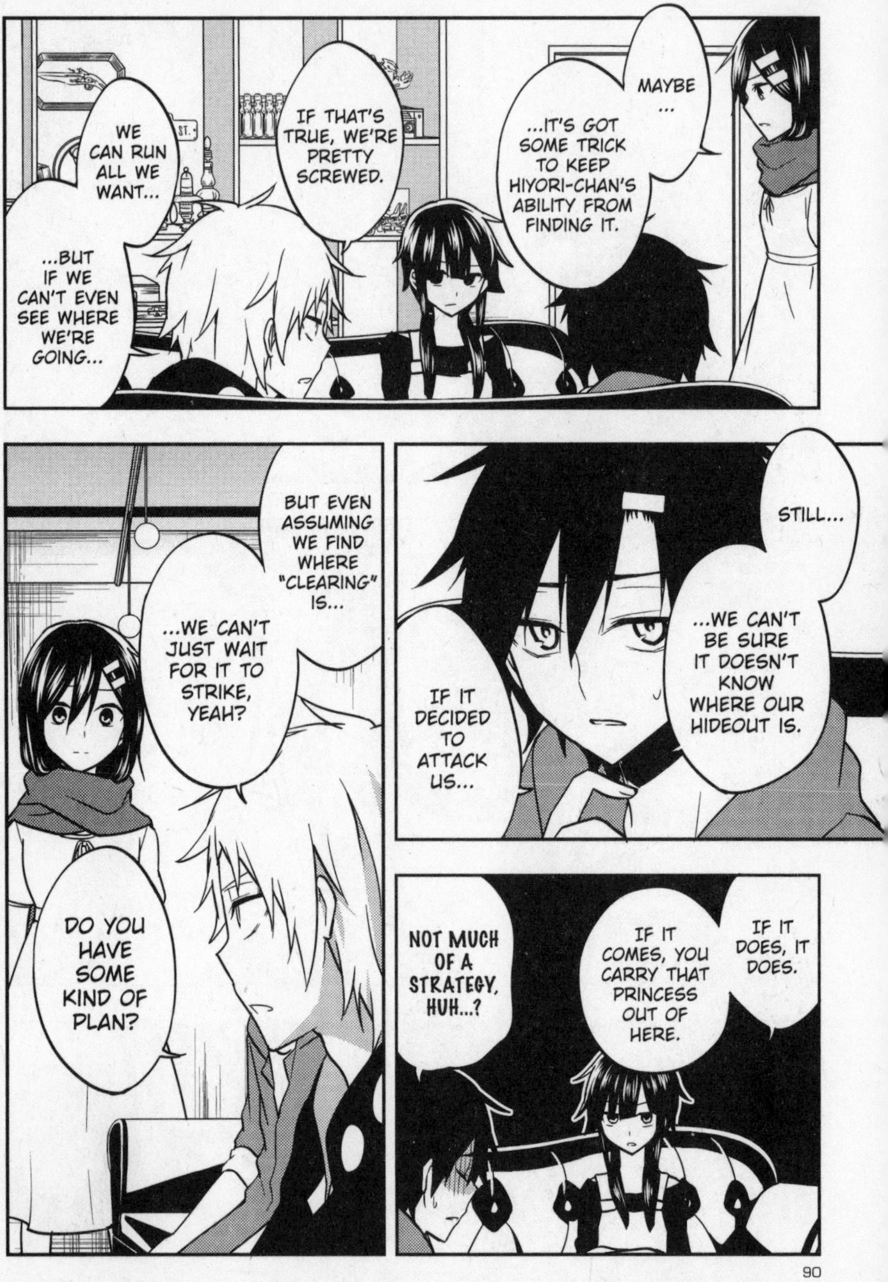
MAYBE ...
...IT'S GOT SOME TRICK TO KEEP HIYORI-CHAN'S ABILITY FROM FINDING IT.
IF THAT'S TRUE, WE'RE PRETTY SCREWED.
WE CAN RUN ALL WE WANT...
...BUT IF WE CAN'T EVEN SEE WHERE WE'RE GOING...
STILL...
...WE CAN'T BE SURE IT DOESN'T KNOW WHERE OUR HIDEOUT IS.
IF IT DECIDED TO ATTACK US...
IF IT DOES, IT DOES.
IF IT COMES, YOU CARRY THAT PRINCESS OUT OF HERE.
NOT MUCH OF A STRATEGY, HUH...?
BUT EVEN ASSUMING WE FIND WHERE "CLEARING" IS...
...WE CAN'T JUST WAIT FOR IT TO STRIKE, YEAH?
DO YOU HAVE SOME KIND OF PLAN?

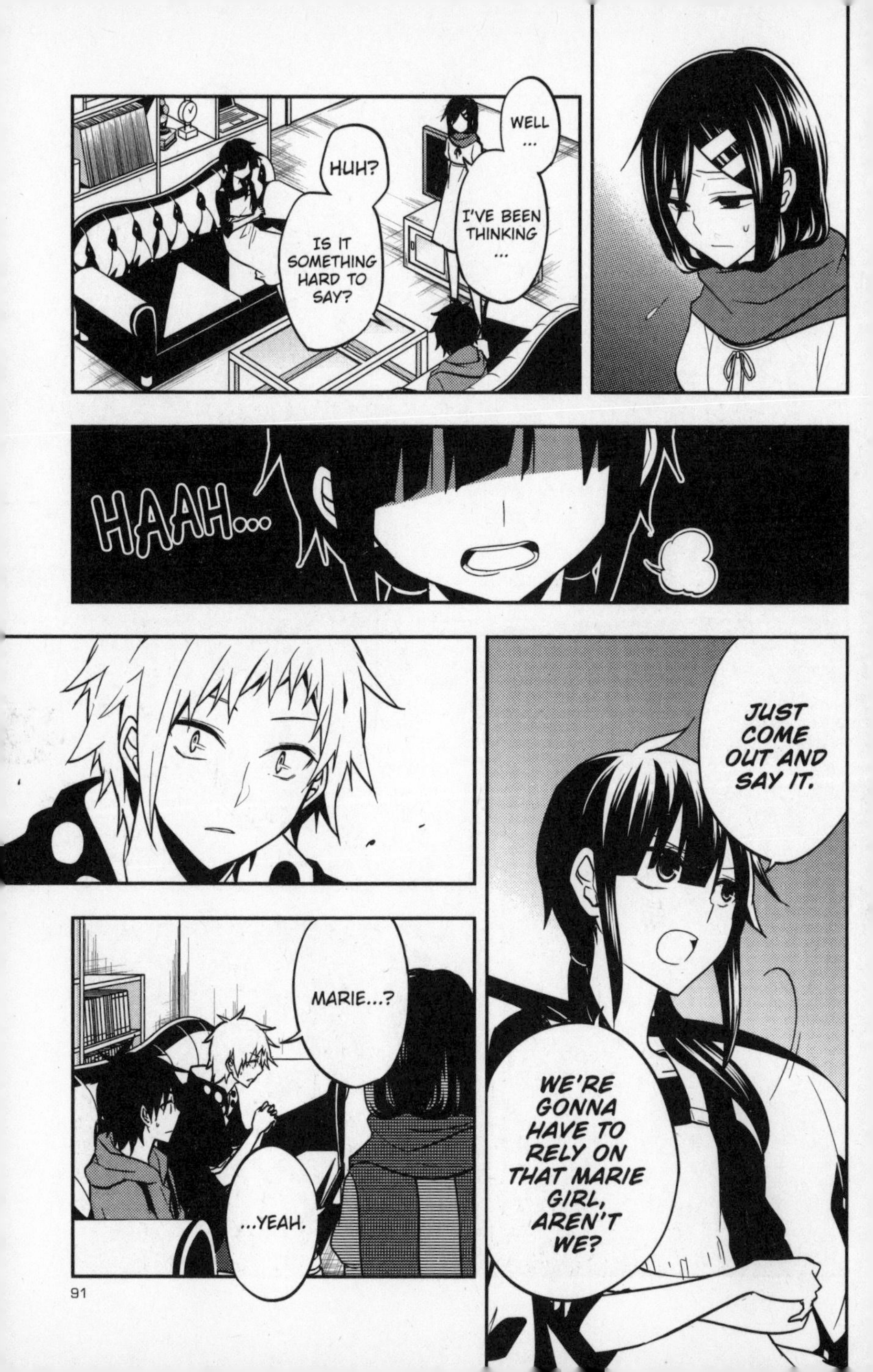
WELL ...
I'VE BEEN THINKING ...
HUH?
IS IT SOMETHING HARD TO SAY?
HAAH...
JUST COME OUT AND SAY IT.
WE'RE GONNA HAVE TO RELY ON THAT MARIE GIRL, AREN'T WE?
MARIE...?
...YEAH.

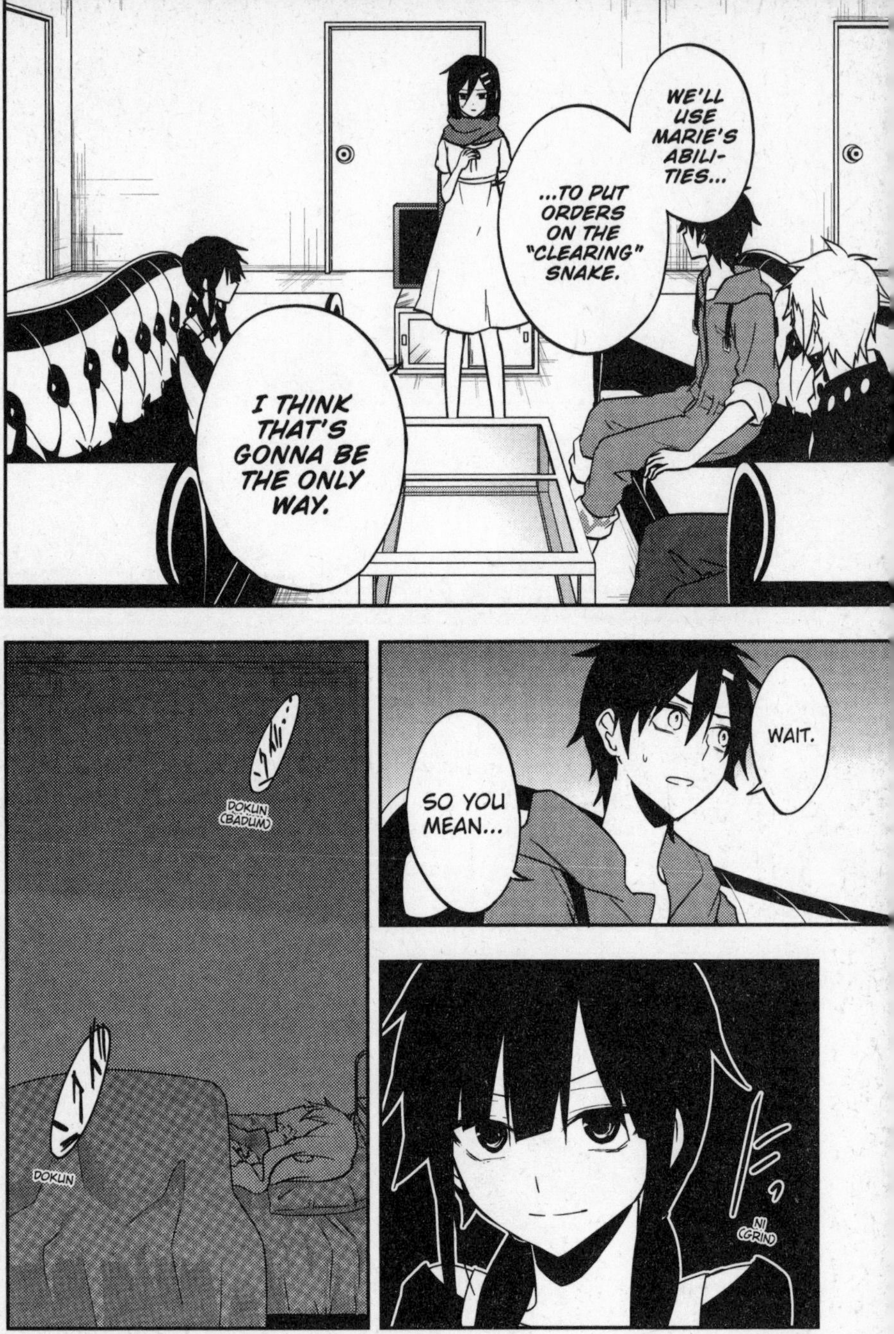
WE'LL USE MARIE'S ABILITIES...
...TO PUT ORDERS ON THE "CLEARING" SNAKE.
I THINK THAT'S GONNA BE THE ONLY WAY.
WAIT.
SO YOU MEAN...
NI (GRIN)
DOKUN (BADUM)
DOKUN

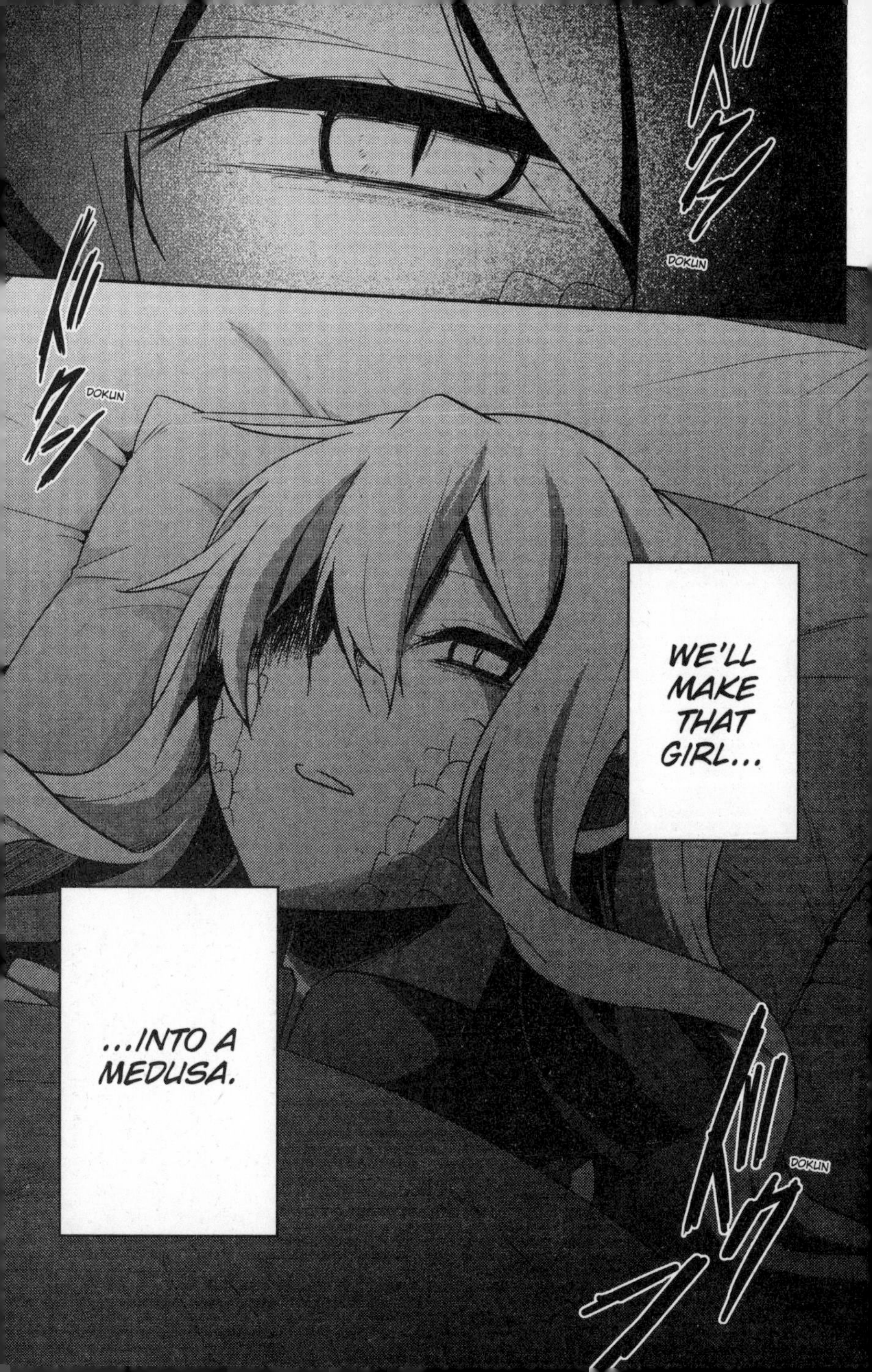
DOKUN
DOKUN
WE'LL MAKE THAT GIRL...
...INTO A MEDUSA.
DOKUN

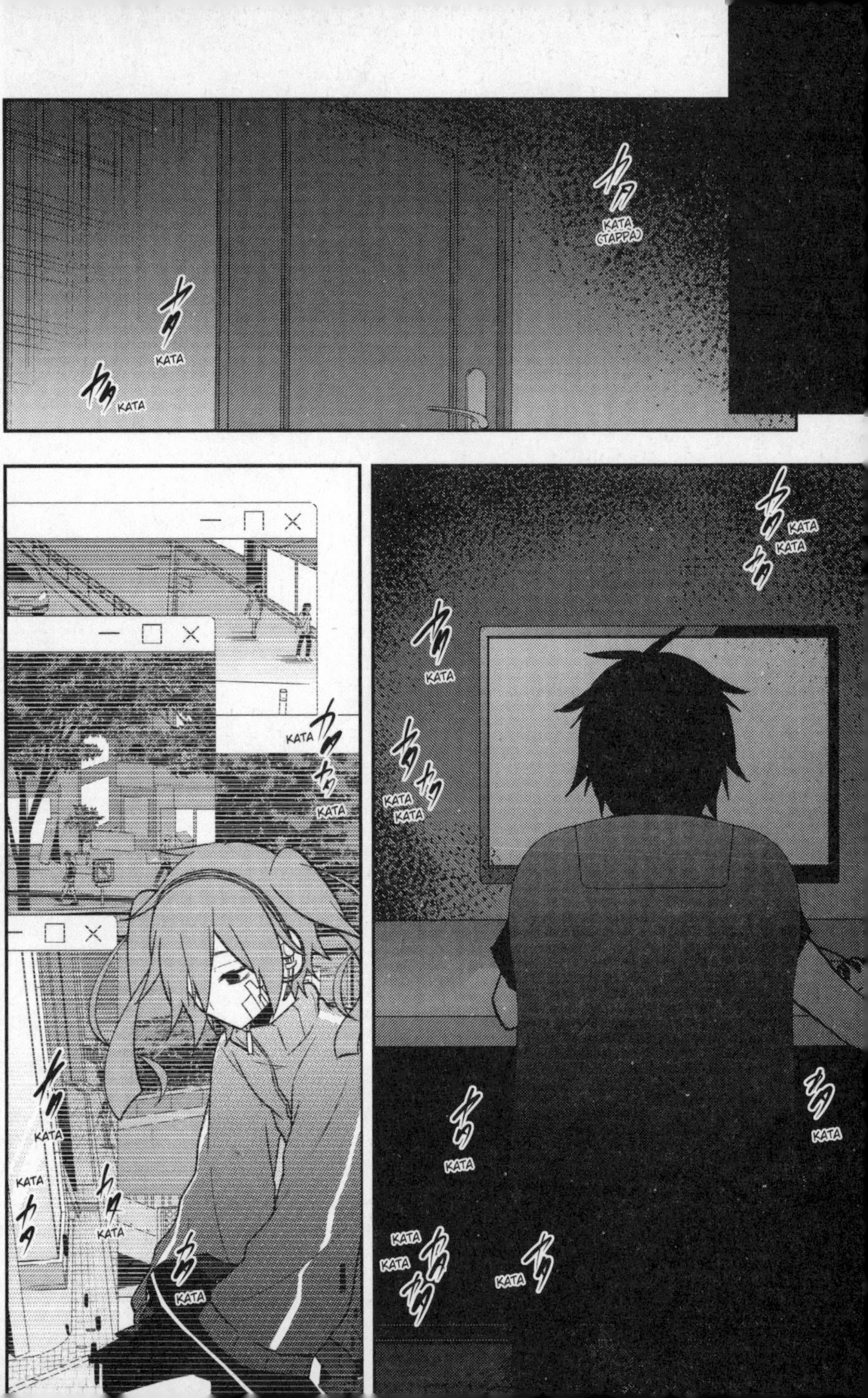
KATA (TAPPA)
KATA
KATA
KATA KATA
KATA
KATA KATA
KATA
KATA
KATA KATA
KATA
KATA
KATA
KATA
KATA
KATA
KATA

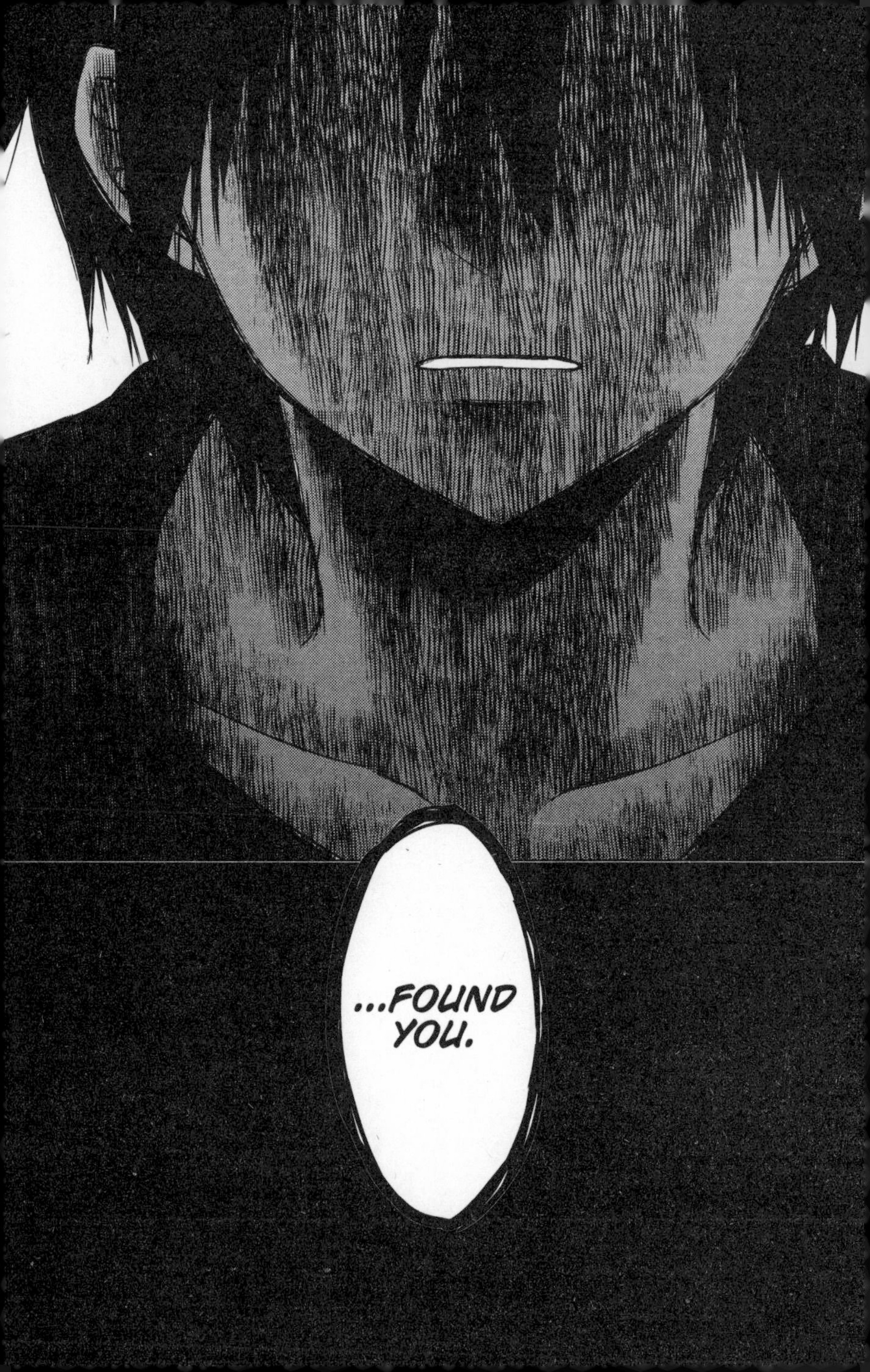
...FOUND YOU.

KAGEROU DAZE

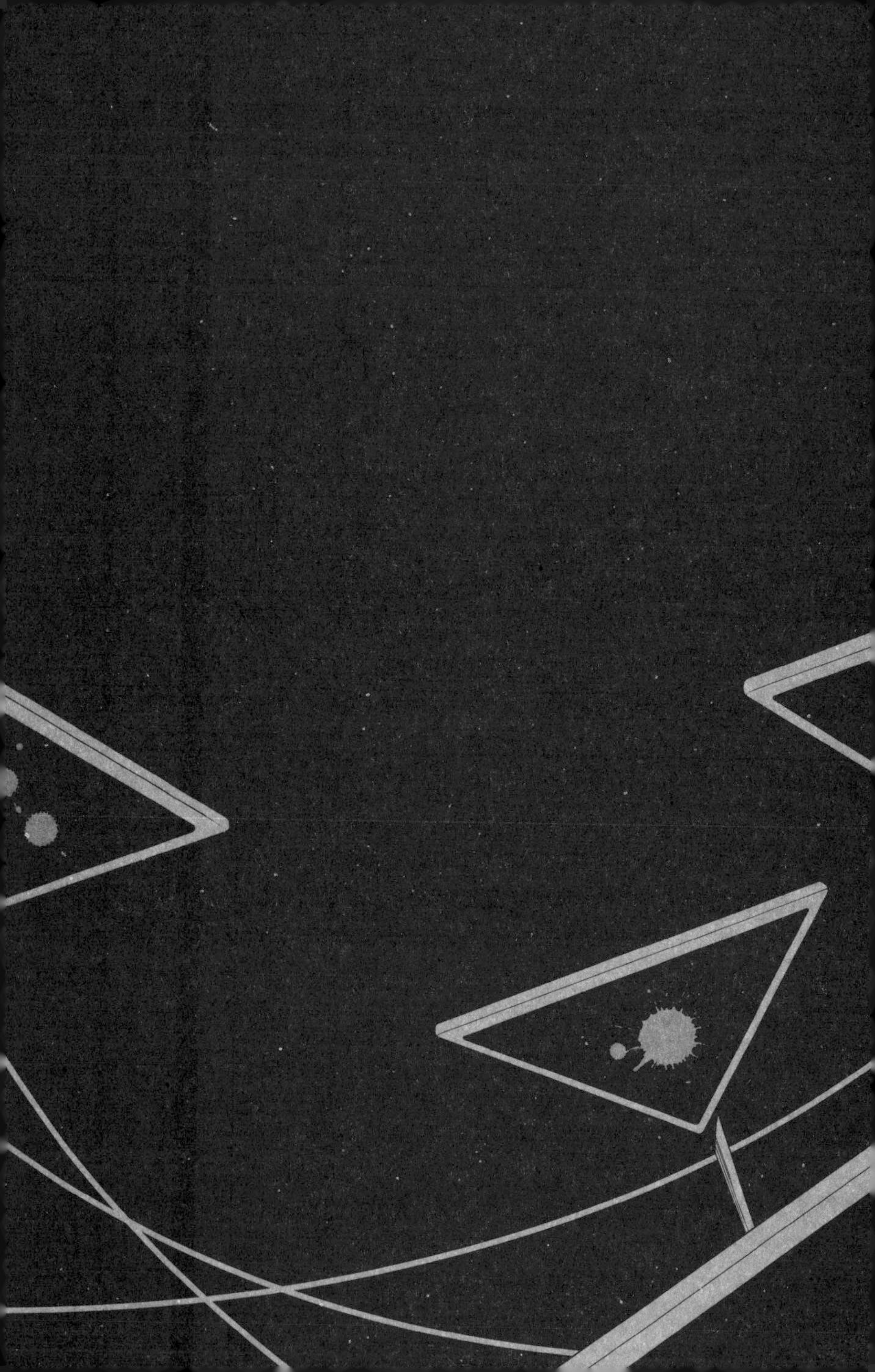

59 >> RED II

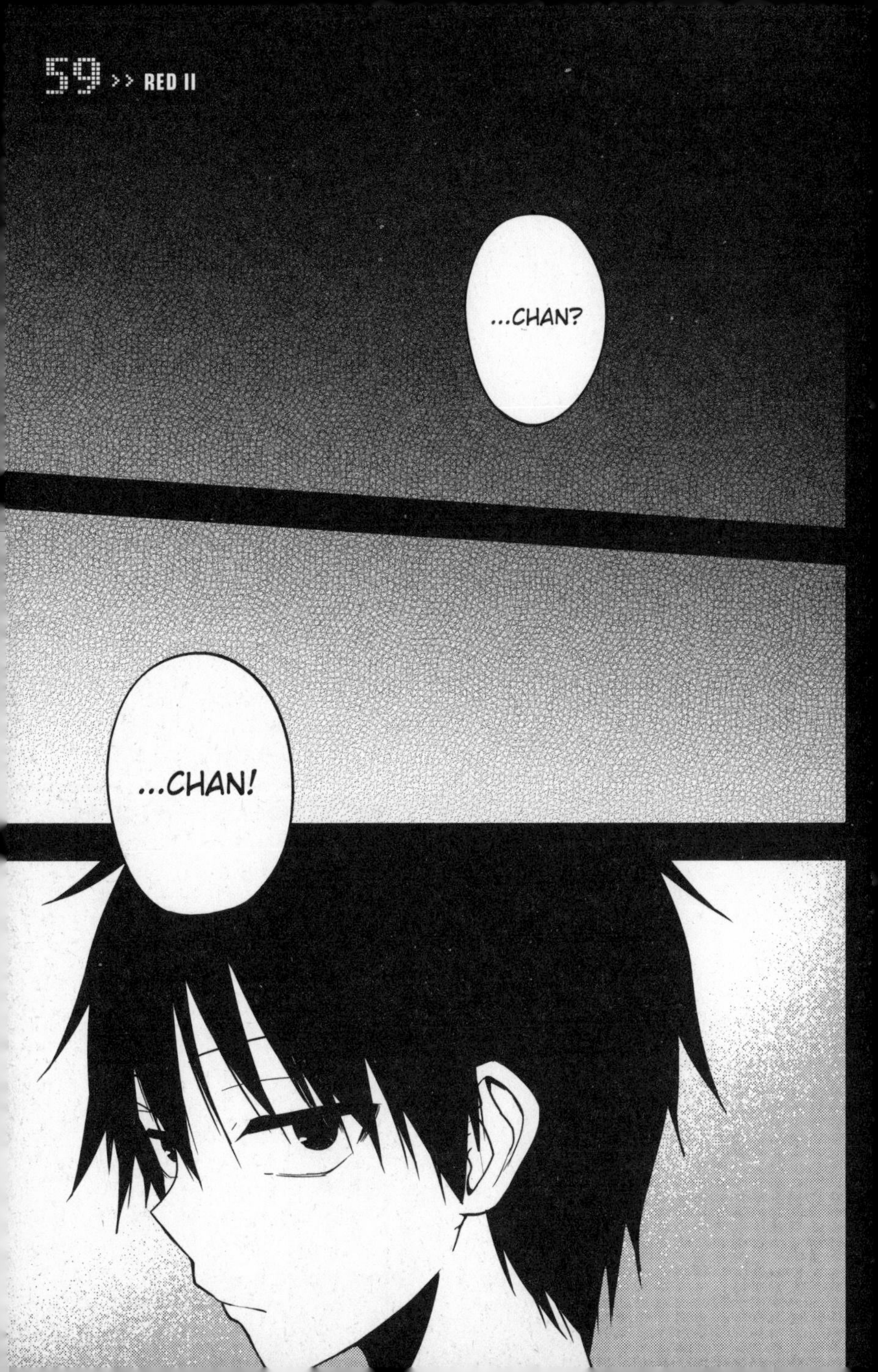
...CHAN?
...CHAN!

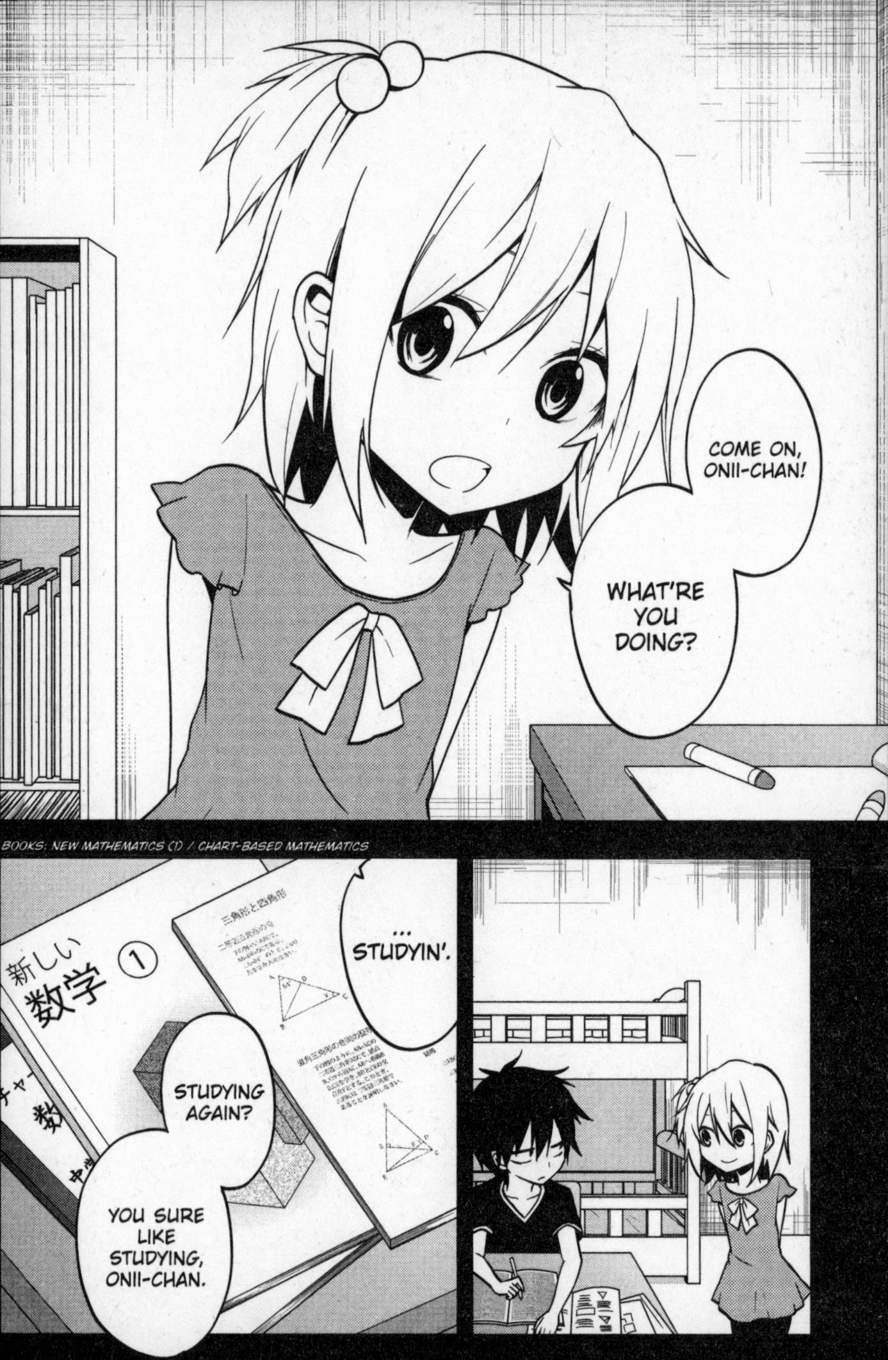
COME ON, ONII-CHAN!
WHAT'RE YOU DOING?
BOOKS: NEW MATHEMATICS (1) / CHART-BASED MATHEMATICS
... STUDYIN'.
新しい 数学 ①
STUDYING AGAIN?
YOU SURE LIKE STUDYING, ONII-CHAN.

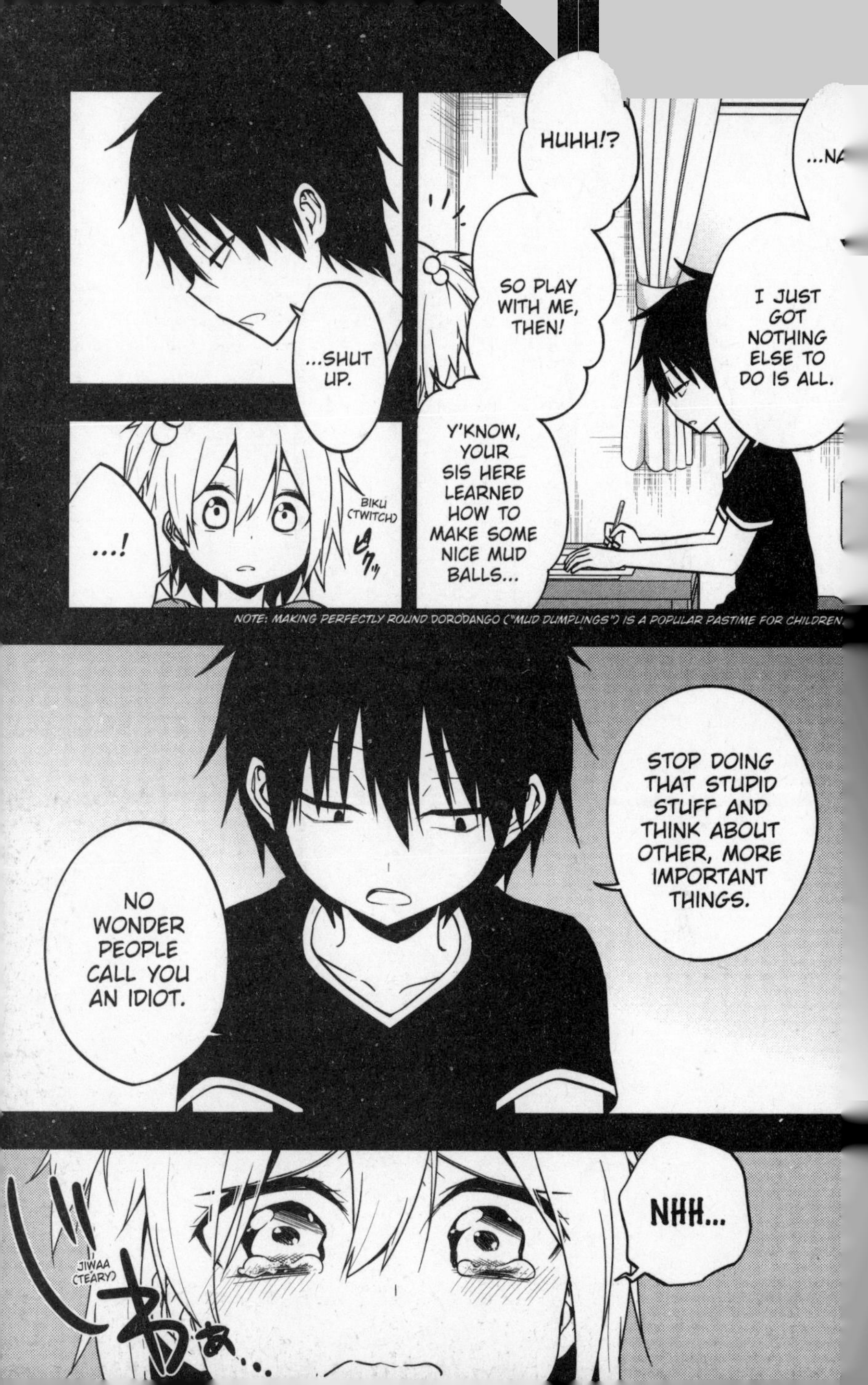
...NA
HUHH!?
I JUST GOT NOTHING ELSE TO DO IS ALL.
SO PLAY WITH ME, THEN!
Y'KNOW, YOUR SIS HERE LEARNED HOW TO MAKE SOME NICE MUD BALLS...
...SHUT UP.
BIKU (TWITCH)
...!
NOTE: MAKING PERFECTLY ROUND DORODANGO ("MUD DUMPLINGS") IS A POPULAR PASTIME FOR CHILDREN.
STOP DOING THAT STUPID STUFF AND THINK ABOUT OTHER, MORE IMPORTANT THINGS.
NO WONDER PEOPLE CALL YOU AN IDIOT.
NHH...
JIWAA (TEARY)

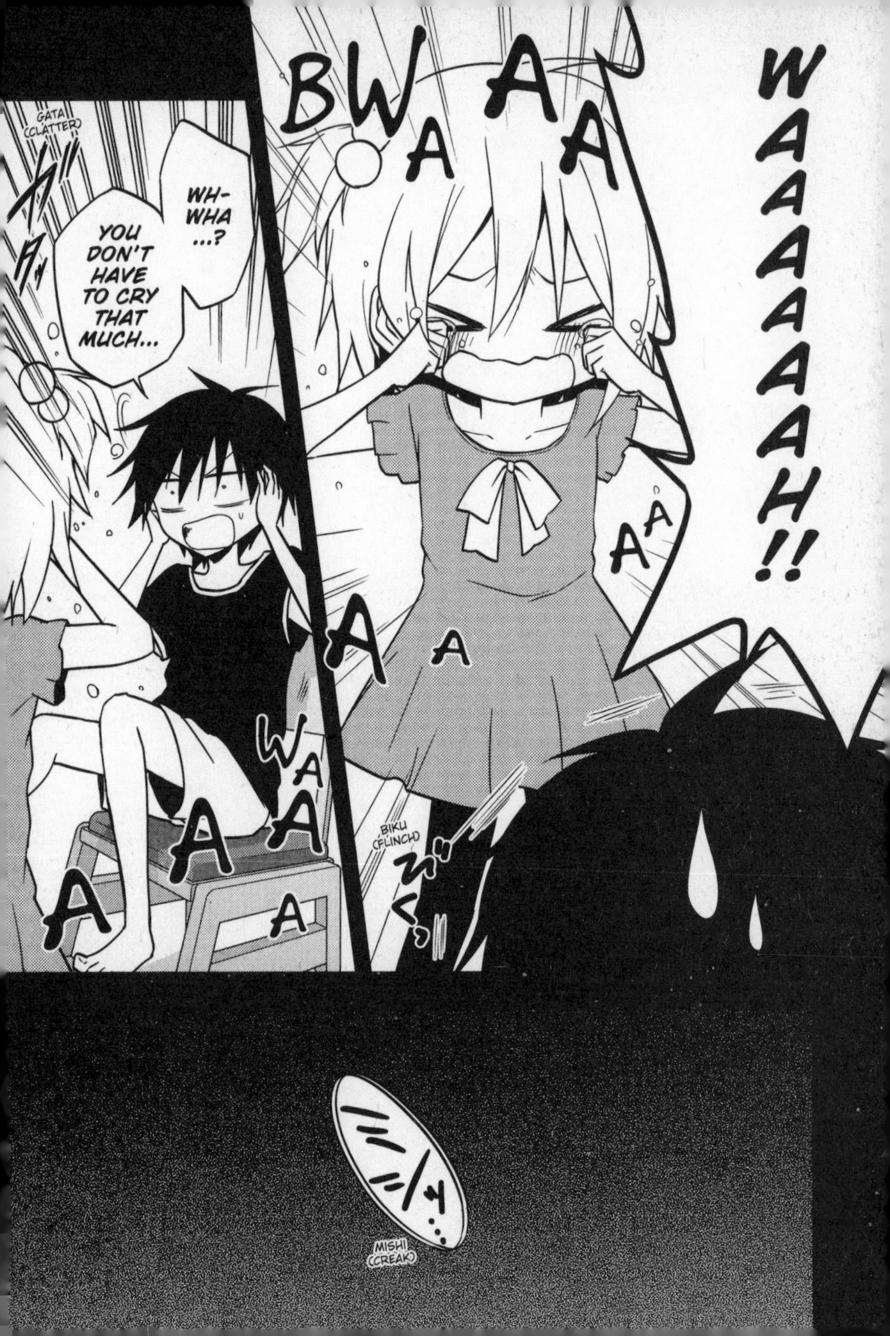
BWAAAA
WAAAAAAAH!!
AAA
AA
BIKU (FLINCH)
GATA (CLATTER)
WH-WHA ...?
YOU DON'T HAVE TO CRY THAT MUCH...
WAAAAAA
MISHI (CREAK)

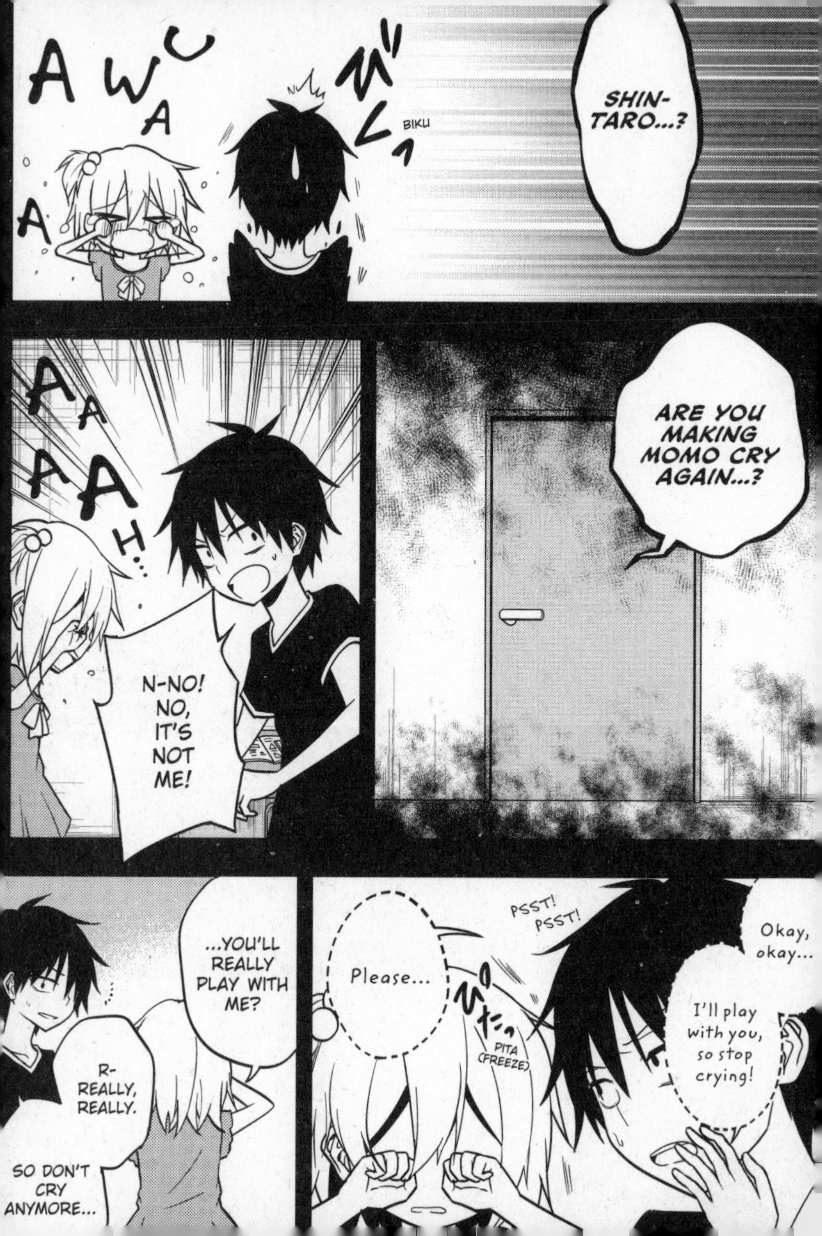
SHIN-TARO...?
BIKU
ARE YOU MAKING MOMO CRY AGAIN...?
AAAAH...
N-NO! NO, IT'S NOT ME!
Okay, okay...
I'll play with you, so stop crying!
PSST! PSST!
PITA (FREEZE)
Please...
...YOU'LL REALLY PLAY WITH ME?
R-REALLY, REALLY.
SO DON'T CRY ANYMORE...

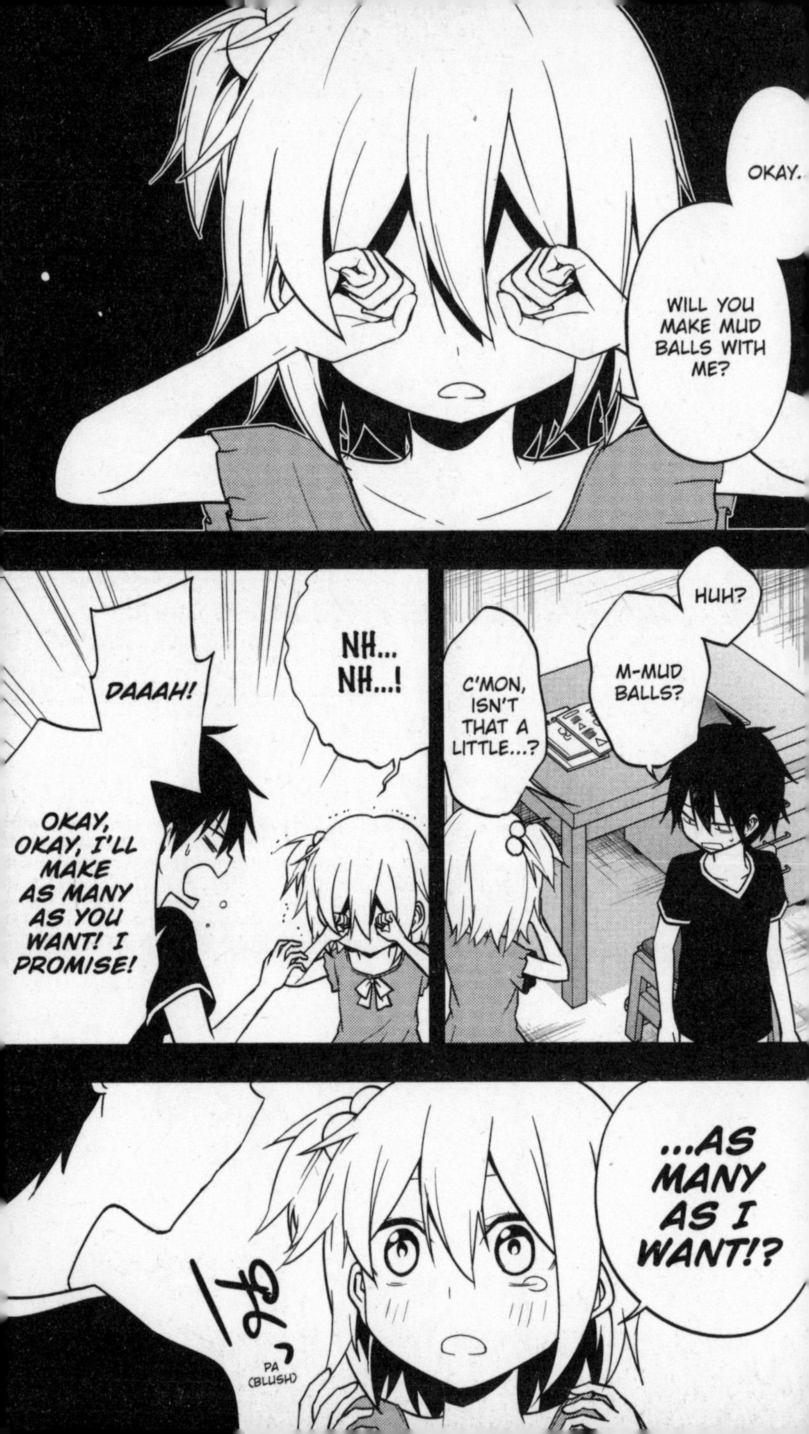
OKAY..
WILL YOU MAKE MUD BALLS WITH ME?
HUH?
M-MUD BALLS?
C'MON, ISN'T THAT A LITTLE...?
NH... NH...!
DAAAH!
OKAY, OKAY, I'LL MAKE AS MANY AS YOU WANT! I PROMISE!
...AS MANY AS I WANT!?
PA (BLUSH)

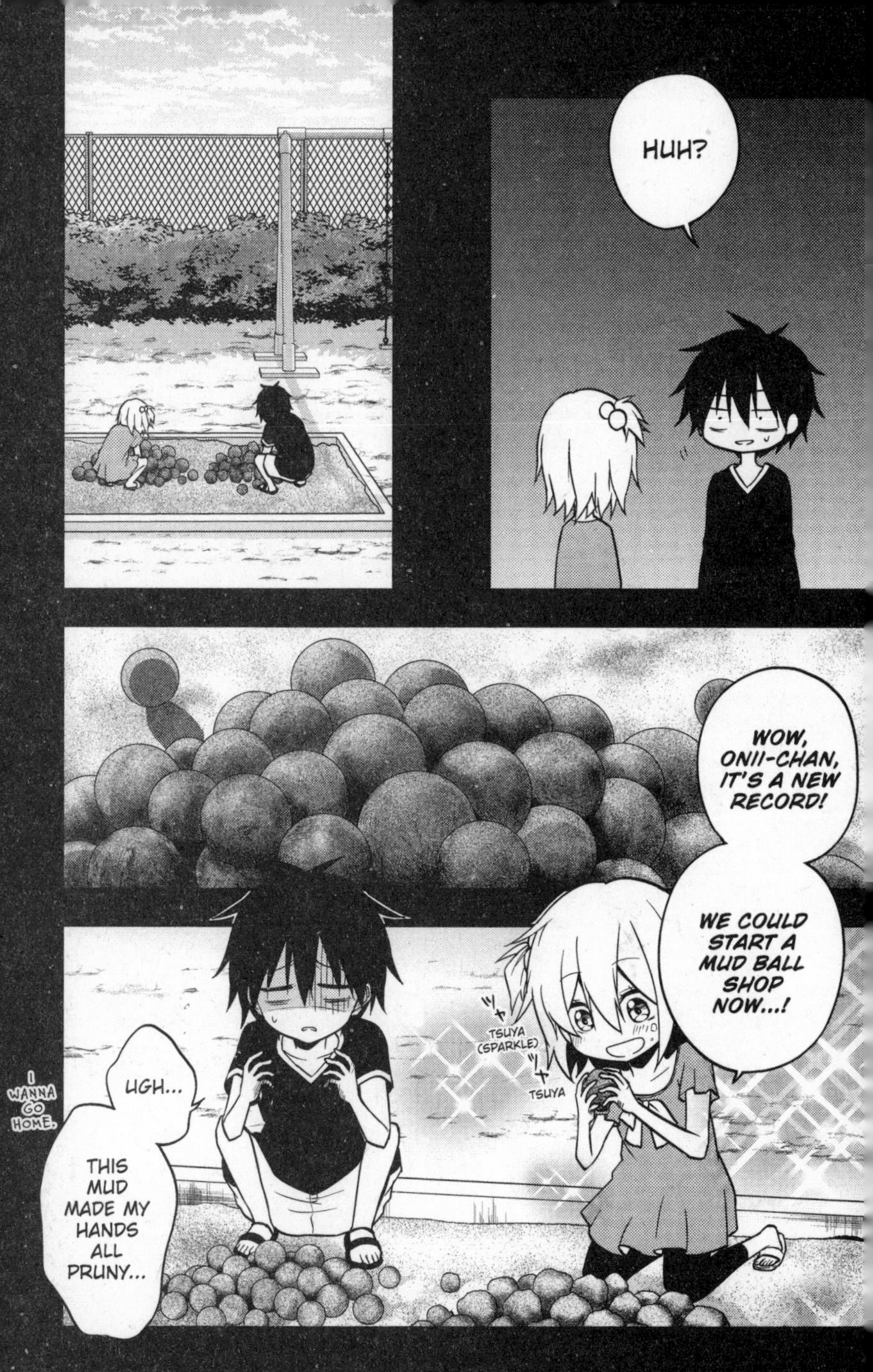

HUH?
WOW, ONII-CHAN, IT'S A NEW RECORD!
WE COULD START A MUD BALL SHOP NOW...!
ツヤ
TSUYA (SPARKLE)
ツヤ
TSUYA
UGH...
THIS MUD MADE MY HANDS ALL PRUNY...
I WANNA GO HOME.

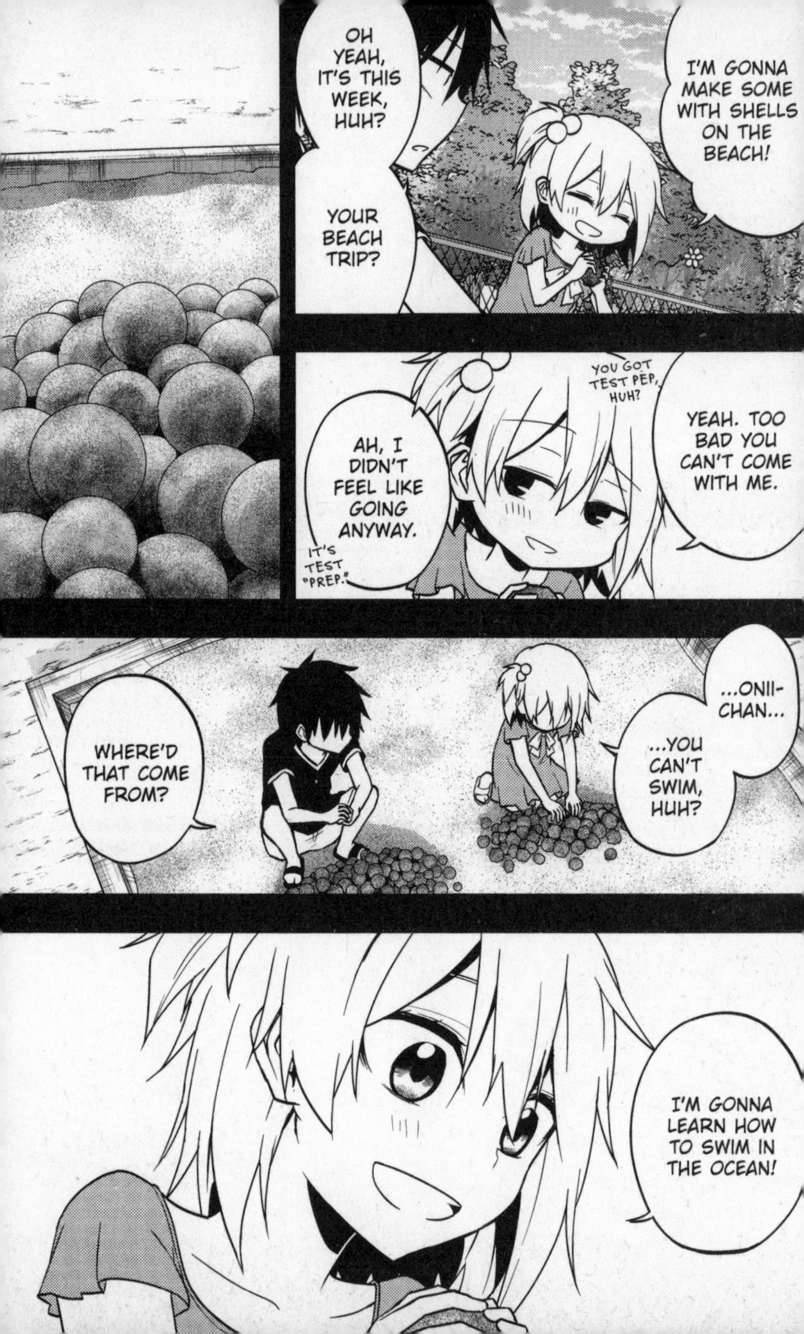
I'M GONNA MAKE SOME WITH SHELLS ON THE BEACH!
OH YEAH, IT'S THIS WEEK, HUH?
YOUR BEACH TRIP?
YEAH. TOO BAD YOU CAN'T COME WITH ME.
YOU GOT TEST PEP, HUH?
AH, I DIDN'T FEEL LIKE GOING ANYWAY.
IT'S TEST "PREP."
...ONII-CHAN...
...YOU CAN'T SWIM, HUH?
WHERE'D THAT COME FROM?
I'M GONNA LEARN HOW TO SWIM IN THE OCEAN!

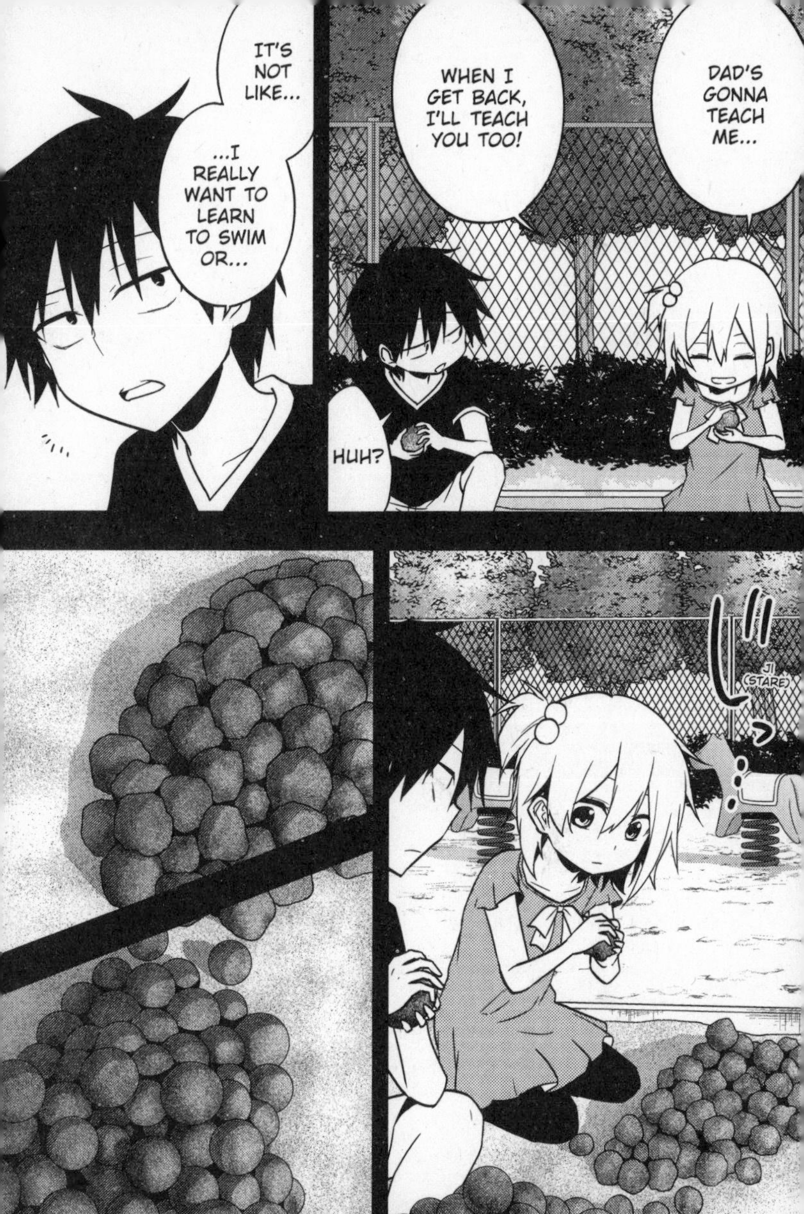
DAD'S GONNA TEACH ME...
WHEN I GET BACK, I'LL TEACH YOU TOO!
HUH?
IT'S NOT LIKE...
...I REALLY WANT TO LEARN TO SWIM OR...
JI (STARE)

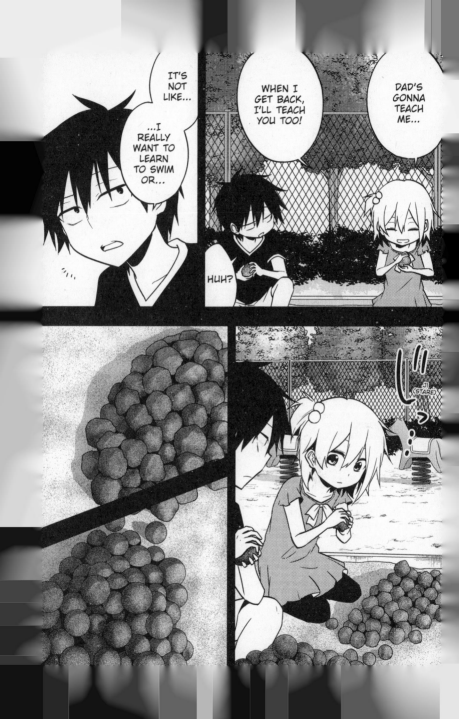

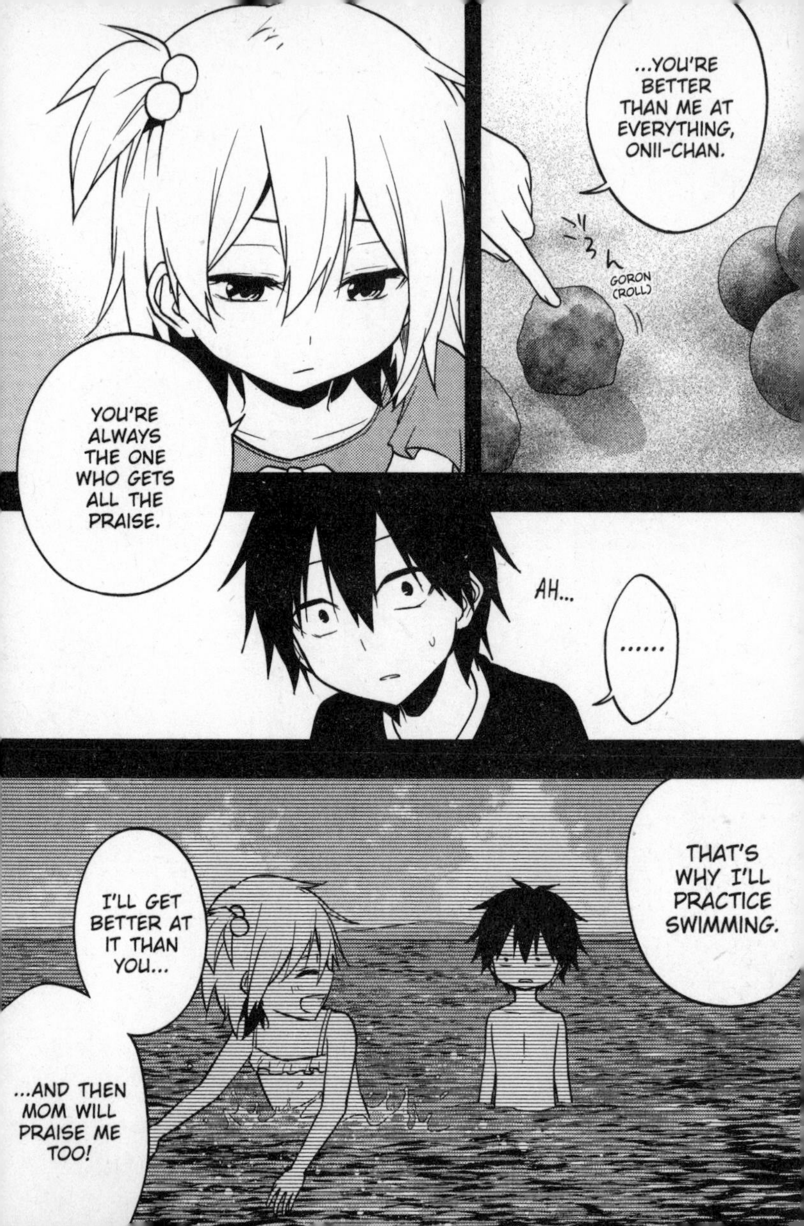
...YOU'RE BETTER THAN ME AT EVERYTHING, ONII-CHAN.
GORON (ROLL)
YOU'RE ALWAYS THE ONE WHO GETS ALL THE PRAISE.
AH...
......
THAT'S WHY I'LL PRACTICE SWIMMING.
I'LL GET BETTER AT IT THAN YOU...
...AND THEN MOM WILL PRAISE ME TOO!

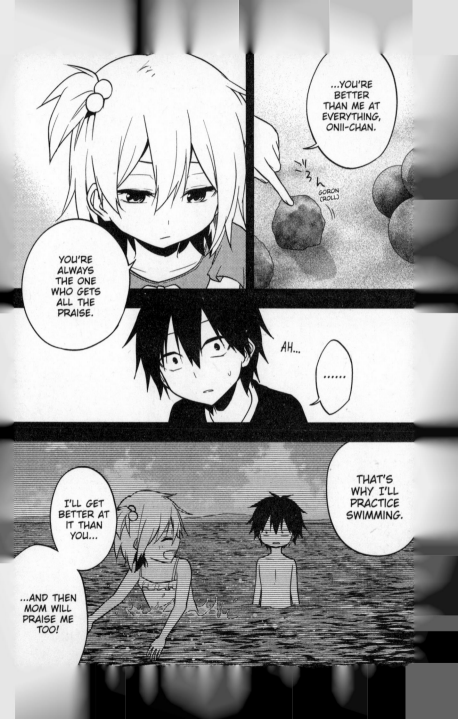

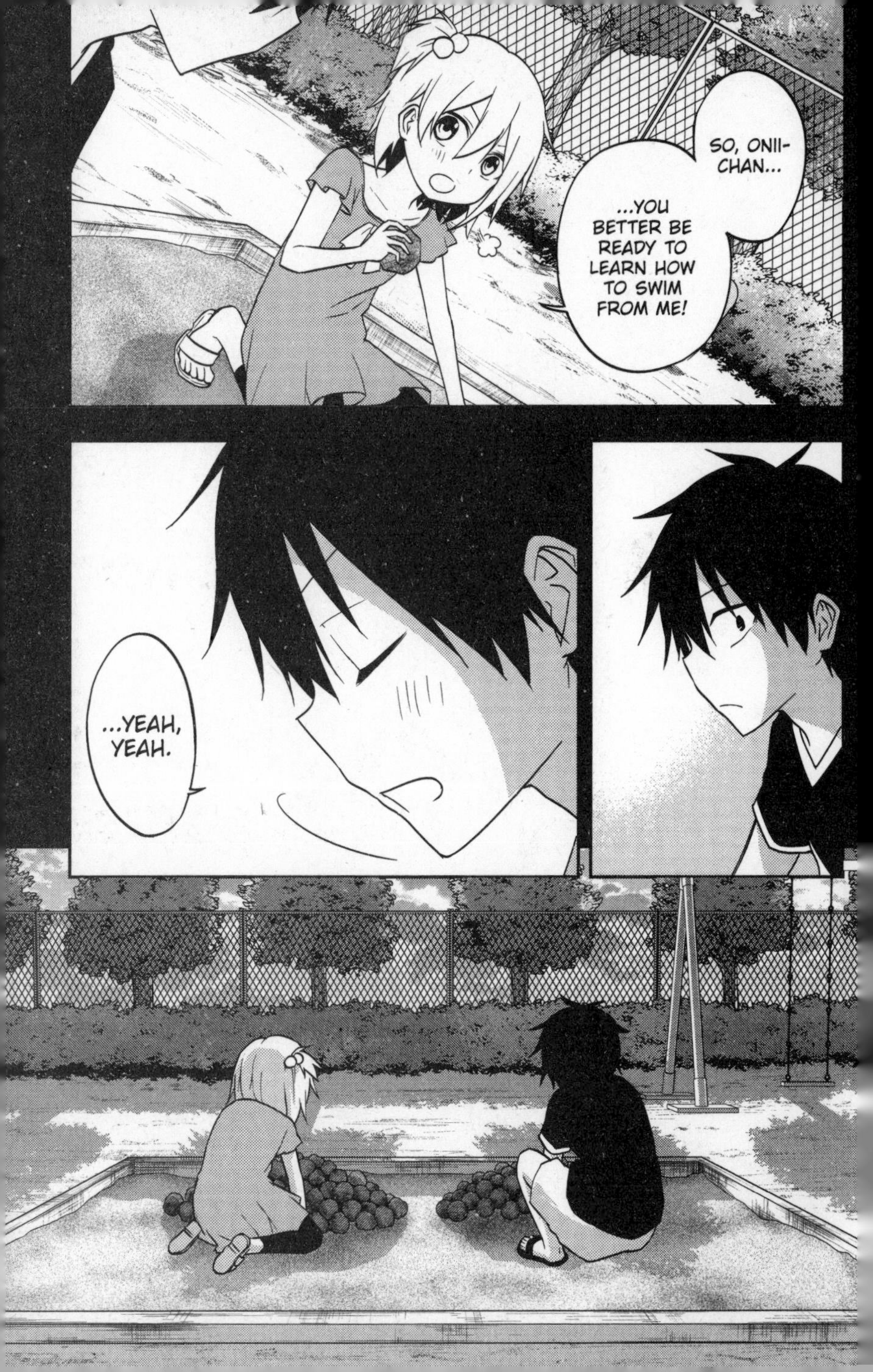
SO, ONII-CHAN...
...YOU BETTER BE READY TO LEARN HOW TO SWIM FROM ME!
...YEAH, YEAH.

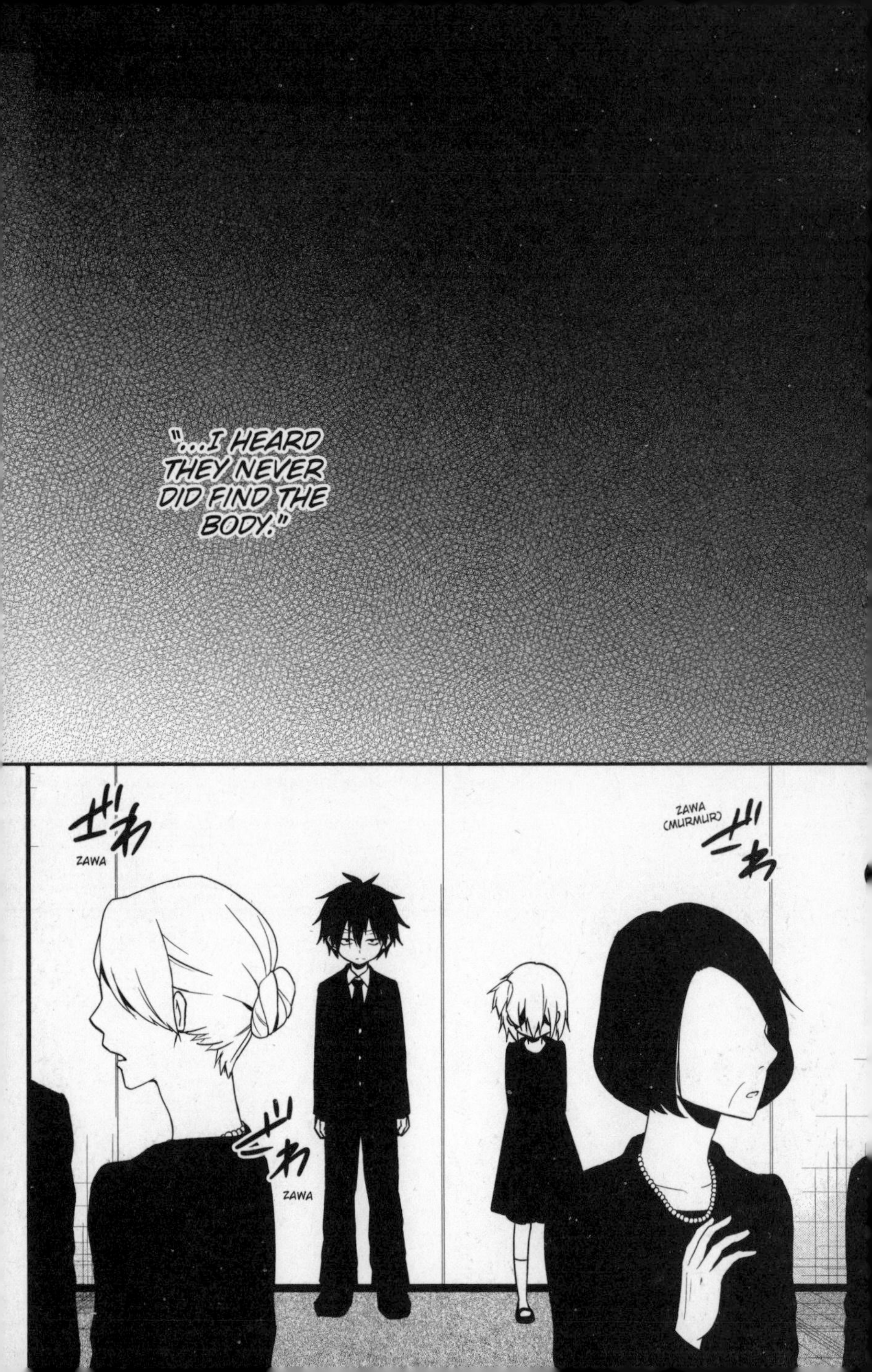
"...I HEARD THEY NEVER DID FIND THE BODY."
ZAWA (MURMUR)
ざわ
ざわ
ZAWA
ざわ
ZAWA

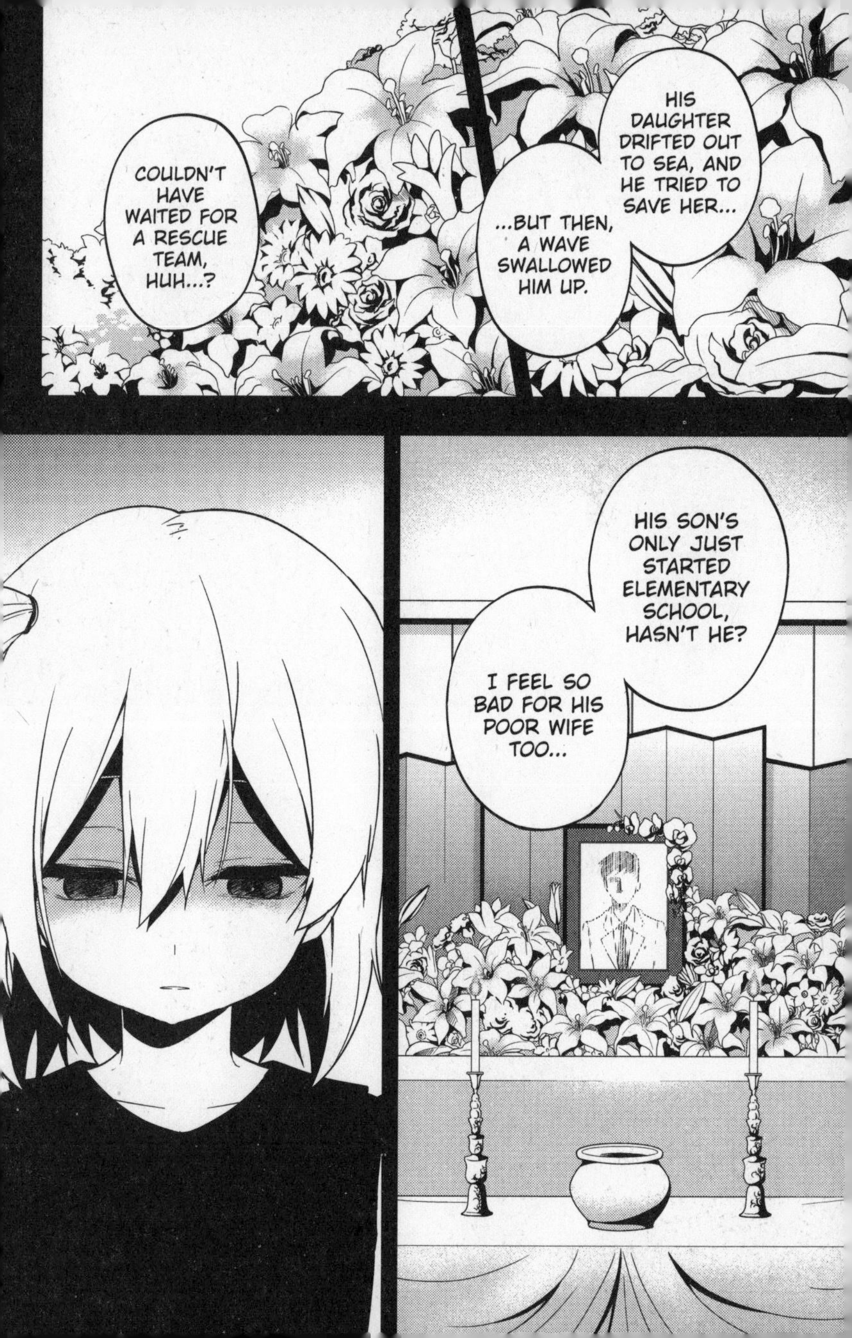
HIS DAUGHTER DRIFTED OUT TO SEA, AND HE TRIED TO SAVE HER...
...BUT THEN, A WAVE SWALLOWED HIM UP.
COULDN'T HAVE WAITED FOR A RESCUE TEAM, HUH...?
HIS SON'S ONLY JUST STARTED ELEMENTARY SCHOOL, HASN'T HE?
I FEEL SO BAD FOR HIS POOR WIFE TOO...

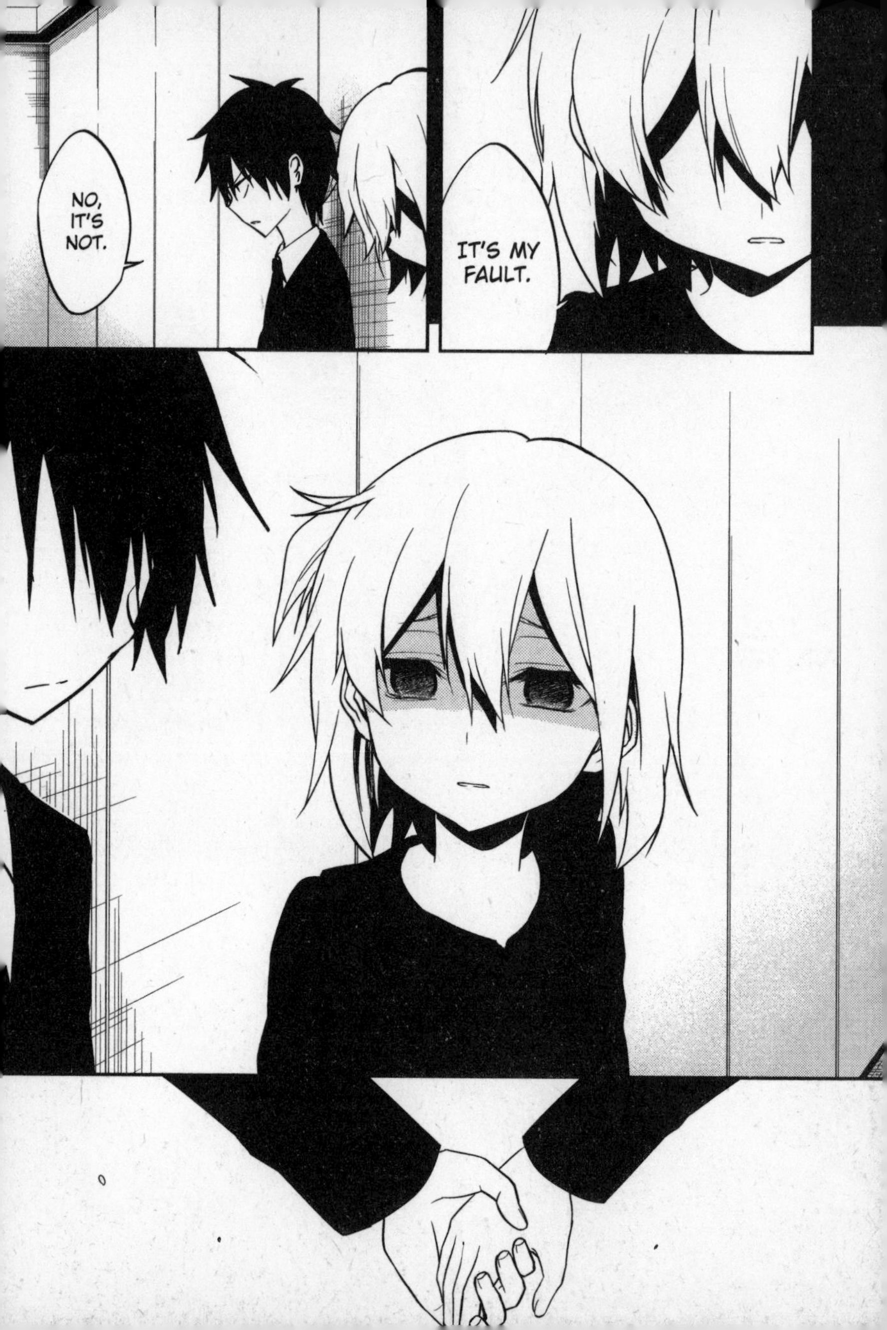
IT'S MY FAULT.
NO, IT'S NOT.

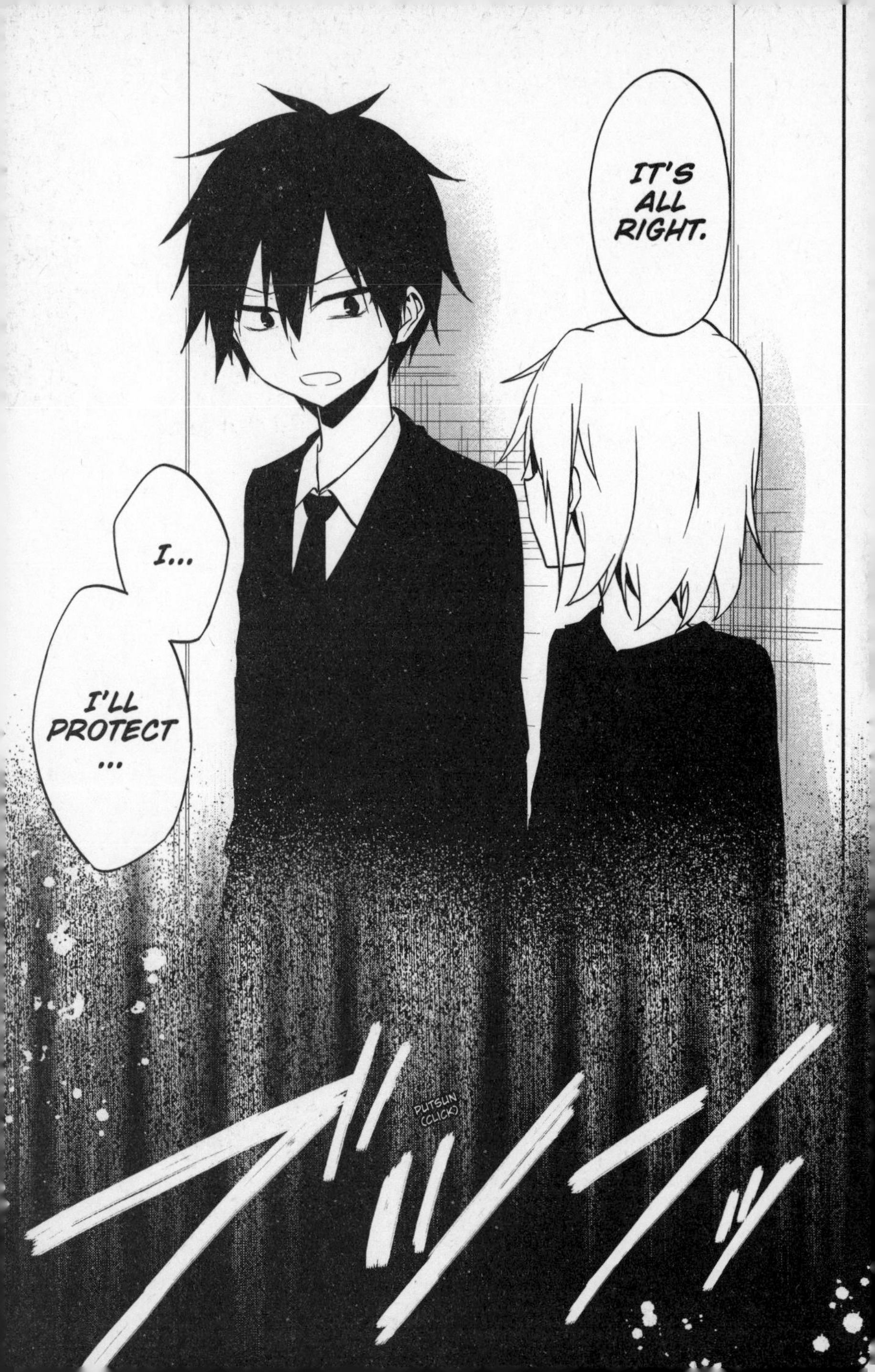
IT'S ALL RIGHT.
I...
I'LL PROTECT ...
PUTSUN (CLICK)

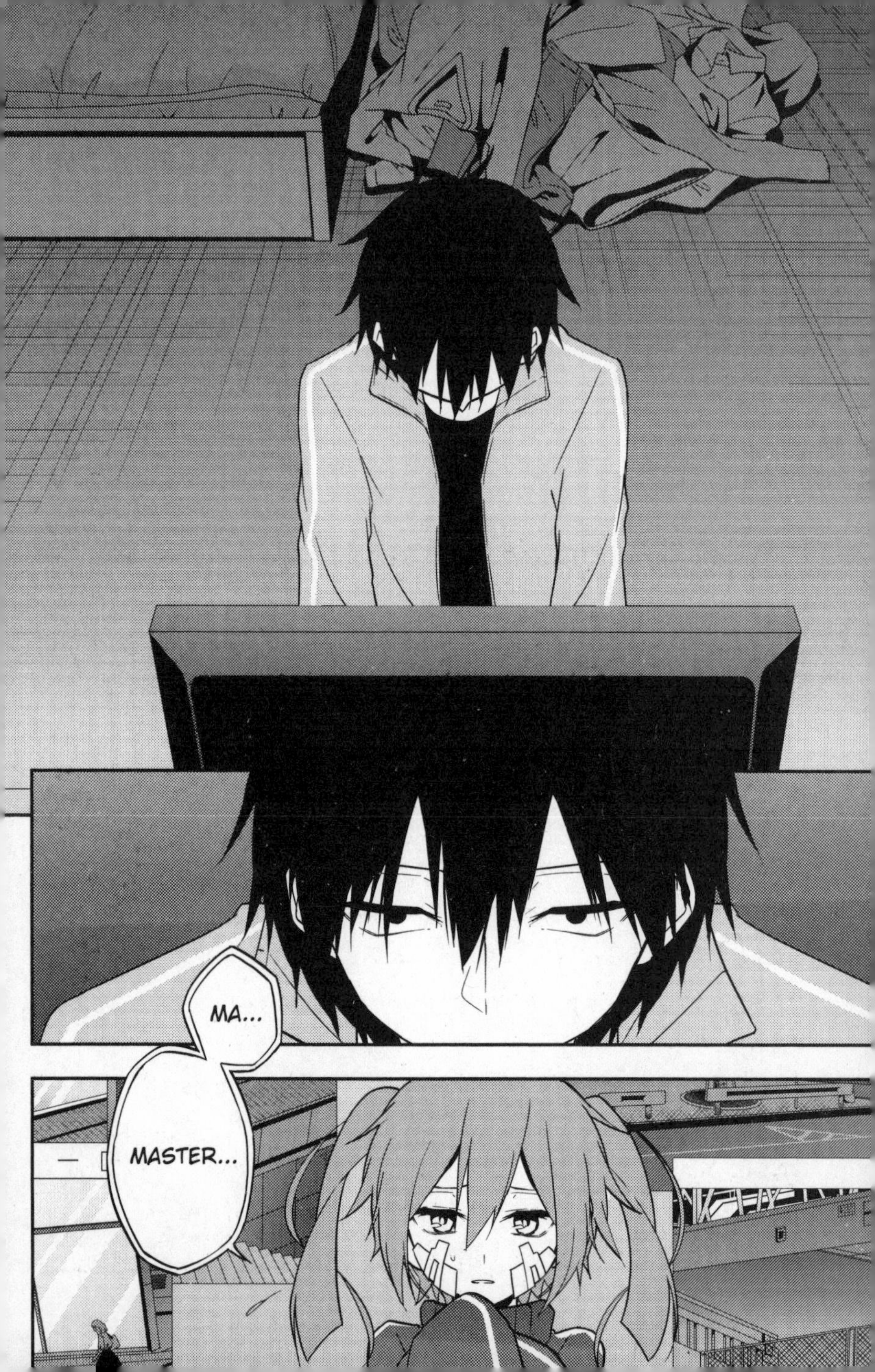
MA...
MASTER...

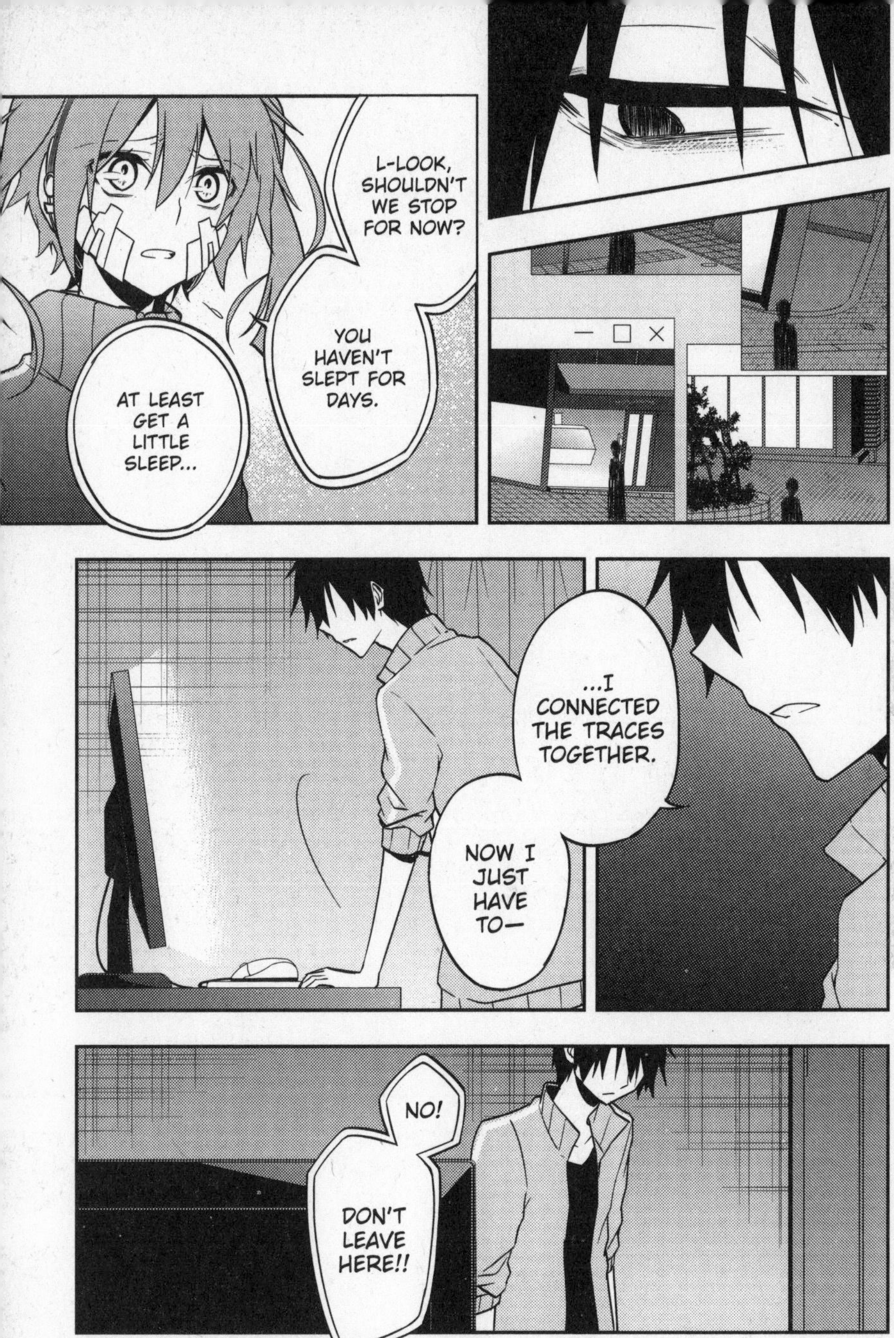
L-LOOK, SHOULDN'T WE STOP FOR NOW?
YOU HAVEN'T SLEPT FOR DAYS.
AT LEAST GET A LITTLE SLEEP...
...I CONNECTED THE TRACES TOGETHER.
NOW I JUST HAVE TO—
NO!
DON'T LEAVE HERE!!

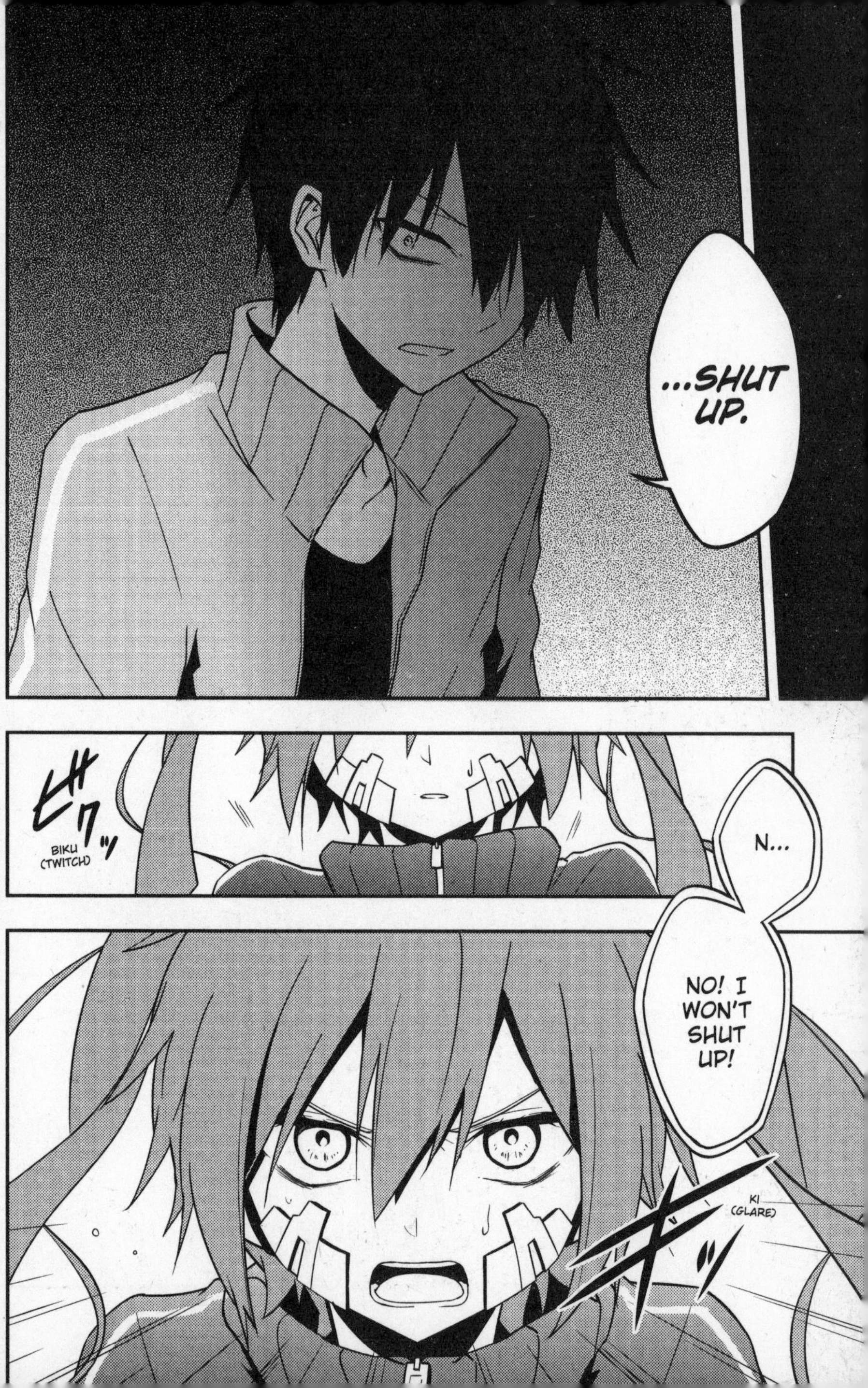
...SHUT UP.
N...
BIKU (TWITCH)
NO! I WON'T SHUT UP!
KI (GLARE)

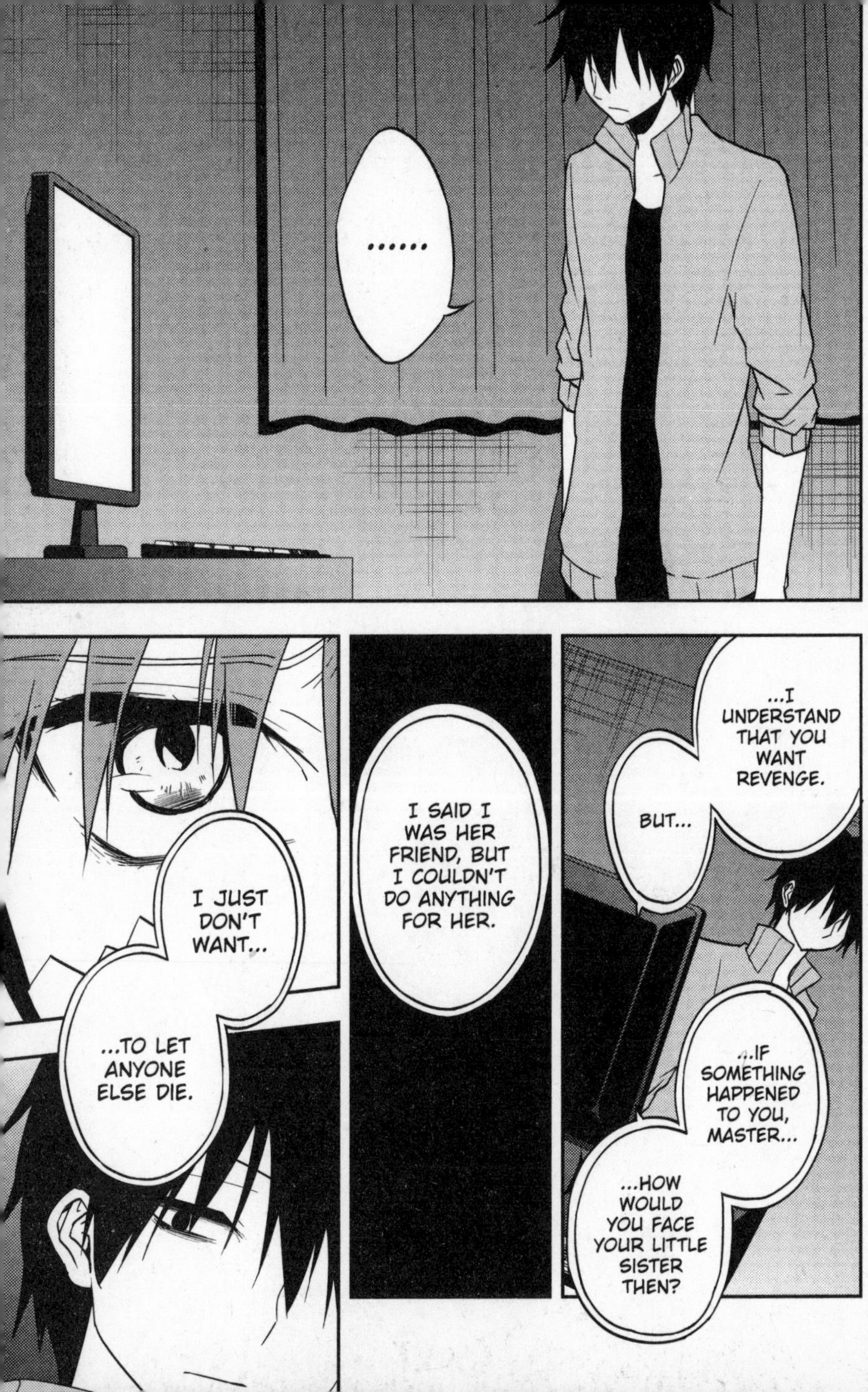
......
...I UNDERSTAND THAT YOU WANT REVENGE.
BUT...
...IF SOMETHING HAPPENED TO YOU, MASTER...
...HOW WOULD YOU FACE YOUR LITTLE SISTER THEN?
I SAID I WAS HER FRIEND, BUT I COULDN'T DO ANYTHING FOR HER.
I JUST DON'T WANT...
...TO LET ANYONE ELSE DIE.

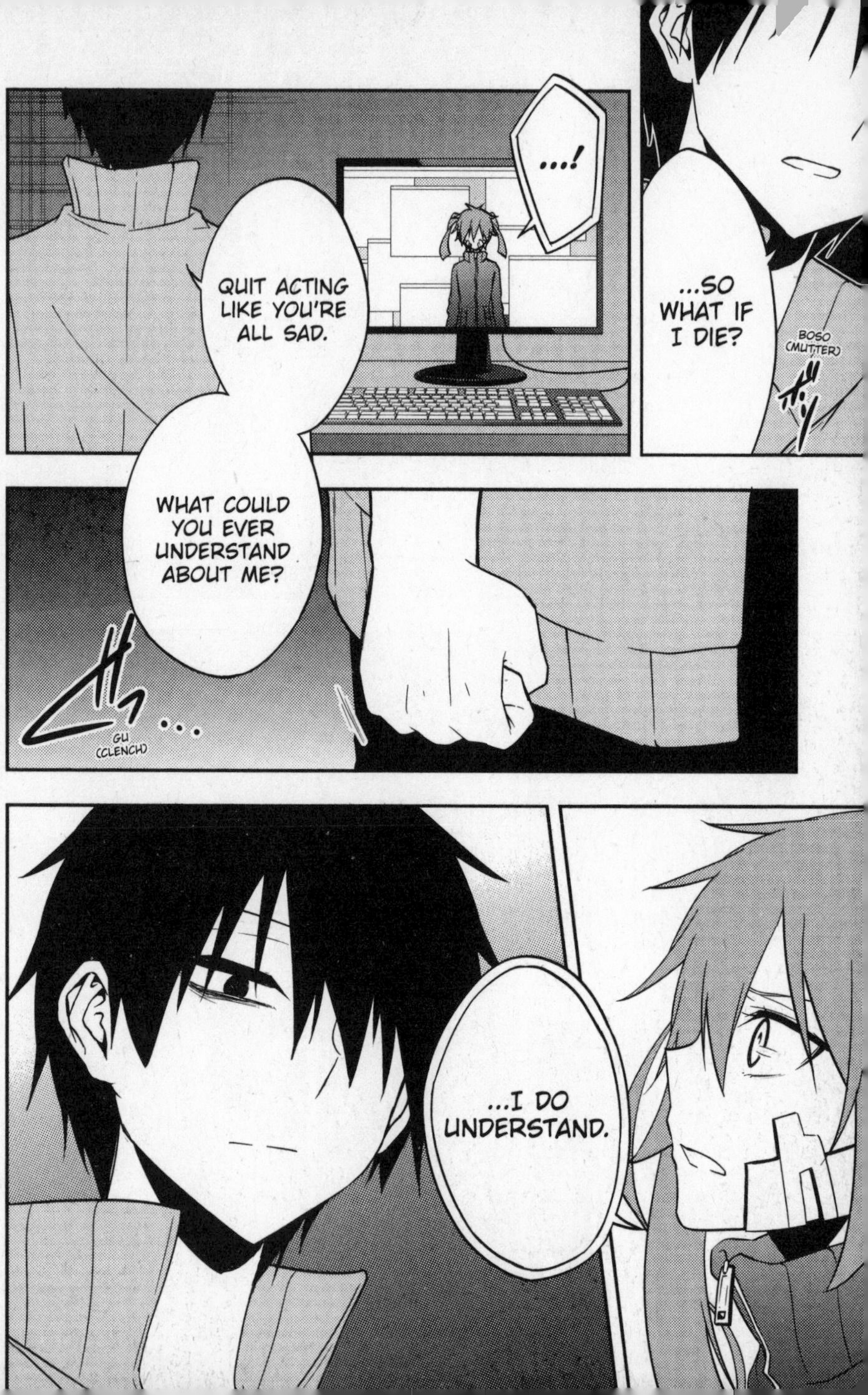
...SO WHAT IF I DIE?
BOSO (MUTTER)
...!
QUIT ACTING LIKE YOU'RE ALL SAD.
WHAT COULD YOU EVER UNDERSTAND ABOUT ME?
GU (CLENCH)
...
...I DO UNDERSTAND.

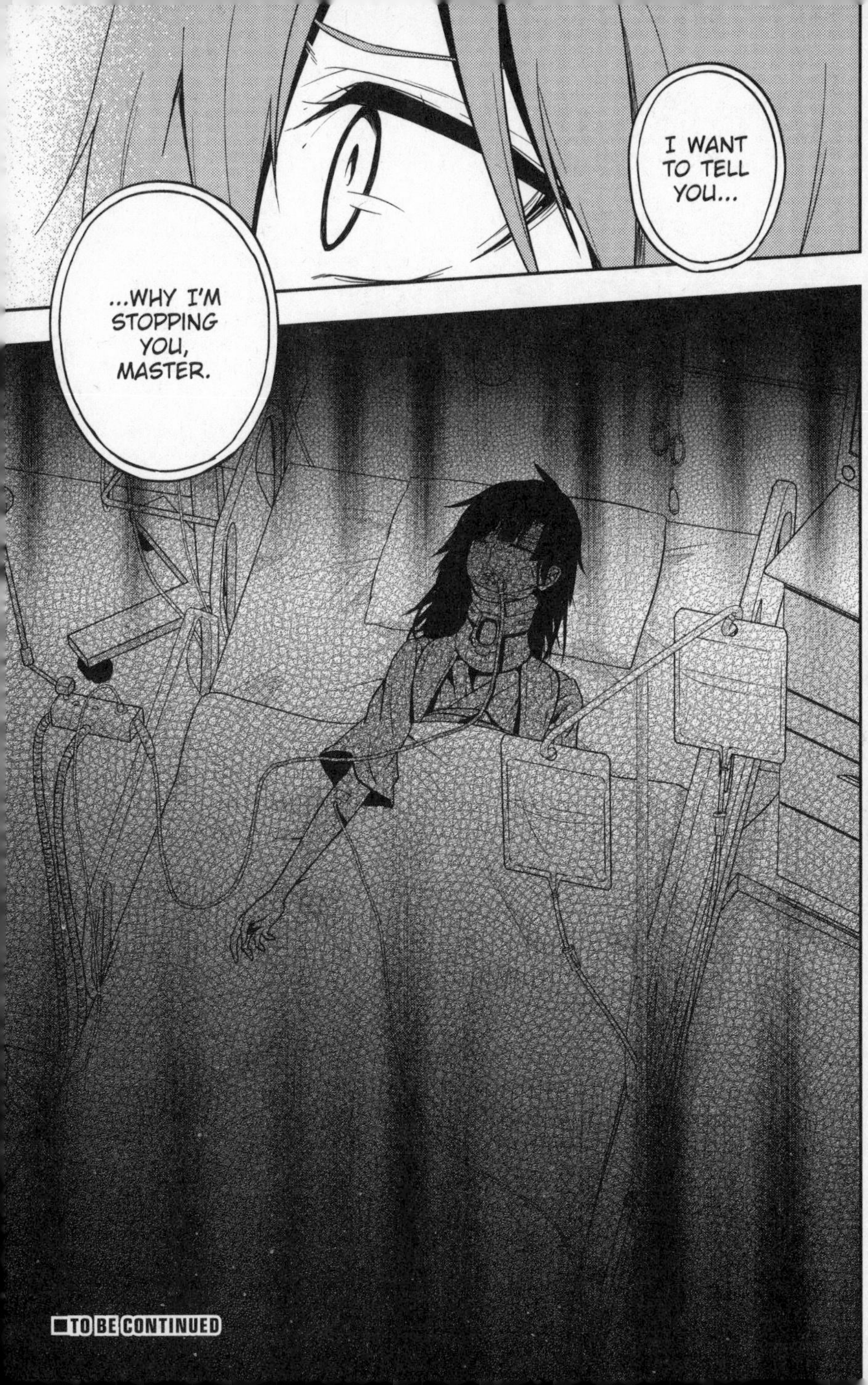
I WANT TO TELL YOU...
...WHY I'M STOPPING YOU, MASTER.
TO BE CONTINUED

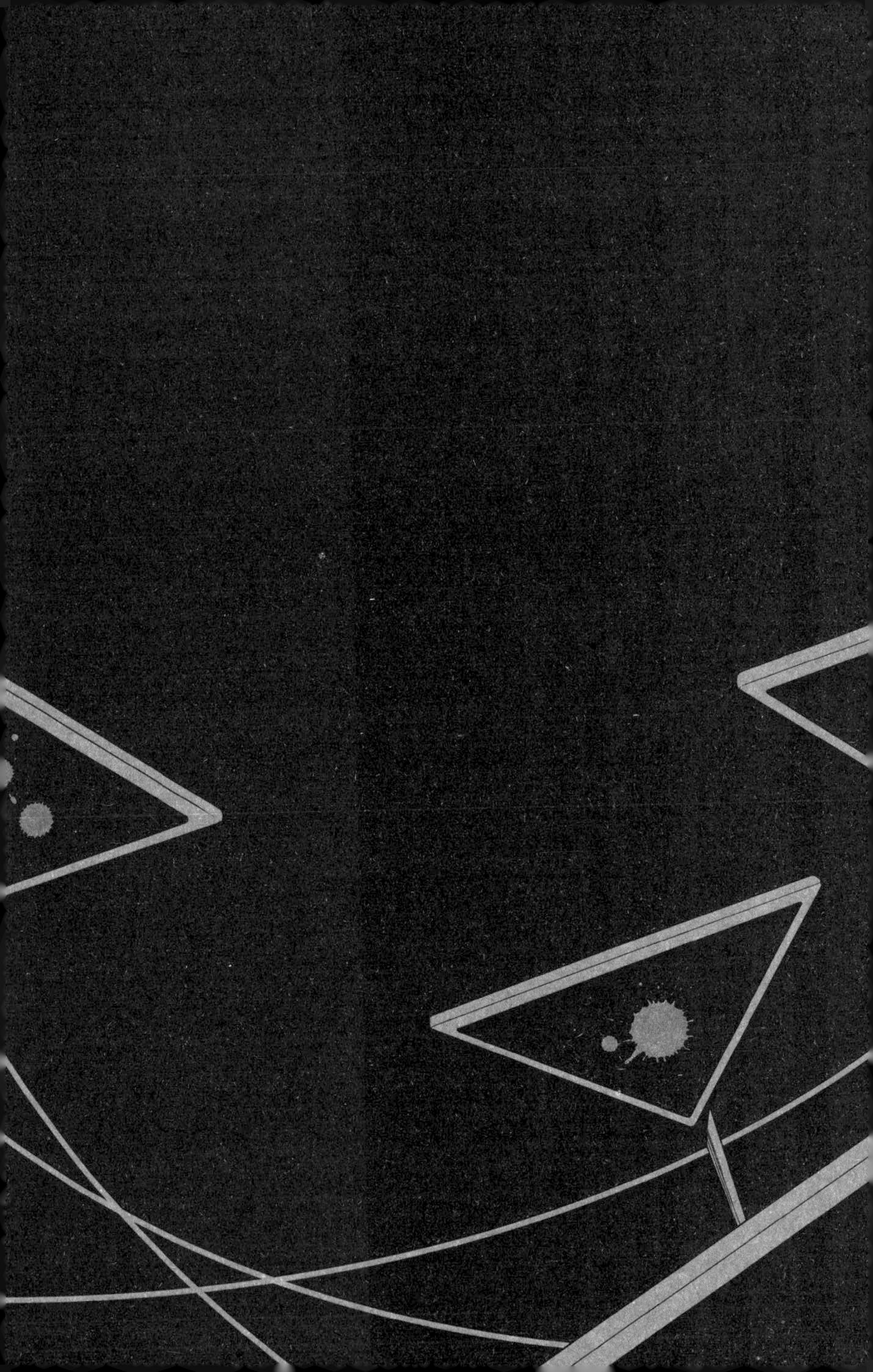

MANGA Vol. 11 IS HERE.

It feels like Volume 10 only just came out, and now we're at number eleven... They sure come fast. The novel version of *Kagerou Daze* is complete, but the manga version continues. What kind of end will there be to the Mekakushi-dan's battle? I'm looking forward to it—very excited even. Things are getting lonelier as the number of characters dwindles, but I'm sure we'll provide you with a red-hot story to the end. Thanks for continuing to support us.

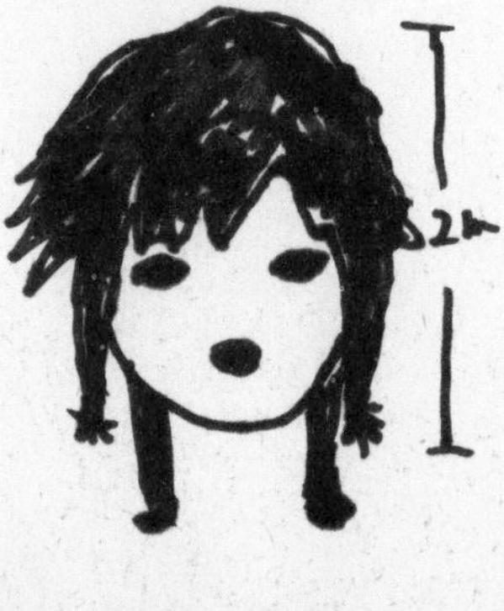
2m

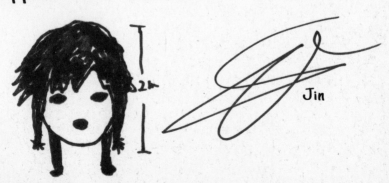

Jin

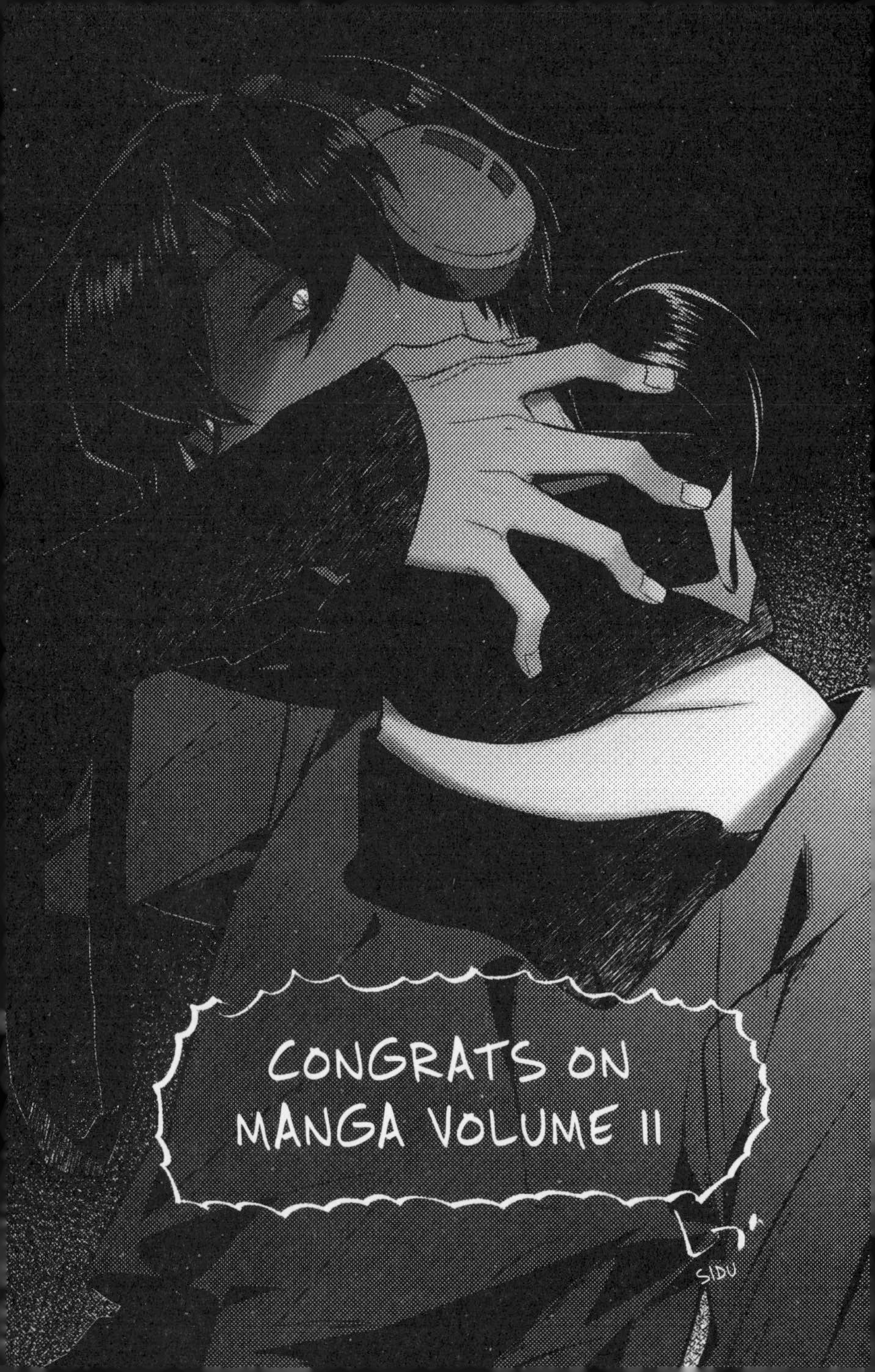
CONGRATS ON MANGA VOLUME 11
SIDU

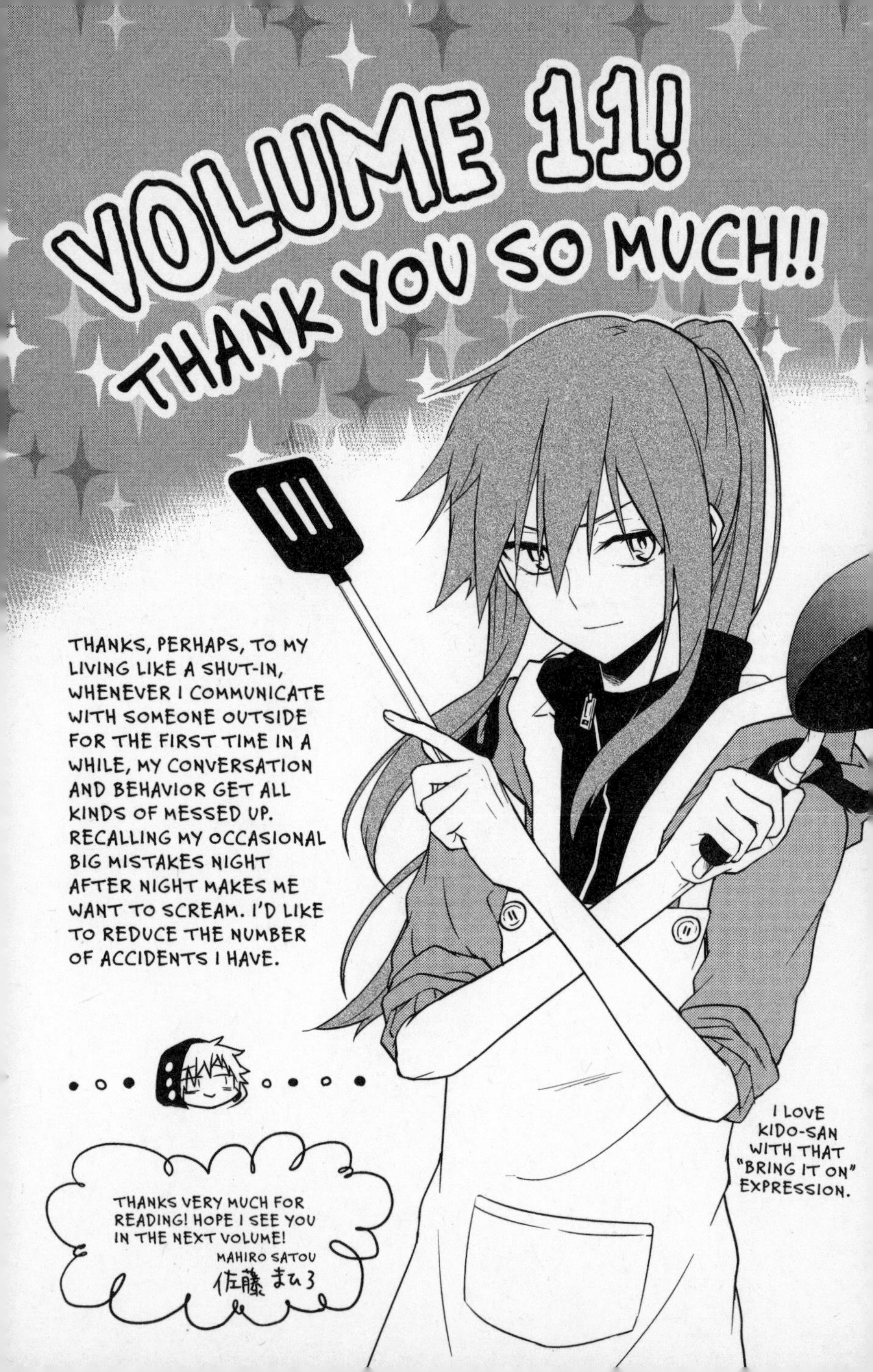
VOLUME 11!
THANK YOU SO MUCH!!
THANKS, PERHAPS, TO MY LIVING LIKE A SHUT-IN, WHENEVER I COMMUNICATE WITH SOMEONE OUTSIDE FOR THE FIRST TIME IN A WHILE, MY CONVERSATION AND BEHAVIOR GET ALL KINDS OF MESSED UP. RECALLING MY OCCASIONAL BIG MISTAKES NIGHT AFTER NIGHT MAKES ME WANT TO SCREAM. I'D LIKE TO REDUCE THE NUMBER OF ACCIDENTS I HAVE.
I LOVE KIDO-SAN WITH THAT "BRING IT ON" EXPRESSION.
THANKS VERY MUCH FOR READING! HOPE I SEE YOU IN THE NEXT VOLUME!
MAHIRO SATOU
佐藤まひろ

KAGEROU DAZE

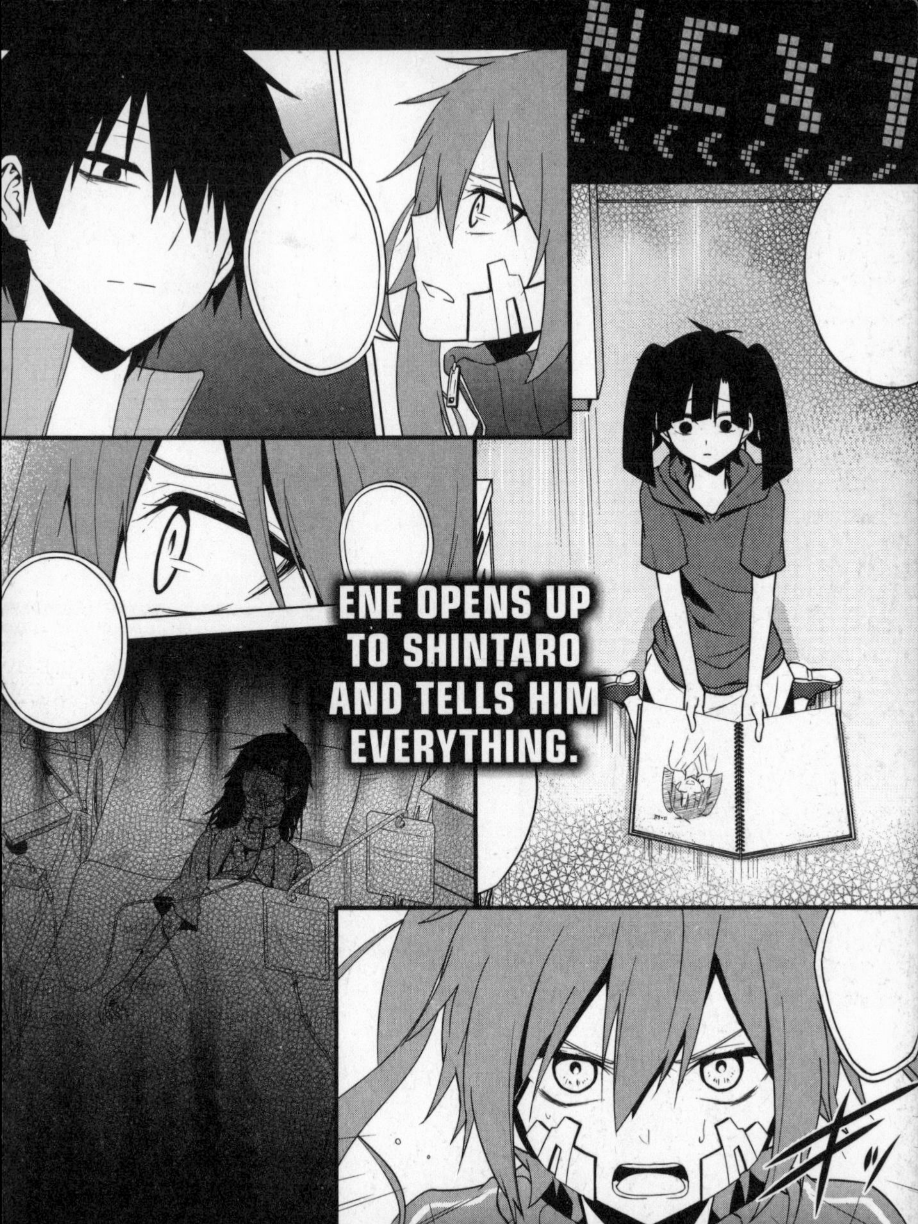
NEXT
ENE OPENS UP TO SHINTARO AND TELLS HIM EVERYTHING.

VOLUME 12

COMING SPRING 2019!!

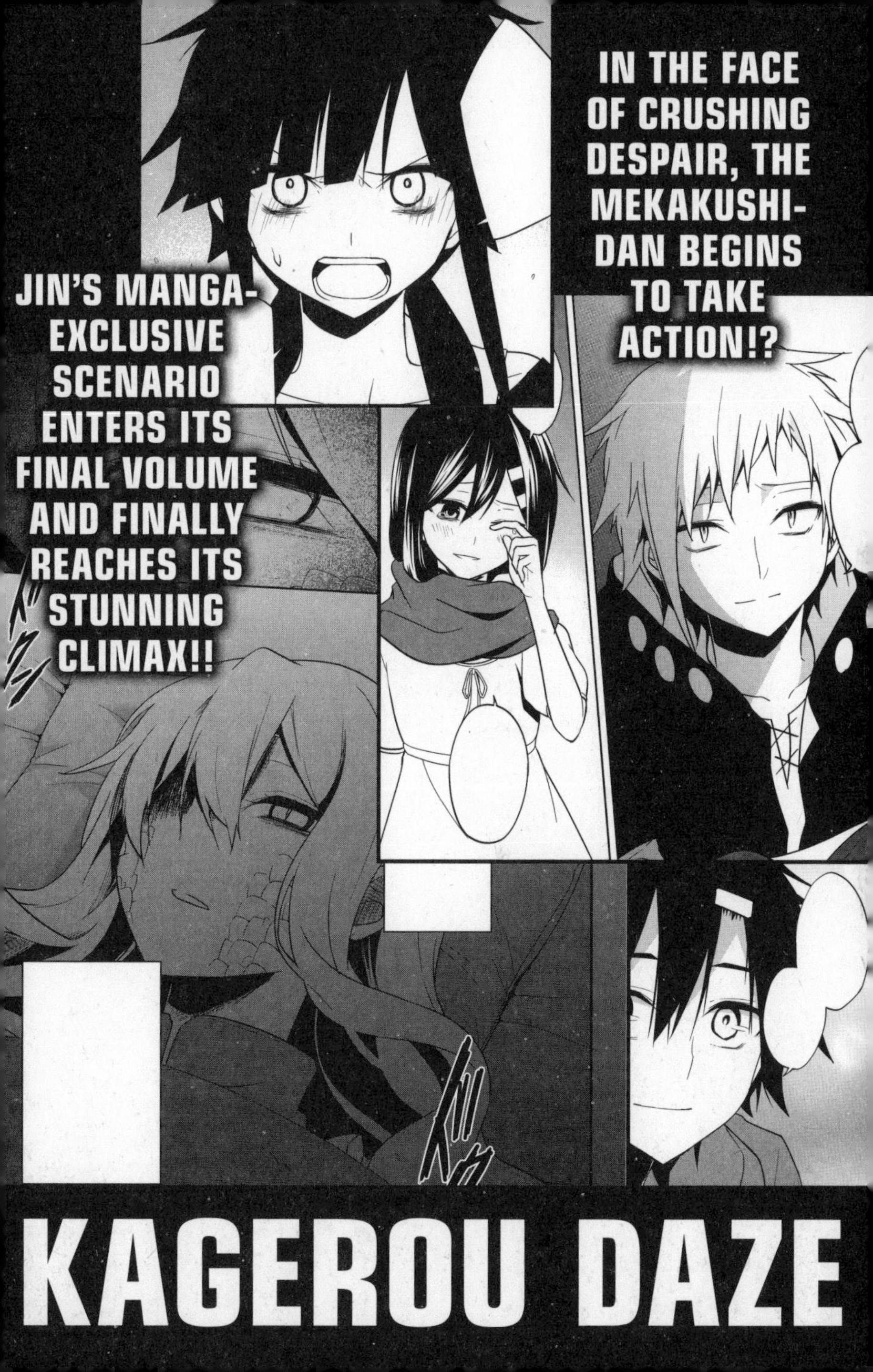
IN THE FACE OF CRUSHING DESPAIR, THE MEKAKUSHI-DAN BEGINS TO TAKE ACTION!?
JIN'S MANGA-EXCLUSIVE SCENARIO ENTERS ITS FINAL VOLUME AND FINALLY REACHES ITS STUNNING CLIMAX!!
KAGEROU DAZE

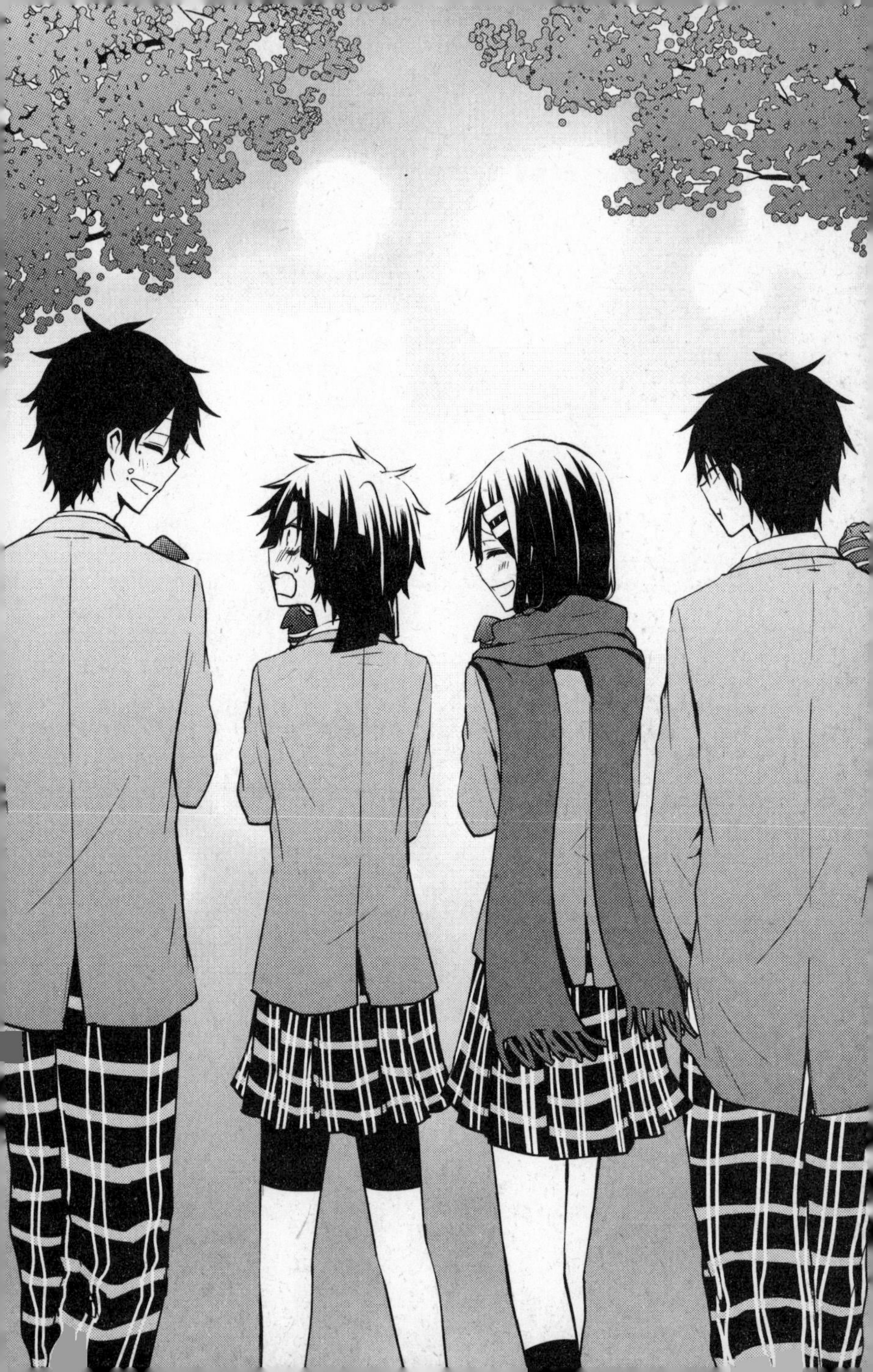

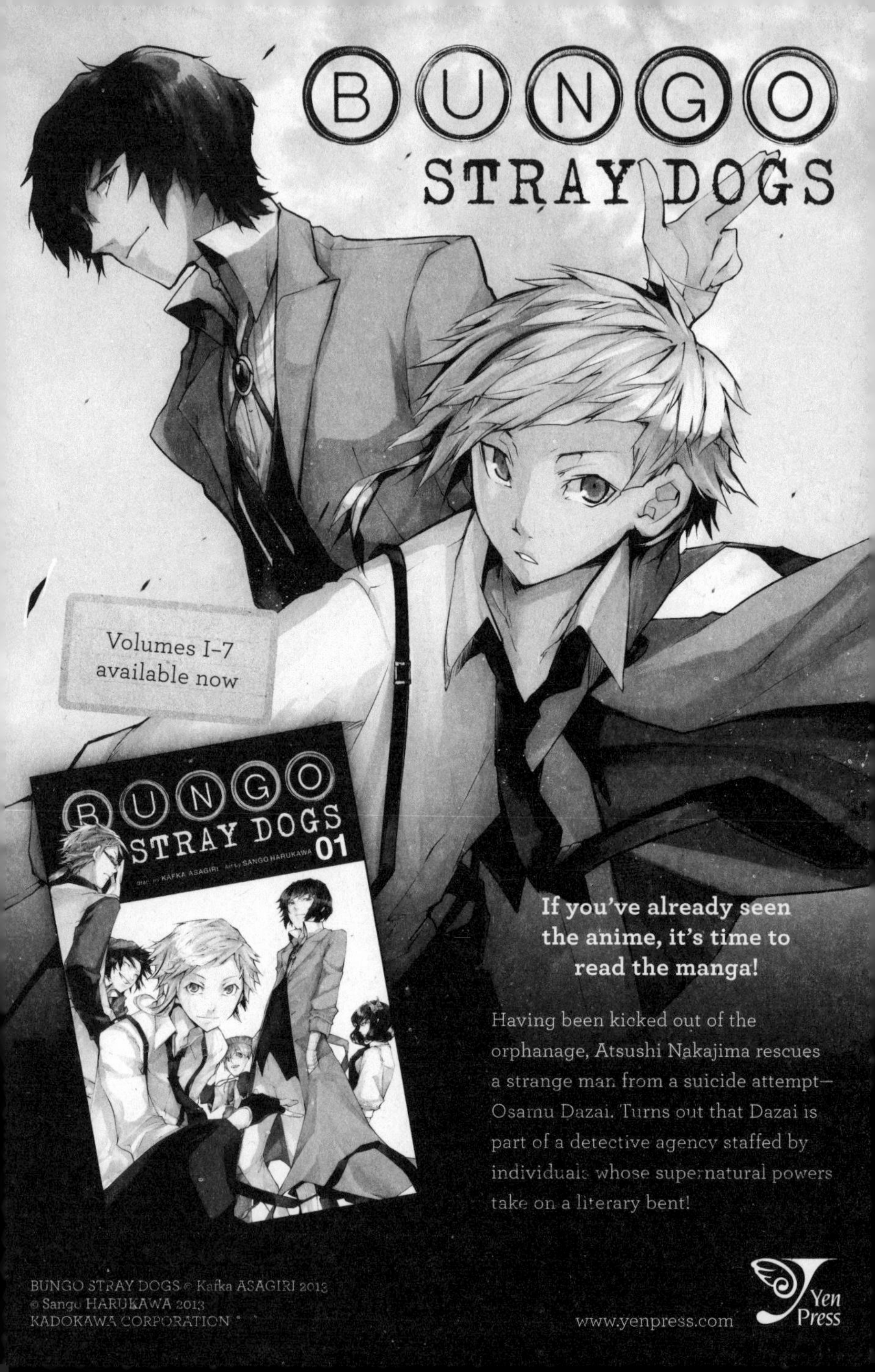
BUNGO
STRAY DOGS
Volumes 1–7
available now
BUNGO
STRAY DOGS
01
KAFKA ASAGIRI
SANGO HARUKAWA
If you've already seen
the anime, it's time to
read the manga!
Having been kicked out of the orphanage, Atsushi Nakajima rescues a strange man from a suicide attempt—Osamu Dazai. Turns out that Dazai is part of a detective agency staffed by individuals whose supernatural powers take on a literary bent!
BUNGO STRAY DOGS © Kafka ASAGIRI 2013
© Sango HARUKAWA 2013
KADOKAWA CORPORATION
www.yenpress.com
Yen
Press

KAGEROU DAZE 11

MAHIRO SATOU
Original Story: JIN
(SHIZEN NO TEKI P)
Character Design: SIDU, WANNYANPOO

Translation: Kevin Gifford • Lettering: Abigail Blackman

KAGEROUDAZE Vol. 11
© Mahiro Satou 2018
© KAGEROU PROJECT / 1st PLACE
First published in Japan in 2018 by KADOKAWA CORPORATION, Tokyo.
English translation rights arranged with KADOKAWA CORPORATION, Tokyo through TUTTLE-MORI AGENCY, Inc., Tokyo.

English translation © 2018 by Yen Press, LLC

Yen Press
1290 Avenue of the Americas
New York, NY 10104

Visit us at yenpress.com
facebook.com/yenpress
twitter.com/yenpress
yenpress.tumblr.com
instagram.com/yenpress

First Yen Press Edition: December 2018

Yen Press is an imprint of Yen Press, LLC.
The Yen Press name and logo are trademarks of Yen Press, LLC.

Library of Congress Control Number: 2016297061

ISBNs: 978-1-9753-2908-2 (paperback)
       978-1-9753-2909-9 (ebook)

10 9 8 7 6 5 4 3 2 1

WOR

Printed in the United States of America